WHAT WOULD BE DIFFERENT

WHAT WOULD BE DIFFERENT

Figures of Possibility in Adorno

Iain Macdonald

STANFORD UNIVERSITY PRESS
STANFORD, CALIFORNIA

Stanford University Press
Stanford, California

Printed in the United States of America on acid-free, archival-quality paper

Library of Congress Cataloging-in-Publication Data

Names: Macdonald, Iain, 1966– author.
Title: What would be different : figures of possibility in Adorno / Iain Macdonald.
Description: Stanford, California : Stanford University Press, 2019. | Includes bibliographical references and index.
Identifiers: LCCN 2019004069 (print) | LCCN 2019008421 (ebook) | ISBN 9781503610644 | ISBN 9781503610279 (cloth : alk. paper) | ISBN 9781503610637 (pbk. : alk. paper)
Subjects: LCSH: Adorno, Theodor W., 1903–1969. | Possibility. | Critical theory. | Sociology. | Philosophy, Modern.
Classification: LCC B3199.A34 (ebook) | LCC B3199.A34 M24 2019 (print) | DDC 193—dc23
LC record available at https://lccn.loc.gov/2019004069

Cover image: © 2019 Sara Morley and Salvatore V. Barrera
Cover design: Rob Ehle

To my mother
and to the memory of my father

CONTENTS

ACKNOWLEDGMENTS

So many colleagues, students, and friends—near and far and in very diverse ways—have contributed something vitally important to this project: comments, criticisms, research opportunities, technical and archival support, or simply gestures of friendship. Thanks are therefore due to Salvatore Barrera, Don Beith, Jay Bernstein, Karen Borrmann, Isabelle Boucher, Ian Chuprun, Karl Côté, Jérôme Cotte, Jen Cressey, Marie-Hélène Desmeules, Martin Desrosiers, George di Giovanni, Olivier Dorais, Gordon Finlayson, Liz Foley, Maxime Fortin-Archambault, Thierry Gendron-Dugré, Christoph Gödde, Peter Gordon, Vincent Grondin, Espen Hammer, Firmin Havugimana, Olivier Huot-Beaulieu, Thomas Khurana, Kathy Kiloh, Sonja Kleinod, Bianca Laliberté, Samuel-Élie Lesage, Henri Lonitz, Olivier Mathieu, Rocky McKnight, Laetitia Monteils-Laeng, Christoph Menke and the members of his *Kolloquium* at the Goethe-Universität Frankfurt am Main, Ludvic Moquin-Beaudry, Dominic Morin, Marie-Eve Morin, Sara Morley, Pierre-François Noppen, Brian O'Connor, Max Pensky, Darío Perinetti, Henry Pickford, Scott Prentice, Dirk Quadflieg, Karl Racette, Gérard Raulet, Elizabeth Robertson, Yasemin Sarı, Michael Schwarz, Xander Selene, Dirk Setton, Martin Shuster, Jamie Smith, Gabriel Toupin, Roseline Vaillancourt, Nick Walker, and Krzysztof Ziarek. In particular, I thank two people without whose support this project never would have seen the light of day: Laurence Ricard and William Ross.

For institutional support of various kinds, I thank the Social Sciences and Humanities Research Council of Canada, the Exzellenzcluster "Die Herausbildung normativer Ordnungen" at the Goethe-Universität Frankfurt am Main, the Forschungskolleg Humanwissenschaften in Bad Homburg, the Adorno Archive in Frankfurt am Main, and the Walter Benjamin Archive in Berlin. For permission to quote from Adorno's unpublished writings, I also thank the Adorno Archive and the Hamburger Stiftung zur Förderung von Wissenschaft und Kultur.

Some passages appearing in Chapters 2 and 3 were based on parts of my "Adorno's Modal Utopianism: Possibility and Actuality in Adorno and Hegel," *Adorno Studies* 1, no. 1 (2017). An earlier, and shorter, version of this article also appeared in French as "Un utopisme modal? Possibilité et actualité chez Hegel et Adorno," in *Les normes et le possible: Héritage et perspectives de l'École de Francfort*, ed. P.-F. Noppen, G. Raulet, and I. Macdonald (Paris: Éditions de la Maison des Sciences de l'Homme, 2013).

Finally, some parts of Chapter 4 are based on ideas first sketched in my "'What Is, Is More Than It Is': Adorno and Heidegger on the Priority of Possibility," *International Journal of Philosophical Studies* 19, no. 1 (2011), and in two articles that first appeared in French: "L'autre pensée: La possibilité de l'autre commencement et la critique de l'effectivité dans les *Beiträge zur philosophie*," in *Qu'appelle-t-on la pensée? Le philosopher heideggérien,* ed. C. Perrin (Bucharest: Zeta Books, 2014); and "Vers une démodalisation du possible: Heidegger et le clivage de l'estre," *Philosophie,* no. 140 (2019).

ABBREVIATIONS

BGS   Benjamin, Walter. *Gesammelte Schriften*. Edited by Rolf Tiedemann et al. 7 vols. Frankfurt am Main: Suhrkamp Verlag, 1972–1989.

GA   Heidegger, Martin. *Gesamtausgabe*. Edited by Friedrich-Wilhelm von Herrmann et al. Frankfurt am Main: Vittorio Klostermann, 1975–.

GS   Adorno, Theodor W. *Gesammelte Schriften*. Edited by Rolf Tiedemann et al. 20 vols. Frankfurt am Main: Suhrkamp Verlag, 1970–1986.

HGS   Horkheimer, Max. *Gesammelte Schriften*. Edited by Alfred Schmidt and Gunzelin Schmid Noerr. 19 vols. Frankfurt am Main: S. Fischer Verlag, 1985–1996.

MEW   Marx, Karl, and Friedrich Engels. *Werke*. 43 vols. Berlin: Dietz-Verlag, 1956–.

W   Hegel, G. W. F. *Werke*. 20 vols. Edited by Eva Moldenhauer and Karl Markus Michel. Frankfurt am Main: Suhrkamp Verlag, 1969–1971.

WHAT WOULD BE DIFFERENT

CHAPTER 1

WHAT WOULD BE DIFFERENT

Ab esse ad posse valet, a posse ad esse non valet consequentia.

I don't think I can give up on possibility, on the thought of
possibility. Without it, we would be unable to think at all and
indeed, in the strictest sense, nothing at all could even be said.
— Adorno to Arnold Gehlen[1]

Right Life

"What would be different has not as yet begun."[2] This is how Adorno describes
the possibility of a redeemed life in relation to the suffering that stems, in this
life, from the perpetuation of ancestral social injustices. This possibility raises a
number of questions. One might wonder first of all what precisely *would* be different? Adorno mentions indications such as the satisfaction of material needs,
the elimination of senseless suffering, the redemption of the hopes of the past,
the happiness of unborn generations, a humanity that has never yet existed,
freedom, peace, and reconciliation.

But how are we to articulate such possibilities without lapsing into a vague and
naïve utopianism? The answer is far from obvious. The apparent pessimism of the
often-quoted claim that "wrong life cannot be lived rightly"[3] would seem to prevent
us from gaining access to such a redeemed future.[4] Indeed, Adorno elsewhere seems
to imply that wrong life condemns us to remaining trapped in false consciousness:
"If wrong life really cannot be lived rightly [*richtiges Leben*], then for that very reason
there can be no correct consciousness [*richtiges Bewußtsein*] in it either."[5]

It should be noted, however, that there is an ambiguity in the impossibility
of "right life" and "correct consciousness." Does Adorno mean that there is simply no way to escape wrong life, no really possible right life that would belie the
apparent necessity of various forms of suffering and injustice? Or does he mean
that the problem of wrong life cannot be solved by a consciousness that takes

itself to be *correct*? In the latter case, Adorno would not necessarily be ruling out the possibility of right life. He would merely be saying that the alternative to wrong life is not to be found in "correct" life or consciousness, understood in terms of some norm of rectitude to which we must adjust.

The second line of interpretation is the more promising, not least because Adorno explicitly criticizes the notion of correction as rectification, as though a simple adjustment to some available, normatively charged model of existence could set everything right: "False opinion cannot be transcended through intellectual rectification alone but only in relation to reality" (where "reality" refers to concretely given material existence).[6] The meaning of this statement begins to come into focus when we consider that tenacious adherence to theoretical correctives can all too easily cause us to lose sight of the evolving processes that underlie the realities that call for such correctives. The point would be to avoid fetishizing specific theoretical correctives, while continuing to infer from reality the patterns that inform its historical development—a development that may invalidate such correctives along the way. If right life is possible at all, it does not follow from our adherence to any singular vision but only from a renewable critical examination of a life that persists in its wrongness. This is one important way in which socialism failed in its historical incarnations, according to Adorno: it once set about establishing a practical corrective to the very real problem of structural social injustice but then effectively banned any serious renewal of theoretical reflection on the persistence of injustice, especially within the very institutions that were meant to set things right.[7]

No single "image" of right life can be a substitute for right life itself.[8] It is in this sense that Adorno's materialism can be said to be "imageless" and to participate in something akin to a ban on graven images.[9] The adherence to correctives that become ends in themselves can lead to their becoming static images of a reality that has since moved on. In this respect, they become "photographs" that no longer correspond to the view they once depicted and "the content of such images [thereby] becomes a bulwark against reality."[10] Consequently, we are called upon to demolish such barriers: "The powers that be set up façades into which consciousness crashes. It must strive to break through them."[11]

If this exhortation is not in vain, perhaps it is because the trouble with wrong life lies not so much with reality's inherent and insurmountable wrongness but at least in part with the limitations placed on our capacity to get beyond the declining correctives to which false consciousness continues to cling.

To frame the issue modally, and to return to our point of departure, the problem is the following: If we cannot limit ourselves to correctives taken as ends in themselves, then how *should* we conceive of possibilities of liberation and redemption, such as satisfying material needs and eliminating socially unnecessary suffering—or what Adorno sometimes calls "senseless suffering"?[12] What is the status of such possibilities in respect of actuality and wrong life?

The expression "what would be different" refers to these possibilities, while guarding against the production of static images of redemption, for the "different" may also differ from what we currently take to be the way forwards. This insight structures the relation of history—that "fatal continuity"[13] or "heinous continuum"[14]—to a redeemed life, a "right" life that is not merely "correct." However, we need to better understand the relation of such possibilities to the actuality they inhabit. Of course, the question of right life cannot be reduced to mere metaphysical reflections on modal concepts, but neither can we dispense with a metaphysical typology of possibilities in our attempts to understand the processes by which they wax and wane as real or objective. Further questions arise: Can we be utopian without being "unrealistic"? And if so, where should the line be drawn that separates utopian thinking from unhinged fantasy?

The most central metaphysical distinction in this regard is no doubt the one that separates "formal (or abstract) possibility" from "real possibility," on Hegel's use of these terms. This distinction can be summarized rapidly while leaving to one side, for the moment, the question of how it unfolds dialectically. (The next chapter provides more detail.)

Hegel

According to Hegel, *formal* possibility contains a number of determinations. It refers, for example, to that which is thinkable without contradiction, considered entirely independently of whatever may or may not be the case (e.g., unicorns or "the sultan may become the pope"[15]). But it can also refer to contingent actuality, understood as that which could also have been otherwise (e.g., the number of species of parrot[16]). And most importantly for present purposes, it contains the "ought" (*Sollen*) or that which ought to be actual but is powerless in the face of actuality and what actuality in fact produces (e.g., the claim that society ought to be organized differently).

The ought assumes various forms in Hegel. In its full-fledged modal form—in the sense of being explicitly related to actuality, possibility, and necessity—

the ought is a special case of non-being or non-actuality: it names that which is non-actual in the mode of merely purported actualizability.[17] Hence it is included in the broad category of formal possibility, within which there are several specific determinations, including the Kantian ought: acting in accordance with the moral law. Hegel's critique of Kantian morality is well known and can be summarized as an attack against the idea that complete fitness or conformity of finite human willing to the moral law is in fact unattainable. For Kant, morality as it is lived can only take the form of a "*progression* unto *infinity* towards that complete fitness."[18] Indeed, Kant thinks that this requires us to postulate the immortality of the soul, for it is only on this basis that such a progression would not be in vain. Hegel repeatedly subjects these claims to strenuous criticism because they contain "the contradiction of a task that remains a task and yet which must be fulfilled, of a morality that no longer has to correspond to an *actual* consciousness."[19] Moral duty is thereby reduced to "something non-actual,"[20] or to what Hegel elsewhere calls an "impotent"[21] and "perennial"[22] ought.

The criticism of Kantian morality is merely one version of Hegel's critique of the ought, but it encapsulates and exemplifies the general problem. For Hegel, the ought names a renunciation of actuality in the form of clinging to something that actuality cannot produce. Or to put it another way, the ought is the result of a restriction that we cannot transcend. It therefore applies to any situation in which some possible state of affairs is considered desirable or even necessary but cannot be brought about. In short, the ought is the possible, but under the shadow of the impossible. It is for this reason that Hegel includes it in the category of formal possibility, wherein the focus is on the mere *form* of the possible because the question of actualization has been suspended or indefinitely postponed.

Real possibility, on the other hand, is that which does not abstract away from real actuality but takes it as its criterion and content. What is *really* (not merely formally) possible is circumscribed by the concrete inner determinations of real actuality, as Hegel puts it: the sum total of real circumstances that are at the same time the real conditions for the further development of actuality. Whereas formal possibility is a capacious category, real possibility is confining. Hegel's approach here takes actuality to refer to a *totality* of circumstances that are simultaneously the conditions of future actuality. Thus, if it is really possible for an acorn to grow into an oak, the reason is that all of the circumstances-conditions obtain in which this will occur and an oak tree will be the inevitable result. Strictly speaking, no real possibilities (possibilities that correspond to real circumstances qua conditions) go unactualized.

Hegel's view is as simple as it is extreme: from a metaphysical point of view, non-real possibilities are merely formal and so have no claim on actuality. This may be fairly uncontroversial as regards unicorns, but Hegel goes further. For him, it makes no sense to use the category of what merely *ought to be* as a criterion by which actuality may be judged. On the contrary, he suggests that such attempts are entirely misguided and fail to grasp how possibility is related to real actuality and to the absolute. Philosophy "deals only with the idea—which is not so impotent that it merely ought to be, yet is not actual—and further with an actuality in relation to which . . . objects, institutions, and states of affairs are only the superficial outer shell."[23] In other words, philosophically speaking, how a state of affairs develops is never a question of how it *ought* to develop but of what actuality *really* contains in the form of real possibilities. "What is actual *can act*; something announces its actuality *by what it produces*."[24] In other words, the actual is that which is in fact *at work* within history (up to and including reason and the idea itself, according to Hegel), although we may not recognize it at first.

Within Hegel's typology of possibilities, it is difficult to find room for a real possibility that would correspond to the claim that "what would be different has not as yet begun" except to place it in the category of the ought. To speak of inexistent, wished-for, but perpetually unactualized states of affairs is to remain at the level of formal possibility; and to cling to the hope that they should come about—if the circumstances of actualization are not at hand—is to become mired in unreality. For this reason, Hegel's categorization of the ought under the heading of formal possibility provides one of the key battlegrounds for understanding the Adornian alternative. Indeed, the status of "what would be different" will be decided partly on the basis of a struggle over the validity of the Hegelian critique of the ought: Might there be a subset of oughts that can be considered real and not merely formal possibilities?

On Adorno's view, Hegel's approach is a "slap in the face" to possibility:[25]

> According to Hegel's distinction between abstract [i.e., formal] and real possibility, only something that has become actual is, in fact, possible. This kind of philosophy sides with the big guns. It adopts the verdict of a reality that constantly buries what could be different.[26]

Or to put things the other way around, the unachieved right life is no merely formal possibility. According to Adorno, it is a *real* albeit *socially suppressed* possibility. The central modal category is therefore not actuality understood as a totality of circumstances-conditions, as it is for Hegel, but rather *blocked possibility*. As Adorno puts it in relation to the dialectic of theory and practice:

> The possibility of right practice presupposes the full and undiminished consciousness of the *blockage* of practice. If we immediately set about judging a thought by the criterion of its possible actualization [and thereby disqualify thoughts that are not immediately actualizable], then we place fetters on the productive force of thinking. In all likelihood, the only thought that can be made practical is the thought that is not restricted in advance by the practice to which it is meant to be immediately applicable. I would tend to think that the relation of theory and practice is really that dialectical.[27]

Thus, the blocked possibility of right life cannot be said to be a full-fledged real possibility in Hegel's use of the term, since the circumstances-conditions of actuality have not produced it and do not seem on the point of producing it. Yet, for Adorno, right life is not for that reason a vain hope or a mere ought. Rather, it should be understood as a real possibility that has been "cheated" of its actuality.[28] In other words, it is a *real ought*—to coin a phrase—that contests its status as mere formal possibility. However, this line of reasoning requires a reworking of the boundaries of the modal categories at issue.

The Ought beyond the Image

To summarize: Right life is conceivable provided we renounce static images of redemption, but Hegel's typology of possibilities deprives us of a dialectically cogent way of talking about such blocked possibilities, that is, those historically developed yet sadly suppressed, liberating potentialities by which society can and ought to transform itself. For example, how should we understand the call to end socially unnecessary suffering, such as hunger in an age of hitherto unthinkable wealth?

Adorno's thought is an attempt to answer such questions. In fact, it is one of his chief aims to encourage us to face up to blocked possibilities and to lay claim to their status as *real*, in spite of what actuality in fact produces. In due course and in order to provide a fuller picture of Adorno's view, we shall have to take a number of other considerations into account. However, for the moment, it can be said that "blocked possibility" designates a real possibility of progress that is currently obstructed by various social mechanisms and patterns of thinking—including certain approaches to metaphysical thinking. It is a redemptive possibility hobbled and shunted into unreality by real actuality. It is the possibility of saying that actuality is not what it gives itself to be and of discovering that the only criterion by which it can be judged and transformed is, paradoxically, that which it has not yet, but may yet, become.

Adorno is neither the only nor the first thinker to suggest that an enabling perspective on the "potential of what would be different" is worth developing, both theoretically and practically.[29] It could easily be shown that Marx, for example, already paved the way for this sort of reflection, and versions of it can be traced back to figures such as Kant (and his notion of perpetual peace), among several others. But perhaps the best approach to the issue is to lay out a few more immediate counter-examples to the view that will be defended in these pages. If Adorno offers us an alternative to Hegel, then how does he differ from other alternatives to Hegel?

If what we are after is the possibility of the world being remade according to better principles than those which now govern it (which, for Adorno, are principles such as structural social injustices, fear, need, and suffering), then perhaps we should first look to theories that stress historically untapped powers to define and effect radical social change. In this regard, the writings of Georg Lukács and Ernst Bloch—and Adorno's refusal to align himself with either of these figures' views—provide us with a means of taking a first measure of his own concept of possibility.[30]

Lukács

The central modal category of Lukács's *History and Class Consciousness* is no doubt objective possibility—specifically, the objective possibility of the revolutionary actualization of the "correct and authentic class consciousness of the proletariat."[31]

As is well known, Lukács's notion of objective possibility draws on Max Weber's sociological use of this expression, which in turn is based on historiographical considerations. For example, to assess the importance of individual events in the causal chain of history, it is sometimes useful to proceed by constructing "judgements of possibility."[32] The point is not to determine what ought to have happened in history. Rather, objective possibility is "the possibility of what, according to general rules of experience, 'would have' happened if a single causal component was imagined to be absent or modified."[33] In other words, the point is to counterfactually determine the chances (in the sense of "degree of possibility") of decisively different historical consequences if a given historical event had not occurred or had occurred differently. Are our imaginary different event and its consequences "adequately caused,"[34] that is, are they contextually plausible, given what history and experience have taught us? If so, then this can be offered as support for the significance of the event in question. For instance, Weber refers to the Battle of Marathon as historically significant for the development and spread of Greek culture and values. But how can this be shown? The answer lies in the *objective possibility* that a Persian victory would *probably* have stifled what *in fact* occurred, given how other Persian victories played out historically.[35]

However, the concept of objective possibility is not limited to its historiographical use. It can also work within the sociological context of interpreting what Weber calls societized action. Thus, if we begin from the standpoint of social actors contemplating some course of action within a context in which certain behaviors are common, required, or predictable, these actors may form subjective expectations regarding their chances of success. The researcher can first consider these expectations as they relate to the rules and practices of the relevant "instituted order" that orients the actors' behavior, such as a card game or a legal system. However, the researcher can also consider the situation from the standpoint of the *objective* chances of success. This is the standpoint of objective possibility.[36]

For instance, within a given instituted order we can ask questions such as the following: What would be the likely outcome if someone were to act in a particular way? What are the objective chances of success or failure? Is the subjectively planned outcome adequately caused; is it contextually justified and compatible with past experience, the rules and practices of the instituted order, and so on? In this way, the researcher can discover the objective basis for legitimate subjective expectations in relation to factual knowledge of how an instituted order functions. As Weber puts it, objective possibility "can, on average, in terms of its meaning, serve as an appropriate basis for the subjective expectations of the acting persons."[37] As such, objective possibility allows us "to construct connections that our *imagination*, oriented towards and schooled by contact with actuality, *judges* to be adequate."[38]

It is not difficult to see what appealed to Lukács here: objective possibility provided him with a powerful sociological tool for formulating what he took to be the justified expected outcome of revolutionary praxis, formulated on the basis of knowledge of the total process of production qua actuality. To maintain Weber's language for a moment, we might say that, for Lukács, the objective possibility of liberation is precisely "adequately caused" (i.e., neither actual nor necessary but probable) to the extent that it is "subjectively" (through class consciousness) oriented according to the facts of the objective process of production qua instituted order. The *subjective expectation* of liberation can therefore be said to be validated to the extent that it is rooted in the *objective possibility* of liberation, as supported by the researcher's understanding of the governing practices of the instituted order. To put the same thought in more Lukácsian terms, objective possibility is a projection of that of which the proletariat *would* be capable once it has overcome the illusions under which it previously labored.[39] It is thus a historical possibility "imputed" to the proletariat by objective historical forces and within the overall process of production, in opposition to the proletariat's *actual* self-understanding, which is contaminated with ideology or too focused on immediate struggles (e.g., trade-union consciousness).[40]

That said, Lukács takes Weberian objective possibility in a new direction, inflecting it not merely with Marxist but also with Hegelian language, such that one might legitimately wonder: What is the status of objective possibility in relation to real and formal possibilities on Hegel's use of these terms? On the one hand, Lukács does not want to turn the actualization of class consciousness, and so the actualization of the proletariat's objective historical mission, into a mechanical necessity: the objective aspiration to correct consciousness "only *yields the possibility. The solution itself* can only be the fruit of the *conscious* deeds of the proletariat."[41] Or again: "In view of the great distance that the proletariat has to travel ideologically it would be disastrous to foster any illusions."[42] (And Weber too warns against this in the context of Marxist ideal-typical theoretical constructions.)[43] On the other hand, he refuses to allow the actualization of the revolution to collapse into a mere "ought" whose actualization lies in an indeterminate and uncertain future:

> For the ultimate goal is not some "future state" awaiting the proletariat somewhere independent of the movement and the path leading up to it. It is not a condition which can be happily forgotten in the course of daily struggles and recalled only in Sunday sermons as a stirring contrast to workaday cares. Nor is it

an "ought," an "idea" designed to regulate the "actual" process. The ultimate goal is rather that *relation to the totality* (to the whole of society seen as a process), through which every aspect of the struggle acquires its revolutionary significance. This relation informs every aspect in its simple and sober ordinariness, but only a consciousness-in-becoming makes it actual and so confers actuality on the day-to-day struggle by manifesting its relation to the whole. Thus it elevates mere existence to actuality.[44]

This passage makes it clear that Lukács remains quite Hegelian on the question of the ought: the latter implies non-actualization or, at best, the postponement *ad Kalendas Graecas* of an envisioned outcome. Instead of a mere ought, he offers us an *objective image of real possibility*, endowed with sociological validity. Such is the true meaning of his notion of objective possibility. It is a bridging concept that is meant to bind real actuality in its totality to a specific and differently organized real actuality, while maintaining that the second is already objectively latent in the first. Objective possibility is thereby not an impotent ought, according to Lukács; it is the *real, emergent* tendency towards a future that would break with the prevailing bourgeois insistence on the inevitable continuation of the present state of affairs: "Only once human beings are capable of grasping the present as becoming, of recognizing in it those tendencies whose dialectical opposition renders us capable of *making* the future, only then will the present as becoming become *our* present."[45]

However, due to the very fact that this future has yet to be made, Lukács understands that he cannot make use of the full-fledged Hegelian concept of real possibility; hence the alternative expression "objective possibility." The reason is clear: universal liberation is present only in the form of a *quasi-real* possibility—a real possibility in the process of its objective emergence, which is currently hindered by the deficient actual self-understanding of the working class, among other things.[46] The future must yet be made, starting out from revolutionary judgments of possibility and adequate causation; it is not metaphysically necessary. The word "objective" is thereby something of a fig leaf for a not-quite-real "real" possibility, to which we can help ourselves—on credit (or perhaps in the manner of an Aristotelian "first actuality"), as it were, because, in spite of the defects of the proletariat's actual self-understanding, it is adequately caused.

Objective possibility is therefore neither an impotent ought nor a real possibility properly speaking, on Hegel's use of these terms. But it is not entirely distinct from them either. It has features of both. Like the ought, it goes beyond what is factually given without being able to lay claim to imminent actualization. However, like real possibility, the mediated transcendence to which it refers "is not something (subjective) foisted onto the objects from outside, a value judgement or an ought opposed to being. *It is rather the manifestation of their authentic, objective structure itself.*"[47] In other words, it is composed of the inner determinations of real actuality and is therefore a true manifestation of the social totality—but one that only an increasingly self-aware proletarian class consciousness can properly discern and develop in concrete practice. In this sense, it is starkly *opposed* to the ought. Objective possibility is therefore the possibility of "what would be different," where this is understood as the transition to another, better actuality that is truly latent within contemporary actuality, no matter how hidden it may seem to be. For Lukács, what would be different is therefore something like the true form informing history's difficult-to-understand unfolding. It is, in short, an expression of the "developing tendencies of history, [which] constitute a higher actuality than merely empirical 'facts.'"[48]

This mention of "higher actuality" is significant—and problematic. In spite of the otherwise interesting emphasis on objective possibility, and in spite of its role in specifying how the "merely empirical 'facts'" can be transcended, Lukács nevertheless defends the priority of actuality over possibility: objective possibility serves a higher actuality. Moreover, this subordination is carried out along Hegelian lines insofar as Lukács repeats Hegel's rejection of the ought. He is speaking in favor of a dynamization and sublation of what is immediately given into its own higher form.

The trouble with this view, according to Adorno, is that it seeks to dissolve given reality into a whole—or rather a theoretical *image* of the whole—that is taken to be adequate to it.[49] Or to put it differently, in spite of Lukács's criticism of idealism, he defines an essence to which existence is called upon to correspond. To this Adorno replies: "The one . . . who would like to dynamize everything into pure [consummate] actuality tends to be hostile towards the other, the strange—whose name resonates in estrangement, and not in vain, and whose non-identity would guide the liberation not just of consciousness, but of a reconciled humanity."[50]

That is, the intransigence and strangeness of the real is suppressed by Lukácsian correct consciousness, which sets its sights on a truer, higher actuality. Yet this neglects that it is precisely this strangeness that prompted and gave shape to revolutionary attempts to transform the world in the first place. For example, without the experience of the strangeness of the persistent and, indeed, increasing wealth gap in a society that produces so much wealth, there would be little motivation to breach the façade of the apparent impossibility of eliminating poverty. That something appears to us as "strange" is the sign of something that remains to be understood, conceived, deciphered.

While Adorno's emphasis on "strangeness" may seem like little more than a technicality or an idiosyncrasy, it becomes more important once we remember that the actualization of proletarian consciousness misfired, became mired in totalitarian politics, and finally betrayed the promise of universal liberation that Lukács had articulated under the rubric of objective possibility. For from where should emancipatory practice draw renewed vigor if the strangeness of reified reality has been submerged within a fixed vision of the social totality? Following the failure of universal liberation, is it not obliged to return, however sheepishly, to this strangeness—or, more precisely, to the strangeness of a reality that did not produce what was expected of it? As mentioned, for Adorno, "false opinion cannot be transcended through intellectual rectification alone but only in relation to reality"—that is, we need to know how to react if a given corrective fails the test of realization. Or to put the emphasis on strangeness:

> No reconciled state of affairs can come about by annexing strangeness in an act of philosophical imperialism. Rather, the happiness of such a state of affairs would lie in the fact that strangeness, in the proximity that is granted it, [would nevertheless] remain distant and different—neither fully heterogeneous nor fully appropriated. [Lukács's] relentless condemnation of reification blocks the dialectic, and this indicts the philosophical-historical constructions that this condemnation produces.[51]

The problem, on Adorno's view, is therefore not reification or false consciousness as such—although he does not deny that they must be overcome. It is rather that Lukács's account of dereification puts us in thrall to a singular vision of higher actuality that then failed to come about. And the more we cling to this image of higher actuality, or the more we cling to metaphysical, higher actualities *tout court*, the more we rob ourselves of the experience of what would be different. We have therefore to understand how mere reality can become a depotentialized and repotentialized actuality, not how we can remain faithful to the static image of an objective possibility that has been historically thwarted and whose obsolescence condemns us to impotence.

It is with the analysis of this impotence, along with its symptom, the experience of reality as strange, that theory has to diagnose; its purpose should not be to produce "correct consciousness." One might therefore say that for Lukács, what is central is the actualization of the *unique* objective possibility concealed by reified social relations, whereas for Adorno it is the formulation of objective possibilities of which we are deprived, *whenever this becomes necessary,* without fetishizing a specific image of correct consciousness. That is, the formulation of objective possibility requires an exact experience of the refractory and enigmatic strangeness of things, not the submission of all things to some higher actuality. Redemption comes from repotentializing the real at the first sign of the persistence of strangeness (e.g., socially unnecessary suffering), not from the adherence to some graven image of correct actuality or from the zealotry of the correct consciousness that is said to give us access to it.

One might retort that Lukács pursues precisely the same goal: the repotentialization of the real. Does he not say that "the task is to discover the principles by means of which the 'ought' is *in general able* to modify being"?[52] To some extent, yes: Lukácsian objective possibility is meant to describe how a new possibility can emerge and gain reality within history. Indeed, Adorno himself sometimes uses the expression "objective possibility" to frame his notion of what would be different. But ultimately, as we have seen, Lukács prefers to turn objective possibility towards a higher actuality, towards a whole that includes everything, excludes nothing, and to which reality and experience must conform: "the total process . . . represents the authentic, higher actuality, over against the facts."[53]

Where, in this higher actuality, is the experience of strangeness—of nonidentity—that first drove Lukács to speak of the concrete objective possibility of universal liberation? Perhaps if he had not subordinated objective possibility to a higher actuality, or, more specifically, if he had been more attentive to the persistent strangeness of what *ought not to be* (which can include static theoretical images of redemption), then the increasingly evident failure of the proletarian revolution might not have left theory and practice in such disarray. By contrast, Adorno suggests another path, which focuses on the experience of strangeness and non-identity as potentializing—as productive of a *real* ought—instead of on keeping faith with a presumed higher actuality that is guaranteed by its purported correctness rather than by the non-identity from which it arose. So, as Adorno remarks of the later Lukács, "we are left with the feeling of a person who rattles his chains hopelessly, imagining that their clanking is the march of the *Weltgeist*."[54] Absent strangeness, objective possibility becomes dogmatic, a mere image whose process of construction has been forgotten and that exposes itself to the danger of idolatry.[55]

In short, the enemy of freedom is not the recalcitrant strangeness of reality but the inability to think what is unthought or remains to be thought within reality: "It is up to philosophy to think that which differs from what is thought, and which alone makes it into a thought, while at the same time its demon tries to persuade it that [the different] ought not to exist."[56] Or as Adorno also puts it: "Dialectic is the *consistent* consciousness of non-identity,"[57] not the *correct* consciousness of some allegedly higher actuality.

Bloch

The case of Ernst Bloch in some ways resembles that of Lukács, although it also presents a number of important differences. Is Bloch in some related sense guilty of defending a static image of the correct consciousness of a higher actuality? As we have seen, it is not that we should not seek correctives; it is that the search for correctives should be formulated on the basis of a suppleness in relation to experience and to that which is non-identical within it rather than in the name of rectitude in relation to a higher actuality. In general, the appeal to correctness—in the sense of adapting to a putatively corrective norm whose relevance has waned—is one way among others in which society comes to "lag behind its own potential."[58] Indeed, the more Lukács insists on the actualization of his rigid construal of objective possibility in the moment of its manifest blockage and non-actualizability—even its vitiation in totalitarian socialism— the greater the lag.

With Bloch, something similar is indeed at issue. However, unlike Lukács, Bloch delves much more deeply into the structure and status of unactualized possibilities in their relation to actuality and the social status quo. In this regard, his position is much closer to Adorno's than to Lukács's. In some ways, the casual reader may even wonder why Adorno is so critical of Bloch when they are both clearly interested in undoing the influence of Hegel's "actualism" and his restrictive typology of possibilities. Understanding Adorno's peculiar concept of possibility therefore requires distinguishing it from Bloch's.

The first and most important factor for understanding the relevance of

Bloch lies in his attempt to redraw the line separating formal from real possibility and, more specifically, his defense of the ought against Hegel's criticisms of it. Unlike Lukács, and to his credit, Bloch seeks to salvage the ought. In *Subject-Object*, for example, Bloch argues that Hegel's philosophy, in spite of its manifest critical potential, illegitimately undermines our hope for a future that would be different and free of the contingent but systemic causes of suffering.

He begins by admitting that Hegel's critique of the ought is on target in some cases—for example, in relation to Kant and the question of endless progress towards the complete correspondence of the will to the moral law. But Hegel's criticisms "would be even more compelling had they not eliminated the ought in general, the surplus of the legitimate-yet-unattained [*den Überschuß des Geltend-Unerreichten*]."[59] This line of reasoning leads Bloch, quite rightly from an Adornian perspective, to the following conclusion:

> The will grows weary when the ought is entirely eliminated, when it is taken to be something utterly and eternally endless. This is the price—all too high—that Hegel pays and it is entirely unnecessary. The alternative to endless progress toward the future is not to block it off entirely.[60]

In light of such passages, Adorno is sometimes fairly indulgent in relation to Bloch, although in the end he is perhaps even more harsh with him than with Lukács. The reasons were no doubt various, but Adorno reports that during a notable rupture between 1942 and 1958 their "severely strained relations" were due to their "political differences,"[61] and more specifically to Bloch's "obstinate" commitment to "the dreadful state of affairs . . . that passes for communism in the East."[62] However, in the second half of the 1950s, Bloch came into conflict with the East German Communist Party and was ultimately forced into retirement—an episode that surely paved the way for a temporary renewal of their friendship.[63] No doubt with this in mind, Adorno acknowledges and praises Bloch's anti-authoritarian, anti-deferential stance in a text from 1960: "He does not infer from the fact that [domination, hierarchy, and so on] have not yet been abolished the perfidious maxim that they could not and should not be abolished."[64] Everything that Adorno and Bloch have in common intellectually gravitates around this point: redemptive possibilities are not legitimated by factual reality but by their systematic suppression within it.[65]

Nevertheless, at around the same time, when asked whether he might consider writing a review of *The Principle of Hope* (in which Bloch deals with precisely these issues), Adorno firmly declined, citing the "gravest of reservations" he had regarding that "gargantuan tome."[66] He does not go into great detail about his reservations, but what he does say is telling:

> Bloch belongs precisely to those philosophers—and God knows I don't want to say anything disparaging—who is entirely consumed in living communication, in speech, and whose writing, by comparison, is like a residue of living thought—and often enough a residue that is not all that pure.[67]

Whatever his stated intention, Adorno's remark is disparaging enough, especially once we spell out the alchemical metaphor. Bloch's writings are a residue of living thought, in the manner of the alchemist's *caput mortuum*: the useless by-product that can be compared with the skull from which all spirit and life has departed. Such reservations, which take aim at the way in which Bloch falls short of the philosophical mark, are already present in a much earlier letter to Horkheimer, in which he regrets "*a certain irresponsibility in his style of philosophical improvisation*."[68] Furthermore, Adorno would later add "coldness" to the list of charges leveled against Bloch—no doubt the most damning word he could have used, indicating "the historical *and* psychological failure of the subject."[69]

"Residue," "irresponsibility," "coldness": such are the keywords of Adorno's critique. To what philosophical content do they point? At first glance, it is far from clear. With regard to the concept of possibility, it might still seem that Bloch's thought, his recovery of the ought from Hegel's criticisms, and especially the account of modality that he provides in his monumental *Principle of Hope* should have been of more interest to Adorno, rather than taking on the character of nearly useless by-products and symptoms of coldness. But here as elsewhere, "the decisive differences between philosophers are always to be found tucked away in nuances; and [those positions] which are most irreconcilable are [precisely those which are] similar, but which thrive on different centers."[70]

Bloch certainly provides the reader with a fascinating model of possibility in *The Principle of Hope*. Indeed, his approach is manifestly redemptive and points to a decisive break with existing actuality, from within its apparent confines.[71] More importantly, Bloch explicitly distinguishes between competing orders of formal and real possibility within the framework of a multiplicity of modal concepts, culminating in the anti-Hegelian "objectively-real possible," which is articulated on what he calls the "Front of the world process," that is, within the context of historical socialism.[72] The objectively-real possible is said to be

> a future-laden determinateness in the real itself. There is thus a real-partial conditionedness of the *object* that represents in the latter itself its real possibility. Human beings are the real possibility of everything which has become of them in their history and, above all, which can still become of them if their progress is not blocked. The human being is therefore a possibility that is not merely exhausted like an acorn in the closed actualization of the oak, but which has not yet ripened the whole of its internal and external conditions and condition-determinants.[73]

To complete this rapidly sketched portrait, we need merely add that, according to Bloch, the most radical and concrete "objectively-real possible" is defined by Marx, "the essential teacher" of the transformation of the world.[74] In this way, Bloch provides a kind of modal underpinning to the political front of socialism and thus shares with Lukács the notion of a very specific objective possibility that breaks with the familiar real possibilities of capitalism. As Bloch himself puts it, the road to the abolition of base deprivation "is and remains that of socialism, the practice of concrete utopia. Everything that is non-illusory, really-possible about hope-images leads to Marx. . . . Becoming happy was always what was sought after in dreams of a better life, and only Marxism can initiate it."[75]

It would be too simple to say that it is Bloch's *political* stance that is the core of the problem—although Adorno sees something "Stalinesque" at work in *The Principle of Hope* and is generally very critical of Bloch's attachment to historical socialism.[76] It would be more accurate to say that there is something about Bloch's *philosophical* stance, albeit as it relates to his Marxism, that Adorno finds untenable. The criticism can be formulated, at least initially, in terms of an exaggeration of which Adorno does not fully approve:

> He competes with the barker at the unforgotten annual fair, he screeches like an orchestrion in an empty restaurant waiting for customers. . . . His oral exaggeration confesses that it itself does not know what it is saying, that its truth is untruth when judged by the criterion of what exists. The narrator's self-congratulatory tone is inseparable from the substantive content [*Gehalt*] of his philoso-

phy, [that is,] the rescue of illusion. Bloch's utopia nestles into the empty space between illusion and what merely exists. Perhaps what he aims at, an experience that has not yet been honored by any experience, can only be represented by way of exaggeration. The theoretical rescue of illusion is how Bloch himself would defend his view.[77]

Now, as is often remarked, Adorno too makes frequent use of exaggeration. In fact, he thinks that it is essential to philosophical thinking: "All thinking is exaggeration, insofar as every thought worthy of the name goes beyond its confirmation by the given facts."[78] More particularly, Adorno's philosophy, like Bloch's, gives us to understand that merely factual reality is not a criterion by which we can measure utopian possibilities that aim to transcend it. A certain exaggeration, *Übertreibung*—thought driving itself beyond that which exists or is recognizable within reality—can sometimes reflect the meaning of this transcendence. To carry out such exaggeration successfully is precisely to rescue or redeem illusion: to go beyond that which merely *seems* immutable. To do so coherently and consistently is just to demonstrate the illusoriness of the "facts"— not in a gesture of disdain with respect to reality but to show us what might yet become of it.[79] To rescue illusion is to give a future to the insufficiency of the real. It is to find within indigent reality that which bears the traces of a redeemed actuality to come. It is, in other words, to outline "an experience that has not yet been honored by experience." In this way, Bloch quite legitimately tries to give voice to "something that would finally be different."[80]

However, Bloch's attempt to enact this rescue fails. To say that his thought nestles into the space *between* factual reality and illusion is to say that he remains on this side of illusion, that his transcendence remains *caught* on something illusory. Consequently, he ends up resembling the carnival barker or the orchestrion, both of which tout the value of something that does not live up to the appealing patter or the soulless music that gesture towards it. In short, there is exaggeration . . . and then there is exaggeration.

Adorno returns to this problem a little later in the same text. Bloch's "historico-philosophical impulse holds onto the perspective of subjective experience even where he has transcended it in the Hegelian sense," he says.[81] But Bloch also goes "beyond what forms the basis of his experience; in this respect, he is an idealist *malgré lui*."[82] What he means is that Bloch's theorization of redemptive possibility, although initially and legitimately developed out of the experience of the political ferment of the period around the Russian and German Revolutions, never again opened itself to living experience in the same way. Bloch never successfully repeated that initial moment of experience exceeding what experience had understood about itself until then (e.g., the worker's realization that subjective poverty is the socially mediated result of contingent—and thus changeable—relations of production). Concretely, Bloch insists on keeping faith with the historical socialist ideal and the conformity of existence to that essence, in spite of its near-total historical undoing and relapse into barbarism. If he is an idealist, then, it is because he prefers to insist on an essence to which existence does not or can no longer correspond rather than revise the alleged essence. To effect this revision, however, he would have to once again give free rein to the "primary experience" of the contradictions of given reality.[83] Primary experience: another name for the emphatic "experience [of that which] has not yet been honored by experience," that is, the experience that does not limit itself to existing concepts and that is therefore expressive of something that stands opposed to and seeks to transcend the difficulties that afflict ordinary experience.[84] Instead, Bloch tells us what primary experience *once was* and how it came to shape the front of the world process.

On Adorno's reading, then, Bloch's utopia, as well as the stories he tells, takes on the status of a "fairy tale." It is not that such fairy tales are without value, but perhaps only as a transcription of primary experience into fantasy or into the mode of memory and legend—in the manner of antique objects that have lost their luster.[85] It is the negativity and loss inherent in such transcriptions that Bloch does not adequately judge, according to one of Adorno's numerous left-handed remarks: "The person who tells fairy tales saves them from the fate of having outlived their time."[86]

By seeking refuge in such images and fragments of past experience, now become obsolete, Bloch deprives himself of the means to think the failure of the proletarian revolution that was taking place at the level of lived actuality. Consequently, he winds up telling

> stories [about suppressed forces winning the day] as though he were speaking about a foregone conclusion, presupposing the transformation of the world, so to speak, unconcerned about what has become of the revolution in the [last] thirty years . . . and what has happened to its concept and possibility under altered technological and social conditions. The absurdity of the status quo suffices for his verdict; there is no question as to what ought to happen.[87]

It is for this reason that Bloch comes under criticism first of all: in spite of his emphasis on recovering a real ought from history, he ends up lagging behind it, unable to understand that the moment of philosophy's revolutionary actualization was missed. All that remains is the exaggeration: the carnival barker, the cloying orchestrion. That history has often acted to restrict the domain of the possible is, of course, something of which Bloch was well aware, but his theory of blockage does not extend to what he himself takes to be objectively-really possible.[88]

Contrary to Bloch's "militant optimism,"[89] which keeps him committed to historical socialism even in the moment of its dilapidation, Adorno recommends that experience remain open—even to the possible ruin of that which was at one time its promise of salvation. Anything else is "coldness" and "irresponsibility." To Bloch's optimistic thinking, Adorno replies: "You should've thought more!"[90] In the absence of this "more" of thought, Bloch comes to designate another species of "correct consciousness": obstinate rectitude. Bloch, for his part, proudly lays claim to this rectitude, this "uprightness": "If the world collapses," he says, "I will stand firm amidst the falling rubble."[91] However, from Adorno's perspective, such rectitude is not the sign of hope's persistence. It is just the opposite: a theoretical pseudo-activity that denies the falling rubble.

However, the waning historical relevance of that rectitude is itself a moment of the historical process that theory can try to decipher and that it can therefore integrate it into its constructions. The "vantage point from which philosophy once appeared to be obsolete has itself become obsolete in the meantime; and in turn it would be ideological, i.e., dogmatic, were we not to acknowledge this fact from the outset."[92] Such moments of baffling defeat and unexpected blockage—that is, of non-identity—are the common spur to much-needed theory and future practice. But they are not decipherable once and for all in the form of a static image of redemption or reducible to the rectitude of any given theoretical stance. As such, Bloch's thought is the residue of the failure of the world process and so a symptom of the missed moment of philosophy's actualization rather than its theoretical consummation. In contrast, Adornian possibility includes the renewable attempt to understand how experience falls "beneath the level of history," as Marx puts it, not merely how a specific objectively-real possible can rise above it.[93]

Towards Blocked Possibility

The preceding remarks on Lukács and Bloch are meant to serve not just as criticism but also as signposts indicating the way towards Adorno's peculiar interest in blocked real possibilities, or—what amounts to the same—real, emphatic oughts. When Adorno says, for example, that "no one ought [*soll*] to go hungry anymore,"[94] he does not take that thought to express a vain hope; he means that society is at once a condition of possibility and impossibility of the elimination of needless suffering: we possess all the means required to end world hunger, yet it persists.[95] Such real oughts and the social riddles in which they are couched deserve to be better understood.

To relate this claim to what we have seen thus far, we might say that Adorno's thought is, first of all, an attempt to criticize the continuum of real actuality in the name of what *ought to be*. However, what ought to be in this sense does not lapse into mere Hegelian formal possibility—if by this is meant that which is entirely separated from real actuality and the problem of actualization. On the contrary, Adornian possibility resembles Lukácsian objective possibility, but only provided we turn the latter around, orienting it away from its static image of higher actuality towards the ought from which Lukács tries too hard to distinguish it.[96] Similarly, Adornian possibility resembles Bloch's objectively-real possible but only provided that we uncouple it from historical socialism and its manifest failures. In other words, it must be understood as a possibility whose reality is attested experientially. Yet such an attestation, even in its highest theoretical forms, is not enough if we are unable to adequately think such possibilities *as blocked* rather than celebrate the correctness or uprightness of the consciousness that thinks these forms. Primary experience is not the experience of the correct, but the experience of non-identity, which drives us not only beyond the false, but beyond the correct as well.

In other words, the opposite of wrong life is not correct life or consciousness but a life that would truly live, where this would mean, at the very least, a renewable capacity for primary experience. If the notion of correct consciousness is to participate in living actuality, then it can only be in the form of the distinction between "a consciousness that is appropriate to the current state of society and one that conceals it."[97] Wrong life is not set right in relation to any specific corrective but rather in the capacity to articulate the experience of real, non-formal oughts that respond to what ought not to be. It is in this sense that "dialectic is the ontology of the wrong state of things."[98] Or as Adorno elsewhere puts it, again focusing on the negativity of right life as distinct from correct consciousness, on the form of its possibility as distinct from any rectitude:

> The only thing that can perhaps be said is that right life today would consist in resistance to the forms of wrong life that have been seen through and critically dissected by the most progressive consciousness. Other than this negative directive no guidance can really be envisaged.[99]

"What would be different" begins with this negative directive: to experience the blocked real possibilities of liberation that connect wrong life to one that would be right.

However, the precision of this directive depends, in part, on the extent to which Adorno can respond to perhaps history's greatest critic of blocked possibilities—namely, Hegel, to whom we shall now turn.

CHAPTER 2

HEGEL'S FALLACY

Possibility and Actuality in Hegel and Adorno

> How could I pretend that the method that I follow in this system of logic, or rather the method that this system follows of itself, would not be capable of greater perfection, of greater elaboration of detail?
> —Hegel[1]

The Trick

In his 1960–1961 lecture course *Ontology and Dialectic,* Adorno pauses for a moment in his critique of Heidegger to comment on a flaw he sees in the Hegelian dialectic. He first says that Heideggerian being involves a "trick" whereby the conceptualization of the non-conceptual is ontologized.[2] The problem does not lie with the attempt to conceptualize something non-conceptual. For Adorno, philosophy can quite legitimately refer to the non-conceptual in the sense of that which is lacking an adequate concept—whether because some existing concept has proven insufficient or because something hitherto unrecognized presses experience and seeks adequate expression within it. That is, the "non-conceptual," on Adorno's use of the term, does not imply that what is at issue *cannot* in principle be conceptualized, only that it *has not* been conceptualized or appropriately conceptualized.[3] Indeed, this is just what he means by the "non-identical"; and the task or "interest" of philosophy—understood as dialectical thinking—is to make explicit such moments of experiential, conceptual non-identity or need: "What is most urgent, conceptually, is that which the concept fails to attain, what its mechanism of abstraction eliminates, or what is not already a case of the concept."[4] Whereas ordinary experience is characterized by its reliance on familiar concepts, primary experience registers something non-conceptual, non-identical.

At first glance, Heidegger seems to respond to the need to conceptualize the non-conceptual by laying claim to being (*Sein*) as the true essence or essential deployment (*Wesen, Wesung*) of beings—an essence that has been obstructed and distorted by misleading metaphysical concepts, including the metaphysical interpretation of essence itself, from which thinking must liberate itself. The truth of being is "that which, unthought, is worthy of thought."[5]

However, the central problem lies not with the tension between the conceptual and the non-conceptual (or unthought) but with Heidegger's treatment of it: the fact that the non-conceptual is taken to be something ontologically unique and supreme—the true essential deployment of being, in which human existence participates and to which it is called upon to conform in authenticity. Adorno asks: Can we legitimately reduce the non-conceptual to *being itself*, as Heidegger does? Should we not instead think the non-conceptual in a more open fashion, allowing it to retain something of its negativity? Should we not allow it to stand for *whatever* content relevantly resists existing concepts?

Chapter 4 returns to the question of the incompatibility of Heideggerian being and Adornian dialectical thinking. For now, we can simply say that for Adorno the ontologization of the relation of concepts to the non-conceptual means that the negative (i.e., the non-conceptual) is illegitimately rendered positive (i.e., given specific content in Heidegger's concept of being). This reduction of existence to a pre-determined essence, of the negative to the positive, is said to be one of Heidegger's "aporetic errors of reasoning."[6]

It is at this point that Adorno claims that Hegel is guilty of a similar offense:

> Naturally, I can't really take knowledge of Hegel for granted here, but, for those who've worked on Hegel, I'd like nevertheless to say that the issue arises in the transition from essence—or more precisely: in the transition from ground to existence in the second book of the *Logic*, where existence is likewise dissolved into pure thinking, by virtue of the fact that existence itself is taken to be conceptually mediated.[7]

Adorno goes on to say that Hegel's error amounts to a "sophism" and a "fallacy."[8] On a very general level, he clearly means to say that Hegel, like Heidegger, too quickly turns the non-conceptual into something conceptual or reduces something inherently negative to its positive form. And in Hegel's particular case, this general problem expresses itself in the way in which the transition from essence to existence is conceptually carried out.

However, from the outset, we should perhaps admit that Adorno is asking *quite a lot* of students whose knowledge of Hegel cannot be taken for granted; indeed, he is asking a lot of anyone, even of those whose knowledge of Hegel *can* be taken for granted. What exactly does he have in mind here, and what, specifically, is the aporetical error of reasoning, or "sophistical leap,"[9] of which he is accusing Hegel? It is not immediately clear what Adorno has in mind, so it is far from obvious how exactly the accusation applies or what the implications might be for dialectical thinking. The task here is to address the question "what fallacy?" and to draw out the philosophical aspects of Adorno's claim.

Hegel: Three Clues

Adorno gives us a few clues as to his meaning. The first is his own explanation of the charge, which is unfortunately very brief. Expanding slightly on his initial point, he says that both Hegel and Heidegger

> get into endless difficulties in the transition to beings out of absolutely posited thought or pure being, a difficulty that cannot in general be overcome by mobilizing some apparatus, such as the one we are presently considering [the logical passage from essence or ground to existence]. This is probably to be explained by the fact that even the most significant philosophical conceptions—and here I am really thinking of Hegel in particular—are, in the way they are individually worked out, shot through with sophisms, with fallacies.[10]

This passage may not clarify the exact nature of the fallacy, but Adorno seems to be saying that Hegel cannot simply help himself to some of his concepts and conclusions, as he seems to do. Moreover, the passage confirms on what aspect to focus our attention: the problem of how to theorize the emergence of actual states of affairs from out of their apparent conditions.

A second clue can be gleaned from a note, dating from 1959, which consolidates some of the preceding points (including the analogy with Heidegger):

> *Regarding ontology and dialectic.* In the transition to real ground, Hegel perfectly well saw the problem of the non-identical: it appears under the heading of "realization" [*Realisierung*]. But really he just "mediates" it. On this one issue, Kierkegaard was in the right against Hegel. The situation is quite analogous to [the ontological concept of] historicality or to the ontological privilege of the ontic in Heidegger: Hegel believes that the non-identical can be tidied away,

brought under identity, because it can only be determined conceptually. True, the non-identical is nothing immediate—it is mediated—that much we can grant him. But on precisely this point, Hegel was not dialectical *enough*. The non-identical is identical *and* non-identical; and the characteristic concept of the non-identical, which transforms it into something identical, or into something self-identical, has non-identity as its *content*. There can no more be identity without non-identity than there can be non-identity without identity. And yet identity is accorded ontological priority within the totality. Such immanent critique is the only adequate critique of Hegel. The absolute system is at the same time its own negation.[11]

Much remains to be clarified, but this passage provides further detail and corroboration. The non-conceptual or non-identical should not be understood solely according to its conceptual determinability or as a mere incitement to revise our conceptual assumptions. It cannot be "tidied away" by mediation or reduced to a mere transitory moment in the movement towards conceptual identity and totality. Thus, in his neglect of the non-identical, Hegel commits an error that forms the basis for an immanent critique of his thought—and the eventual collapse of systematic totality. If the non-identical *persists* in some way, then the system will have failed to achieve its goal.

A third clue is to be found in the "Skoteinos" essay from *Hegel: Three Studies,* where Adorno makes another accusation of fallacy.[12] What he says there corresponds quite neatly to the passages from the *Ontology and Dialectic* lecture course:

> For all his emphasis on negativity and diremption, Hegel knows non-identity only from the side that faces identity, knows it only as an instrument of identity. . . . As in a gigantic credit system, every individual is indebted to others—non-identical—and yet the whole is supposed to be free of debt—identical. This is where the idealist dialectic commits its fallacy. It says, with pathos: non-identity. Non-identity ought to be determined on its own terms as something heterogeneous. However, by determining it [as it does], the dialectic imagines itself to have gone beyond non-identity and to be assured of absolute identity. What is non-identical and unknown might well become identical in being known; and in its conceptualization, the non-conceptual might well become the concept of the non-identical. But the non-identical itself does not simply become a concept by virtue of such reflection; it remains the substantive content [*Gehalt*] of the

concept, distinct from it. There is no transition to existence out of the logical movement of concepts.[13]

Once again, unfortunately, Adorno does not quite name the fallacy committed by Hegel, but he does underscore the fact that there is an illegitimate attempt undertaken in Hegel's thought to sublate the difference between essence and existence, or between non-identity and identity, in the name of their ultimate identity. It also adds a few elements. Hegel acknowledges the non-identical only in the moment of its submission to a new conceptual identity rather than in the moment of its resistance. We can perhaps understand why, from the standpoint of the system, Hegel would say that the heterogeneity of the non-identical is entirely dissolved, without essential remainder. He thinks, for example, that the difference in standpoint or the socially mediated non-identity between Antigone and Creon is entirely sublated in the act of forgiveness of which they were structurally (ethically) incapable; and this incapacity is itself retrospectively overcome from the standpoint of the historical emergence of a rightly conceived forgiveness: "The wounds of spirit heal and leave no scars behind."[14] In other words, what had to be expressed, that which could not be expressed at a previous stage, comes to its adequate expression in the context of the whole and in the completion of the system, which accounts for the basic forms of all such possible tensions. For Adorno, however, such dissolutions of the non-identical into a rational history of the world are clearly problematic.

This is all very characteristic of Adorno's reading of Hegel. Yet it is still far from obvious how this should be spelled out or how the passage from essence to existence is related to the non-conceptual or the non-identical. Thus, if we want to understand Hegel's fallacy, and so the particularity of Adorno's own advanced version of dialectical thinking, then we shall have to consider some specific examples of the problem to which he is alluding. Happily, he tells us roughly where in Hegel we need to begin to look: in the transition from ground to existence.

From Essence to Existence

Rolf Tiedemann suggests that the passage that Adorno has in mind is the following, from the *Science of Logic:*

> *When all the conditions of a fact* [Sache] *are at hand,* the fact steps into existence.

The fact *is, before it exists concretely;* it is, first, as *essence* or as unconditioned; second, it has immediate existence or is determined, and this in the twofold manner just considered, on the one hand in its conditions and on the other in its ground. . . . If, therefore, all the conditions of the fact are at hand, that is, if the totality of the fact is posited as a groundless immediate, then this scattered manifold *internalizes* itself [erinnert *sich*].—The whole fact must be there, within its conditions, or all the conditions must belong to its concrete existence; for *all* of them constitute the reflection of the fact. Or again, immediate existence, since it is condition, is determined by form; its determinations are therefore determinations of reflection and with the positing of one the rest also are essentially posited.[15]

This passage recapitulates what Hegel shows in the immediately preceding chapters and encapsulates the true content of ground, namely, the appearance of something from out of its conditions.

As we shall come to see, Adorno's worry relates to what becomes of essence in its transition to existence or, to put it otherwise, the status of real possibility in its relation to actuality. However, before proceeding, Hegel's language deserves a brief explanation.

Ground—the basis or reason for some "fact" (*Sache,* a thing, a situation, a concept, or whatever is at issue)—is a developed determination of essence or a form that essence metaphysically assumes in relation to appearance. Passing over the more preliminary and formal determinations of ground, what this means is that facts are always grounded, referred to a reason that explains them and manifests itself in the coming together of their real conditions. If something happens, it happens for a reason—this is its ground: I eat *because* I am hungry; hunger is thereby the ground of eating and of my eventual satisfaction.[16] But the ground has to take shape in reality because, while I may feel a pang of hunger, neither the pang nor the hunger it signals actually satisfies the need that is the ground of the pang. *Real conditions* are required: the bread that I eat, not merely the hunger (as mere ground), is the condition of my satisfaction. In this way the ground (hunger) and the conditions of its satisfaction (bread) presuppose each other, as Hegel puts it, in the sense that each requires the other for them to lead to my satisfaction. Hunger aims at bread because bread contains the possibility of its satisfaction.

This process can involve any number of factors that may not be internally related to one another at all. Ground may refer to several independent and even mutually indifferent conditions, such as the ingredients that make up the bread that I eat. For example, in and of themselves, water, yeast, salt, and flour—and the grain from which the flour is milled, as well as the warmth, light, and nutrients that the grain requires to grow, and so on—are just various things, but in relation to a ground (e.g., my hunger), they are gathered up or "internalize themselves" into the bread that satisfies me, that leads to the fact of my satisfaction.

Consequently, just as ground finds expression only within the self-gathering of conditions, my satisfaction is not some additional external thing but a kind of "prospective" fact that animates the relation of ground to conditions, even before satisfaction emerges as a "resulting" fact. That which is grounded (my state of satisfaction) participates anticipatorily in organizing the conditions and is, in that sense, also presupposed and not merely a result. In making bread, I *aim* for satisfaction.

For all of these reasons, the relation of condition to ground is considered a gathering of diverse factors into ground, a "foundering to ground" (*Zugrundegehen*), wherein each loses its particularity in the becoming of some state of affairs.[17] This is how facts come into being. In general, *nihil est sine ratione*.[18] Or to phrase the idea dialectically, every fact is mediated—nothing is given in pure immediacy. Thus, every fact is the result of the interrelatedness of the ground and conditions that it organizes in the process of its own emergence.

The Tautological Movement of the Fact to Itself

On the basis of the preceding, we are perhaps better situated to understand the passage from ground to existence, centering on the assertion that "*when all the conditions of a fact are at hand,* the fact steps into concrete existence."[19] When water, yeast, salt, and flour come together in the bread that I eat, then my hunger will be satisfied.

However, Hegel's assertion may strike us as slightly odd. True, on the one hand, it seems to be an important interim conclusion to a very long chain of reasoning deployed in the Doctrine of Essence; on the other hand, it would seem to be an utter platitude: it really goes without saying that for something to obtain, all the conditions of its obtaining must obtain. Is that *all* we have learned from the overwhelming and agonizingly complex analyses that precede this passage? Might Adorno's accusation of "fallacy" somehow involve the platitudinous or tautological character of this assertion? This may seem likely. Hegel even admits the tautology: The "coming forth [of the fact] is . . . the tautological movement of the fact to itself: its mediation through the conditions and through the ground is the disappearing of both of these."[20] It would seem that we are merely moving in a circle of (prospective) fact to (resulting) fact and round and round again, as various facts become the conditions of realization of further facts. As Kierkegaard sarcastically puts it: Is Hegel's method not just "a brilliant tautology that puts itself at the service of scientific superstition with many signs and wonderful deeds"?[21] (We may also recall that Adorno mentions that Kierkegaard is in the right against Hegel on the issue of the mediation.)

While some of Hegel's many detractors may wish to take the easy way out at this juncture, it has nevertheless to be acknowledged that the end and the beginning of the trajectory are far from *obviously* or *trivially* identical. That is, the identity of prospective and resulting facts or of ground-conditions and existence may well be what is at issue, but to the extent that it *has to be demonstrated,* then there is certainly some important argumentative work to be done. Thus, while apparently platitudinous assertions can indeed be frustrating, we would have to show that the terms in play here are, in fact, flatly or viciously tautological in order to claim that the assertion of the fact's concrete coming into existence is empty.

Indeed, Hegel himself says that tautologies suffer from "tediousness," that is, they offer no real novelty or possibility of forwards movement.[22] Consequently, it seems unlikely that Adorno would be accusing Hegel of an error involving the very tautology to which Hegel himself draws attention and claims to dissipate in the complex context that establishes the identity of the terms in play. On Hegel's view, the self-proclaimed tautology is defused once we understand the nature of the identity: "Now, insofar as ground and grounded have diverse content, the ground-relation has ceased to be a formal one; the turning back to the ground and the procession forwards from ground to posited is no longer a tautology; the *ground* is realized."[23]

In short, there is nothing trivially self-identical about the relation of ground to existence as mediated through real conditions. Yet here again, we encounter the realization that seems to bother Adorno ("the ground is realized")—although, frustratingly, it is still not clear exactly why this is a problem. Consequently, at this stage of the unfolding of the enigma of Hegel's fallacy, we are once again left to puzzle over the (supposedly glaring) problem that Adorno sees in the transition from ground to existence. We need more to go on.

The Troublesome "All"

Regarding "realization," Hegel evidently means to say that we can know that the fact has or will come into *concrete existence* from the givenness of its conditions: to be *real* means to be expressed in an existing state of affairs and not to be merely latent therein. And from the context and Hegel's use of the word "all," we know we are dealing with *necessary and sufficient* conditions: "*When* all *the conditions of a fact are at hand,* the fact steps into concrete existence." Hegel underscores this in the final transition from ground to existence: "The whole fact must be there, within its conditions, or all the conditions belong to its concrete existence; for *all* of them constitute the reflection of the fact."[24] In other words, only a *totality* of relevant conditions is sufficient for a fact's appearance—a totality from which the fact then necessarily emerges.

The "all" that Hegel mentions several times and emphasizes twice in this passage should perhaps give us reason to pause. What real content corresponds to this vaguely and formally defined totality of conditions? Might it be this that catches Adorno's critical eye?

The problem in this case might be construed as follows. It is evident that if a fact does not obtain, then its conditions did not obtain. But how do things stand if some *purported* totality of conditions does *not* produce its corresponding fact? Here the problem is that of the relation between the real totality and the purported totality: from whose standpoint is the "all" accessible? Such questions arise throughout Adorno's writings. In fact, he takes great interest in precisely those situations in which some apparently real possibility or set of conditions fails to produce what it ought to have produced or was expected to produce, as the famous first line of the introduction to *Negative Dialectic* attests: "Philosophy, which once seemed obsolete, lives on because the moment of its actualization was missed."[25] What retains Adorno's attention here is just the idea that the conditions for the revolutionary actualization of philosophy were said to be at hand but did not produce the imagined outcome: theory-infused praxis did not bring about universal emancipation. Philosophy is thereby left to puzzle over the riddle of its non-actualization and to reflect on its future possibility. Adorno frequently mentions related examples of missed opportunities, such as the apparent impossibility of ensuring universal access to food, shelter, and education in an age where the conditions—that is, the forces of production—are manifestly available and sufficient for achieving these goals.[26] Such conditions *ought* perhaps to give rise to the satisfaction of material and intellectual needs, in an emphatic sense that has yet to be made explicit, but actuality is such that they have not given rise to that which they make possible. Indeed, given existing forces of production, "no one ought to go hungry anymore"—yet people do.

Hegel's "all" dissipates such worries with a logical wave of the hand: that someone should presume to specify the determinate and exhaustive content of the totality of conditions for some fact is quite possible, but the indeterminate "all" forever has the upper hand. That some state of affairs should fail to emerge from its *purported* conditions is no more than an instance of the one-sidedness of consciousness and so more or less a matter of indifference to philosophy. Metaphysically speaking, *all* conditions are required, *whatever they may be.* Formulated in this way, Hegel's claim is unassailable. So much the worse for those who claim to know the conditions should things not turn out as expected. The possibility of a subjective, epistemic deficit (e.g., ignorance or a misapprehension of the real situation) is simply not relevant to the metaphysical concerns at issue here. Water, yeast, salt, flour, and so on are required to make a certain kind of bread. If bread on the table is not the result, then that is not the fault of the metaphysics of ground and existence.

Nevertheless, we might well imagine that what bothers Adorno here is the entirely formal notion of a totality of conditions, which guarantees the emergence of the fact but is entirely idle when we find ourselves in the concrete situation of trying—and failing—to actualize a liberation on the basis of existing conditions. More specifically, it may well be a question, for Adorno, of the philosophical perspective we should adopt in relation to the totality and more specifically in relation to what we take to be the corollaries and consequences of Hegel's unassailable claim regarding the emergence of existing facts from their real conditions.

Conflagration of the Possible

The issue as it currently stands can be restated as follows: The totality of existing conditions leaves no room for facts other than those produced by those conditions. That all conditions are required, whatever they may be, just means that, outside an existing totality of conditions, facts are not facts but just vain fantasies. Although we can well imagine utopian futures, what only ought to exist has no bearing or influence on the true structure of total actuality. Hegel's frequent critique of the ought, already presented in the previous chapter, makes this clear: "If one constructs a world *as it ought to be,* then it certainly has an existence, but only within one's opinions—a pliant medium in which the imagination can construct anything it pleases."[27]

We can now perhaps begin to see that Hegel's view relies on quite specific notions of possibility that are directly relevant to Adorno's critique. In particular, the notion of a totality of existing conditions—real possibilities—that excludes certain non-actual facts from consideration refers us directly to a modal reworking of the issues previously discussed. Moreover, there is no need to impose modality on the problem from without, since Hegel himself sees the transition from ground to existence as having necessarily to take on modal form—this is precisely how ground and conditions are further developed from out of their conceptual deficiencies.

As Hegel points out, one central problem with the notion of ground is that grounds are never lacking: we can come up with a reason for practically anything (rationalizations, twenty-twenty hindsight, making excuses, and so on). With pedants and sophists in mind, he says, "In our time, rich as we are in reflection, and given to empty ratiocination, someone who does not know how to advance a good ground for anything whatever, even for the worst and most perverse views, cannot have come far."[28] However, once ground is provided with *real* content (i.e., rooted in *real* states of affairs), it yields to the dialectic of actuality and possibility.

Thus, in the section on "Actuality" in the *Science of Logic,* Hegel returns to the question of concrete coming-into-existence, now treated in explicitly modal terms:

> When all the conditions of a fact are completely present, the fact steps into actuality; the completeness of the conditions is the totality as being in the content, and the *fact* is *itself* this content determined as being equally actual and possible. In the sphere of the conditioned ground, the conditions have the form (that is, the ground or the reflection that stands on its own) *outside them*, and it is this form that makes them moments of the fact and elicits concrete existence *in them*. Here, on the contrary, the immediate actuality is not determined to be a condition by virtue of a presupposing reflection; rather, it is posited that immediate actuality is itself possibility.[29]

The advantage of this way of putting things, as Hegel notes, is that we do not have to account for which ground is responsible for gathering up externally indifferent conditions into a totality or for when or how it does so. Instead, actuality is shown to be dialectically identical to possibility, such that the *reality* of real possibility is just *the same reality* as that of existing actuality. The concept of ground is thereby transformed into an active and modally charged interrelation and alternation of conditions and facts. More precisely, actual facts are not *merely* facts; as a totality, they also constitute a *"complete circle of conditions"*[30]—the whole set of real possibilities—for further facts. And just as the transition from ground to existence involved necessity ("the whole fact must be there, within its conditions"), so too does the dialectical identity of actuality and possibility: "What is really possible can no longer be otherwise; under the given conditions and circumstances, nothing else can follow. Real possibility and necessity are, therefore, only *apparently* distinguished."[31] In short, real possibilities are just actual facts considered as the necessary and sufficient conditions for something. Once again, Hegel seems to be on solid ground, for it is difficult to see how Adorno could object to the way in which possibility and actuality are dialectically interrelated.

However, conversely, Hegel also thinks that, as the fact emerges, real possibility is entirely consumed in its actualization: immediate actuality, understood as a totality of real possibilities, is "destined" to be "consumed" and to "disappear."[32] Or in more technical language:

> [Actuality, understood as the] movement of self-sublating real possibility thus produces *the same moments that are already present,* but each as it comes to be out of the other. In its negative character, then, this movement is not even a *transition* but rather a *mutual dissolution of different moments in their own coming-together.*—In formal possibility, if something was possible, then an *other* than it, not *itself,* was also possible. Real possibility no longer has *such an other* over against it, for it is real insofar as it is itself also actuality. Therefore, as its *immediate concrete existence, the circle of conditions,* sublates itself, it makes itself into the *in-itselfness* that it already is, namely, the in-itself of an other. And conversely, since its moment of in-itselfness thereby sublates itself at the same time, it becomes actuality, hence the moment which it likewise already is.[33]

It would seem, then, that there is a price to be paid for the metaphysical transition from possibility to actuality. Real possibilities do not linger within actuality. (We might think of the way in which the oak "uses up" the acorn from which it emerges and that serves, among other conditions, as its real possibility.) Either real possibilities are coextensive with immediate actuality and are consumed in the emergence of their corresponding facts, or they are relegated to the status of merely formal possibilities. Simply put, there can be no "excess" or unactualizable real possibilities, no oughts that can be considered real because all real possibilities are used up in the actualization of the fact or, more generally, of total actuality itself.

This claim is made in various ways in Hegel's writings but perhaps nowhere more concisely than in the dictum that "essence must appear,"[34] which, among other things, is a way of saying that any purported essence bereft of being or existence—an *ineffectual* essence—is not an essence at all but rather a mere subjective representation or opinion. We can certainly err in our assessment of the determinate content of what is actual, but what is *truly and essentially* actual will necessarily find expression in reality: "What is actual *can act;* something announces its actuality *by what it produces.*"[35] Hegel also phrases this thought more affirmatively and more specifically in terms of ground and existence, that is, precisely those terms that Adorno finds problematic. In the *Propaedeutic,* for example, he writes: "On account of the identity of ground and existence, there is nothing in the appearance that is not in the essence and, conversely, nothing in the essence that is not in the appearance."[36] And in the *Science of Logic* he adds a crowning touch: While the possible should be classified under the general heading of essence, any possibility that does not express itself in being or existence "has no truth" and is, in fact, an "impossibility":

> Minus the ought [that characterizes impotent possibility], possibility is *essentiality* as such; but the absolute form entails this: that minus being, essence itself is only a moment that has no truth. [Formal] possibility is this *mere* essentiality, but *so posited* as to be only a moment that does not conform to the absolute form. It is the in-itself, determined only as something *posited* or, equally, as *not being in itself.*—Inwardly, possibility is therefore contradiction, or it is *impossibility.*[37]

In short, all lingering, unactualized possibilities—and a fortiori any oughts that diverge from actuality—are, in fact, tantamount to impossibilities devoid of truth and reality. Such is Hegel's actualism.[38]

Hegel's Double Error: Marx's Contribution

A slight shift in perspective may yet be needed to bring Adorno's criticism fully into view. From the claim that "when *all conditions* are present, the fact *must* become actual," we have arrived at a second claim, which Hegel apparently considers to be a corollary of the first: All real possibilities are "consumed" in the actualization of the fact and, indeed, of actuality itself qua totality. Since "there is nothing in the appearance that is not in the essence and, conversely, nothing in the essence that is not in the appearance," then there is simply no place in Hegel's metaphysics for real possibilities that remain unactualized. *There are no real oughts.* This leads to a crucial reframing of the original clue regarding the transition from essence or ground to existence. The problem is *not* that all conditions are required for something to come about—that goes without saying. It is that Hegel's view of actuality qua totality shunts all non-actualized possibilities into the category of formal possibility. It is this that forms the basis for Adorno's accusation of fallacy.

To phrase the issue in social terms, Adorno's worry is that the transition to actuality out of possibility, as Hegel sees it, provides metaphysical legitimation to defective social reality, since, metaphysically speaking, things simply could not have been otherwise. Not having bread to eat, even though its conditions are plentiful today, is not the expression of an ought but of a real state of affairs that was produced out of its necessary and sufficient conditions. And while this is not to say that things could not be different in the future, that we should not strive to make them different, or that we should not demand reform where reform is needed, Hegel's understanding of the necessary transition from ground to existence—or from real possibility to actuality—means that present actuality is the only possible result of a linear development of prior actuality; and for him, this means that there is no meaningful gap between "is" and "ought":

> For it is not what is that makes us rage and suffer, but the fact that things are not as they ought to be. But if we recognize that things are as they must be, i.e., that it is not arbitrariness and chance that make them what they are, then we also recognize that things are as they ought to be.[39]

And if this is so, then it is because Hegel thinks that history contains no unactualized real possibilities, that it is rather "a system of events that is ruled by a single spirit,"[40] "all for the good of a single enterprise."[41]

Against this view, Adorno will take specific aim at the notion of a "single spirit" and the corresponding reduction of "ought" to "is" (or, what amounts to the same, the claim that any independent content that the ought may have is necessarily confined to the realm of formal possibility). However, in order to get a clearer picture of Adorno's target in Hegel's thought, we shall have to further explore its sources and motivations.

In relation to the question of how Hegel's categories and dialectical transitions affect—or not—human needs and suffering, Adorno must, at some level, have been thinking of Marx's 1843–1844 criticisms of Hegel, for they come strikingly close to the issues at hand, especially in those passages that deal with Hegel's flawed view of actualization and historical realization. Indeed, in this regard, Marx speaks of Hegel's "double error."[42]

Marx describes the error in a number of ways, but it can be summarized relatively briefly. On the one hand, Hegel's philosophy conceptually *sanctifies* historical institutions by enshrining them as essential determinations of pure thought and its reflection in historical actuality. Marx refers to this as Hegel's "*false* positivism."[43] On the other hand, and correspondingly, while the shapes of historical consciousness presented by Hegel do in fact succeed in grasping something essential—the power of dialectical critique—they also *block* the return to living consciousness and material needs that would allow us to develop and truly actualize the critical potential that lies latent in Hegel's thought. This is what Marx refers to as Hegel's "merely *apparent* criticism."[44]

The two branches of this double error can also be traced back to their common root. Essentially, Hegel's philosophy succumbs to the fundamental problem of religious thinking: it defends "the *fantastic actualization* of the human essence because the *human essence* has attained no true actuality."[45] Consequently, "the sublation of religion as the *illusory* happiness of the people is a demand for their *actual* happiness."[46] The same holds true of philosophy insofar as its description of human actualization shows itself to be incomplete. In other words, to the extent that an *actualizable* true happiness is denied us by a philosophy that reduces history and historical shapes of consciousness to inadequate categories and stunted forms of historical actualization, it remains inextricably bound up with religious abstraction and must therefore be overcome. Happiness must be actualized historically, not merely in a "thought-image that abstracts away from *actual human beings*."[47] These ideas, familiar though they may be, should be spelled out a little more in order to draw out their specific connection with the modal aspect of Adorno's argument.

What is of interest in the present context is that Marx's critique of Hegel turns on the question of a failed or merely conceptual actualization. While Hegel claims that human beings can actualize "the end of reason," Marx will say that this actualization does not in fact occur as promised in bourgeois civil society. We are instead bound to and by laws and institutions that perpetuate injustices. We remain estranged when we should be most at home in the world. It is at this point that "all the illusions of speculation" come to the fore.[48]

One of the most central of these illusions derives from a gap that Marx perceives between Hegel's apparently essential social categories and what we are *now capable* of within history. In other words, Marx perceives a modal "surplus," as it were, that is now historically available but that is immediately recuperated or suppressed by the social perpetuation and philosophical sanctioning of the existing structures of bourgeois civil society. This gap or modal surplus is first expressed in Marx's astonishment that the historical laws and institutions of bourgeois civil society should correspond, on Hegel's view, with human self-actualization *as such* rather than being shameful and "beneath the level of history."[49] Thus, contrary to what Hegel claims, Marx will say that

> reason is at home in unreason as unreason. The human being who has recognized that they are leading an outwardly alienated [*entäußertes*] life in politics, law, etc., is [nevertheless] leading their true human life in this outwardly alienated life as such. Self-affirmation or self-confirmation in *contradiction* with itself—in contradiction both with the knowledge and essence of the object—is thus [presented in Hegel as] true *knowledge* and *life*.
>
> There can therefore no longer be any question about an act of accommodation on Hegel's part in relation to religion, the state, etc., since this lie is the lie of his principle.[50]

According to Marx, then, there is a tension—and, indeed, a contradiction—at work in the very principle of Hegel's view of self- and species-actualization: the social forms that are said to make them possible are, in fact, making them impossible: "Workers become all the poorer the more wealth they produce, the more production increases in power and size."[51]

The substantive content of this contradiction can be presented rather straightforwardly. For Marx, we have now reached a stage in the historical development of the forces of production at which it is possible to overcome the illusory necessity of certain ways of thinking and being, including religious postponements of human happiness and the perpetuation of private property. More concretely, the merely real relations of production act as pseudo-necessary fetters on the actual forces of production.[52] As long as human self-affirmation limits itself to such relations, as though they were a point of culmination in human history rather than a stage in its development, it is in contradiction with itself, with what we are now historically and technically capable of achieving, as compared with what would have been impossible in the past. This historically and theoretically mediated modal surplus is what Marx, true to Hegel's vocabulary if not his conclusions, calls our "essence," which exceeds that which has existed hitherto and which gives us something to do and to be in history. Until such time that this essence is concretely expressed, the surplus possibility of human actualization will remain the modal equivalent of the surplus value surreptitiously expropriated by the capitalist.

In contrast, Hegel seems to overcome historical forms such as religion and private property, but only within *thinking,* that is, by making them relative determinations within a greater whole. Insofar as they are sublated, it is only as *objects of knowledge,* not in their actuality, which Hegel regards as essential to the self-actualization of human existence. They are thereby "left standing," as Marx puts it.[53] The question is why these forms should persist if they perpetuate a suffering that has since become needless. What is it about religion and private property that makes Hegel enshrine them as he does? Why does he not say of them what he says of slavery, namely, that it occurs "in a world in which a wrong is still right"?[54] It is not that Marx thinks that Hegel does not give us the means to answer such questions; it is that Hegel does not seem to consider the possibility of posing them in relation to bourgeois civil society. The task is therefore to think the possibility of an actualization *beyond* the forms of actualization that Hegel describes and to which he limits himself (and once again, the modal charge of Marx's language should not be ignored):

> Atheism and communism are no flight, no abstraction; they are not a loss of the objective world produced by human beings, of the objectivity born of our essential powers; they are no return in poverty to unnatural, undeveloped simplicity. On the contrary, they are much rather the actual becoming, the actualization of our essence and of our essence as actual—an actualization that has emerged as actual for human beings [*das wirkliche Werden, die wirklich für den Menschen gewordne Verwirklichung seines Wesens und seines Wesens als eines wirklichen*].[55]

Thus, for Marx, Hegel's shapes of consciousness and structures of bourgeois ethical life effectively *hinder* the emergence and actualization of ulterior social forms. On this basis, Hegel *ought* to have gone further, to have offered more critical purchase on the sublation of estrangement in its most contemporary forms. Marx's point therefore has to do with the way in which philosophical and social conceptions that lay claim to universality and necessity can conceal and stifle real but nascent social possibilities of the progress of humanity (which he summarizes under the heading "essence"). In general, the satisfaction of material needs may indeed be contingent to the extent that there can be no metaphysical guarantee of satisfaction, but at a time in history when the forces of production are able to provide far more satisfaction than they in fact provide, it is irrational to continue to accept a postponement of happiness rather than consider that bourgeois relations of production have become a means of suppressing the elimination, now become possible, of senseless suffering. The forces of production have now become non-identical with the relations of production. But in this regard, what is most important for present purposes is the modal aspect of Marx's argument. Indeed, *not* to understand the modal aspect would entail not understanding the terms of his critique. This aspect comes out in his insistent use of the language of actualization and of the coming into being of social potentialities. More specifically, it is a question of criticizing the philosophical structures and concepts by which a new actualization—an actualization now become possible—is deferred, defused, delayed, and even denied.

This resonates well with Adorno's worries about the transition to existence from ground or essence. Their common point is this: Hegel erroneously substitutes wrong life for one that could yet be right, an "illusory essence" for the "true essence" that we have now developed for ourselves within history:

> By grasping the *positive* meaning of self-related negation—albeit once again in estranged fashion—Hegel grasps the human being's self-estrangement, the alienated externalization of our essence, our objective privation, and our deactualization [*Entwirklichung*] as self-production, an expression of essence, objectification, and actualization, [respectively].[56]

This series of contrasts is remarkable, culminating in a thwarting of actualization that Marx calls "deactualization," an unusual modal concept that suggests an *undoing* of what actuality would otherwise express—an undoing that here takes the form of the philosophical and social mechanisms by which we lose sight of social potentialities, developed within history, but only negatively expressed therein, for example, in the "fettered" forces of production.[57]

While Hegel readily admits that ethical life may sometimes provoke shocking and destabilizing experiences in which something hitherto hidden comes to expression (e.g., in the Reign of Terror or in the unintentional shockwaves that Antigone unleashes that lead to the destruction of Greek ethical life), there is also a counter-tendency, elevated to metaphysical status in Hegel, to preserve bourgeois civil society, effectively shielding it from the very criticisms on the basis of which ethical life derives its power to evolve. Hegel thereby blocks the possibility of what would be different: the constitution of a society in which the persistence of socially unnecessary suffering, the fettering of the forces of production, and the postponement of happiness would be abolished. To this extent, he perpetuates the antagonisms that Marx names instead of treating them explicitly and dialectically. This is the substance of the double error that Marx diagnoses: the false positivism of existing practices, coupled with the suppression of the critical potential of thinking, which would empower it to name the possibility of a better world.

Strands of Possibility

If we now look at Marx's argument from the standpoint of Adorno's accusation of fallacy, it is most interesting not on the usual questions of humanism, atheism, or communism, or even on the question of the institutions of bourgeois civil society, but rather on the question of the relation of actuality to possibility. In this regard, Marx's conclusions are the concrete expression of the highly philosophical critique that they presuppose. (That they also presuppose other factors goes without saying.) On Marx's account, Hegel's concept of actualization fails to the extent that it finds its point of culmination and completion in forms of consciousness and of society that are "beneath" the level of "an actualization that has emerged as actual for human beings." Hegel's very "principle" is a "lie" to the extent that a gap has opened up between the prior achievements of bourgeois civil society and what we can yet achieve, based on what is now *at work* in society and which Marx understands in terms of proletarian consciousness and the unfettering of the forces of production. However, for this truly to be a problem of *principle,* the error cannot lie with Hegel's personal political views (however construed) nor with dialectical thinking as such since Marx lays claim to its critical potential. What, then, is the principle to which

Marx refers? It is Hegel's modal principle of actualization, which Adorno too considers defective.

At this stage, we need merely recall the metaphysical relation of essence to existence as it plays itself out in the dialectic of possibility and actuality. As we saw previously, Hegel's theory of actuality commits him to the view that real possibility "is destined to be sublated, i.e., to be the possibility of an other"[58]— of a new actuality. Accordingly, there can be no such thing as a real possibility that does not, qua real, become actual. Real possibilities simply "disappear,"[59] or are "used up" and "consumed,"[60] within the process of actuality.

When framed in terms of Hegel's metaphysics, the philosophical principle at which Marx takes aim is clearly the reduction of real possibility to the domain of those which are actualized, relegating those which remain in abeyance, including oughts, to the status of merely formal possibilities. Actuality is total in that no real possibilities are excluded from it. However, this totality is shown to be false,[61] to the extent that the historically new possibility of the elimination of socially unnecessary suffering and domination is socially *deactualized* or shunted into mere formal possibility by the relations of production and by Hegel's social and metaphysical categories, which both take on the appearance of necessity. To put it more starkly, real possibility is conflated with actuality at the level of metaphysical principles so that there can be no non-formal remainder. Marx thus thinks that this principle amounts to a denial or rejection of an actually developed essence.[62]

Returning now to Adorno, we can say that he essentially takes over from Marx this notion of the "lie of the principle" and further develops it both modally and in terms of what he calls the non-identical. He also attempts to sidestep a weakness in Marx's position. A few things are worth pointing out.

First, Adorno explicitly denounces the reduction of possibility to actuality, which he takes, like Marx, to mean the relegation of real possibilities of liberation to the status of merely formal possibilities:

> The critical yardstick that allows reason and indeed compels and obliges reason to oppose the superior strength of the course of the world is always the fact that in every situation there is a concrete possibility of doing things differently. This possibility is present and sufficiently developed and does not need to be inflated into an abstract utopia that then automatically provokes a petulant objection to the effect that it will not work, it will never work. What you can see here is one of the most disastrous consequences of idealist historical constructions. By

equating spirit with everything that is actual, possibility and actuality are rendered identical. It is not only that what is actual is made equal with spirit, but
rather also that spirit is made equal with actuality. The tension between the two
is eliminated, thereby quashing the function of spirit as a critical authority.[63]

In short, contrary to Hegel's modal typology, we cannot simply assume that
real possibility and actuality are dialectically identical. It is one thing to say
that actuality is informed by spirit—for example, that historical forms of consciousness continue to find expression in actuality—for at least this still leaves
room for a critical surplus of spirit over actuality; but it is quite another to
suggest that spirit, the totality of real possibilities that animate unfolding actuality, is somehow *exhausted* in given actuality, is identical with it. Whereas
Hegel says that "there is nothing in the appearance that is not in the essence
and, conversely, nothing in the essence that is not in the appearance,"[64] Marx
and Adorno say that some real possibilities of liberation are suppressed not just
by the apparent necessity of existing laws and institutions but also by the very
principle of actualization that philosophically informs them—the all-too-strict
distinction between merely formal possibilities and the real possibilities that
are supposed to be entirely consumed in emergent actuality. It is on this point
that "Hegel was not dialectical *enough.*"[65]

Second, in a gesture that begins to separate Adorno from Marx, rather than
look on history as having reached a necessary point of culmination and crisis in
bourgeois civil society, Adorno urges us (alluding to Benjamin along the way) to
regard history as a whole from the standpoint of its *multiple* failures and, more
specifically, from the standpoint of its multiple missed opportunities or deactualized moments of possible liberation: "In every situation there is a concrete possibility of doing things differently."[66] One might imagine that what Adorno means
here is that we should not take for granted that a given historical outcome was
necessary, simply because that is what actually happened. But that would be to
misunderstand his target, which is *not* the irrefutable claim that "when all the
conditions of a fact are completely present, the fact steps into actuality." Rather,
the target is the metaphysical assurance with which we speak of the abstraction
or unreality of unactualized possibilities—and not just those that Marx says have
only recently become available to us. Adorno makes this clear: "The entire structure of history will only be free of the single-stranded view [*Einsträhnigkeit*] that
is present in Hegelian and Marxian doctrine once we refuse to accept the dictum
that [a rational organization of humanity] has only now become possible."[67]

Thus, on the one hand, Adorno is clearly seeking, with Marxian inspiration, to rescue essence from existence or, more precisely, real possibilities of liberation from their continual suppression within history. On the other hand, he just as clearly regards Marx as participating in another version of the same philosophical error of seeing history in terms of more or less linear development. To see history as "single-stranded" is to see it as informed by a "single spirit" that unfolds gradually as an actuality that constantly and providentially emerges from the consumed totality of conditions that it already contained within itself. As Habermas succinctly puts it, dogmatic Marxist philosophy of history commits us to "the *unilinear, necessary, uninterrupted, and progressive development of a macro-subject.*"[68] In other words, like Hegel, dogmatic Marxism subscribes to the view that history follows a course—with many dips and turns, detours and dead ends, but all belonging to one great pathway—of ever greater actualization, as each historical possibility of progress is wrested from the context of its emergence and saved from the danger of deactualization.[69] Such universal histories are, for Adorno, nothing more than modern myths.

However, everything changes if we stop understanding history in terms of how it is informed by a "single spirit" that knows of no truly missed opportunities, no lingering real possibilities, and no real oughts. History is not the story of this single spirit's progress but of how this representation of progress veils our repeated failure to eliminate needless suffering at moments when it was possible to do so.

Of course, Adorno does not dispute the social potential that Marxism attempts to name. On the contrary, it is obvious that the forces of production now allow for the actualization of possibilities hitherto unimaginable. But there is nothing special about our era, which Marx and Engels take to be a unique turning point in the development of the forces of production.[70] In all periods of history, the social evidence of gratuitous loss and injustice—the knowledge that there is no Tauris for Iphigenia or the innumerable iterations of *Carthago delenda est*—is overwhelming: things ought not to have turned out as they did; we possessed the means to choose a different path. Socially unnecessary suffering is not limited to the nineteenth century. Barbarism is therefore not a name given to civilization's fraught origins; it is the name given to those instances, whether ancient or recent, of gratuitous loss and injustice, even within so-called civilized societies. Whoever participates unreflectively in the fact that is said to have necessarily emerged from its conditions fails to grasp that the criterion of actuality cannot be actuality itself, but only those moments in which actuality has cheated us of something different and better. To deny the single-stranded view of history is therefore not to engage in wishful thinking, nor is it a purely theoretical reference to possible worlds; it is a reference to the concrete responsibility we bear not to sweep socially unnecessary suffering under the rug of actuality and the assumption that all real possibilities are consumed in the process of its unfolding.

Adorno thereby multiplies the guiding thought of Marx's modal critique of Hegel. Hegel's principle of actualization is a lie not merely to the extent that the forces of production are now artificially fettered; it is a lie in the *more general historical* sense that *countless* possibilities of eliminating socially unnecessary suffering have been suppressed or judged to be unreal at different points in history.

Moreover, it is a lie in the *metaphysical* sense that the inevitable emergence of a fact from its necessary and sufficient conditions does *not* entail that all real possibilities have been consumed in the process. The result is the notion of blocked possibility or the thought of "what would be different"—if we finally come to view history as the precipitate not only of our successes but of instances upon instances of needless loss. As Adorno puts it,

> Confronted with [its internal contradictions], the purpose of society—and this alone is what makes a society of society—demands that it be organized according to what the relations of production relentlessly hinder, here and everywhere, and likewise according to what the forces of production make immediately possible, here and now. The *telos* of such an organization of society would be to negate the physical suffering of even the least of its members, as well as the inward, reflected forms of that suffering.[71]

However, to carry this out, we need a more detailed understanding of what specifically is hindered. Socially, this involves the historical actualization of what the forces of production make possible. Metaphysically, it involves a reworking of the Hegelian typology of possibilities. The boundary line separating formal from real possibility must be redrawn so that certain real, albeit unactualized, possibilities are salvaged from Hegel's critique of the ought. Adorno is asking of us that we begin to think of experience and society in terms of such blocked possibilities, the frayed and unwoven strands of history.

Thus, the problem with Hegel's actualism can now be seen to hinge on an ambiguity in the concept of possibility, which he tries to master by way of a restrictive typology. The ambiguity is the following: While it is quite legitimate to hold that real possibilities are those that can become actual, such a claim, as it stands, is equivocal. Might there be different species of real possibility that fit this general description: some that immediately make the transition to existence, and some that do not? Hegel's approach seeks to eliminate the equivocation by adopting the stronger position: *Only* those possibilities are real that are readily actualizable because compatible with existing actuality, while other possibilities have the lesser status of empty oughts or, more generally, of merely formal possibilities.

There is, of course, a reason for Hegel to take this line, although from an Adornian perspective he goes too far. The reason is simply that real possibility, as a metaphysical category, has to be referred to a criterion that allows us to separate it from merely formal possibility. For Hegel, this criterion is real actuality ("when all the conditions of a fact are completely present, the fact steps into actuality"). The advantage of this criterion is clear enough: By refusing reality to possibilities that are not actualized, he conveniently avoids the nonsense of non-actualizable possibilities. "*Essence must appear*,"[72] for otherwise it is not essence at all. But he cuts away too much and ends up assimilating to the absurdity of non-appearing essences the possibilities that so interest Adorno: those emancipatory possibilities that *can* be actualized (the conditions being, in general, available) but whose actualization is contingently though systematically denied us by the way things are currently organized or considered impossible by heteronomous consciousness, which judges things only by the standard of factual reality.

The Fallacy

On the basis of the preceding, we can finally address the question with which we began. What is the fallacy at work in Hegel's transition from ground to existence and from real possibility to actuality?

As we have seen, the central problem is the denial of blocked real possibilities of liberation and of the elimination of socially unnecessary suffering within the context of a metaphysics that requires all real possibilities to be consumed in the emergent actuality with which they are identical. With Marx, we then saw that our essence is to be construed concretely and historically: what we have to actualize is not exhausted in the existing forms of bourgeois civil society or the modern state, in which this essence is given in its negative form.

However, in a return to Adorno, we also saw that we should free ourselves from all single-stranded views of history, including the one to which Marx to succumbs by taking the proletarian revolution to be the necessary outcome of redressing social injustices. In an era in which this revolution has failed, what is required of us is the primary experience of blocked possibilities within history, without recourse to the myths of total actualization and bourgeois civil society, let alone universal history.

With all of this in mind, the fallacy no longer resists comprehension. Adorno thinks that Hegel *begs the question* of the identity of possibility and actuality by assuming that all real possibilities are consumed in the development and emergence of individual facts and of actuality itself understood as a totality of conditions. In this way, Adorno, with some insight from Marx, asks us to look more closely at that which does not fit this picture—for example, the disjunction between forces and relations of production or, more generally, between the non-identical and the concept that claims to sublate it definitively.

The Objection

It may be objected that the narrative of Hegel's thought, and of the *Logic* in particular, should here be taken into account. One should not insist, as Adorno seems to do, on the transition from ground to existence or, more generally, on the dialectical identity of possibility and actuality, because these determinations are foregrounded only at a certain stage of the unfolding of Hegel's argument—at the level of the Objective Logic. These categories—indebted as they are to the defective metaphysics of the Enlightenment—yield to the higher and truer determinations, richer in content, that make up the Subjective Logic and, perhaps most notably, the dialectic of realized purpose and means and the idea of the good. Adorno's critique therefore misses the mark because his target is lower down the chain in the order of concepts that, higher up the chain, leads to Hegel's true position. In this regard, that "no one ought to go hungry anymore" would—today at least, if not in Hegel's time—be an instance of the rational cognition of a good purpose that has perhaps not made its way into reality quite yet but whose realization is assured insofar as actuality contains both the purpose and the means for achieving it. In short, the Subjective Logic's concept of cognition and the idea of the good provide what is lacking in the Objective Logic's constructions and thereby responds to Adorno's critique.

This objection has the clear merit of challenging Adorno on the objective basis of the explicit structure of Hegel's logic, to which he admittedly does not seem to pay much attention. In response, it may first of all be said that the basis of Adorno's complaint is not invalidated by the progressive structure of the text. He draws attention to a problem that results from a categorial distinction between formal and real possibilities that is neither revoked nor nuanced anywhere in Hegel's writings. This is just as true in the Subjective Logic as in the Objective Logic, although the philosophical context and the terminology evolve over the course of the book. Even the "genuine position of rational cognition,"[73] which is presented towards the end of the Subjective Logic and meant to describe the reconciliation of "is" and "ought," is just another, higher instance of the relegation of the ought to the status of formal possibility, which marks it indelibly with the signs of non-objectivity, perennial deferral, and impotent longing. In fact, it might simply be said that the only good purpose (or ought) that matters for Hegel is the one that is already entirely compatible with and present in existing actuality.

Hegel's starting point is once again the critique of Kantian morality, which sustains its ought only by recourse to the postulate of the immortality of the soul. This mires us in contradiction, according to Hegel, because it means that conformity of finite willing to the moral law is seen as both necessarily actualizable and impossible to actualize in this world. As Hegel puts it, "The idea of the fulfilled good is indeed an *absolute postulate,* but no more than a postulate. . . . There still are two worlds in opposition, one a realm of subjectivity in the pure spaces of transparent thought, the other a realm of objectivity in the element of an externally manifold actuality, an impervious realm of darkness."[74] This contradiction cannot stand.

Its solution requires a shift in perspective. The subjective will should not be abstractly opposed to an actuality taken to be external to it, as though the subject's ought were somehow foreign to actuality. Rather, subjective activity has to be seen as *partaking of* the activity of the becoming of actuality itself. In other words, the will must cease to oppose itself to actuality. The genuine good purpose is one that the will subjectively receives from actuality as that which the latter objectively demands. Only then can the will "appropriate" or "seize hold" of actuality and shape it accordingly.[75] In other words, subjectivity is reflective of objectivity in the moment that objectivity is discovered to be susceptible to changes that may be instigated by the subjective will. In this way, the will is best understood as the agent of actuality; it is not opposed to it. Hence, the only really *good* purpose is the one that is also *true,* that is, the one that corresponds to the world as it *really is* or the one that coincides with a world that *can* be transformed because it provides the real conditions, the real possibility, and the means for its transformation, including the will that enacts it. The correct perspective on the good purpose is therefore said to be based on the identity or reconciliation of the theoretical idea and the practical idea, the "is" and the "ought."[76] The concrete manifestation of this identity is the realization of the good purpose.

It is not difficult to see why this solution to the apparent contradiction of is and ought is merely a more developed version of the same identity of actuality and possibility that appears in the Objective Logic. The good purpose is the possibility (of activity and realization) that lies latent within actuality, just as actuality provides the purpose with its objective circumstances and means of realization. In the language of the Objective Logic, real possibility is to be found nowhere else but in real actuality, with which it is entirely compatible. In the language of the Subjective Logic, "purpose is communicated to actuality without any resistance and is in the simple relation of identity with it."[77] This is so because the good purpose and its means of realization are considered dialectically identical, just like actuality and possibility. In short, the dialectic of purpose and means is the same as the dialectic of possibility and actuality, but reframed in the language of the good.

Consequently, the relation of ought to is—*correctly conceived*—does not refer us to something unrealized or to another world opposed to this one. Quite simply, this world *is constitutively* already as it *ought* to be:

> Unsatisfied striving vanishes when we recognize [*erkennen*] that the final purpose of the world is just as much accomplished as it is eternally accomplishing itself. This is, in general, the outlook of the mature person, whereas youth believes that the world is in an utterly sorry state, and that something quite different must be made of it. The religious consciousness, on the contrary, regards the world as governed by divine Providence and hence as corresponding to what it *ought* to be.[78]

Thus, the correct outlook on the world means that we should not fixate on the frustration of non-realization, should this occur. The common activity of purpose seizing means and means bequeathing to purpose its real, substantive content is self-renewing and ongoing as history unfolds. While Hegel reduces the ought to the is, their identity is dialectical: "This agreement between is and ought is not rigid and unmoving, however, since the final purpose of the world, the good, only *is* because it constantly brings itself about."[79] In a quite restricted sense, it can be said that there are legitimate oughts, namely, those that we receive from the inner determinations of actuality and that the will's activity can bring about. After all, as Hegel says, "Who is not so clever as to be able to discern in our surroundings quite a lot that is not, in fact, how it ought to be?"[80] Nevertheless, the "agreement" between is and ought still entails that no legitimate ought remains unactual: the idea "is not so impotent that it merely ought to be, yet is not actual."[81]

However, talk of legitimate oughts should no doubt be considered an unfortunate mannerism, at least from a rigorously Hegelian perspective. If no legitimate ought goes unactualized (if actuality legitimates the ought by the criterion of its inner determinations understood as available means), then, strictly speaking, there are no oughts at all but only actuality itself and the activity of its unfolding in the dialectical interrelation of purposes and means. That is, the only legitimate oughts are those that dissolve themselves entirely into the category of real possibility and are therefore concretely realizable in the action of a rightly oriented will. But this means that there is no room for an ought that is not already an is, or at least implicit within what is.

What if someone—say, Adorno—should nevertheless lay claim to a legitimate good purpose that, in the face of actuality, remains unrealized? Hegel's answer is clear:

> If it is now claimed that the purpose of the good is . . . not realized, what we have is a relapse of the concept to the standpoint that it assumes prior to its activity, when the actual is determined as worthless and yet presupposed as real. This is a relapse that gives rise to the progression to bad infinity. . . . By this view the concept only stands in its own way, and all that it has to do about it is to turn, not against an external actuality, but against itself.[82]

In other words, if we are not part of the solution, we are part of the problem: the correct view of the world is that "things are as they ought to be."[83] Any remainder or unrealized ought is simply a symptom of relapse to the contradiction—or non-identity—of the good purpose and external actuality.

Adorno, however, will say that in such passages, Hegel "disputes away the contradiction between idea and actuality, [and thereby] sets the tone for his entire corpus."[84] One might say, for example, that it is not philosophy's concern that the solution to Antigone's tragic fate took centuries to be realized, although it was already somehow "actual" in the events of the tragedy. In the meantime, Antigone, Haemon, and Eurydice all die and the social problem that is at the root of all this suffering remains entirely intact. Should philosophy not do more to understand the gap between the actual and the real than simply name it? Are such periods of spiritual delay, and of what Hegel calls the mere "prose of the world,"[85] really not worthy of philosophical scrutiny?

More concretely, if we say, with Adorno, that "no one ought to go hungry anymore," then the modal charge of the claim—its ought—seeks to communicate a contradiction, a case of non-identity: The forces of production are in fact such that we could put an end to needless need. Yet nothing is done, though the conditions are, in general, available and the purpose has been announced. In such cases, is it enough to say that what is actual may not yet be real and then leave it at that or, worse, merely trust that reason or Providence will set things right in the end? For Hegel, it would seem that the realization of the idea of the good as merely posited within thought is sufficient. To this, Adorno will say that Hegel fails to take the problem of realization seriously. Rather, "he just 'mediates' it" and so "tidies away" the non-identical (e.g., the fact that people continue to go hungry). This again is why "Hegel was not dialectical *enough*."[86] To put it bluntly, the problem of the non-identity of the idea of the good and the real state of the world is not solved by affirming the idea of the good as participating in an ongoing realization. Hence, Hegel's view of the realization of the good leads us directly back to Marx's critique: The bad state of affairs is indeed overcome, but only in the mere *thought* of the good fulfilling itself within history. "There is no transition to existence out of the logical movement of concepts."[87]

Indeed, this is just what Adorno suggests in a passage that more or less explicitly takes up the objection mentioned, based on the moment of rational subjective cognition and the willing of the good. He begins by according to Hegel, as he does elsewhere, the importance of determinate negation:

> Like almost all of Hegel's categories, the negated—and thereby positive—negation also has some experiential content—namely, for the subjective progression of philosophical cognition [*Erkenntnis*]. If the knower knows precisely enough what an insight lacks or where it goes wrong, then by virtue of such determinateness they will usually already have a sense of what has been missed.

He then goes on to clearly state that we cannot remain at the level of the Objective Logic, that the subjective moment is necessary. This is just what Hegel himself would say. But he then adds that the metaphysical framework within which Hegel discusses this subjective moment is inadequate. Another kind of metaphysics is necessary:

> But this moment of determinate negation, because it is itself something subjective, may not be credited to the Objective Logic, let alone to metaphysics. Nevertheless, it is that [subjective] moment that makes the strongest claim in favor of the sufficiency of emphatic cognition and its ability to succeed in spite of it all, and this provides a basis for the possibility of a metaphysics beyond the Hegelian one.[88]

We will see in the final chapter what sort of metaphysics it is that Adorno has in mind, but it is already possible to discern its outlines within the present context. What we have just seen is that the structure of realization is indeed correctly described by Hegel: What is initially an ought is determined and shaped by the subjective will, which thereby tries to give itself the real means of bringing it about. But realization *itself* is taken to be a category of thought that paradoxically *may not* find its correlate in objective reality. Philosophy should be able take up the challenge of understanding the structure of such situations. Hence the importance of a theory—call it a metaphysics—of blocked possibility: There is more to say about the persistence of the ought within actuality than Hegel says. To say "things are as they must be" is not enough, and to say that, for that reason, the good cannot remain an ought without being is not a solution to the problem of realizing the good but merely a restatement of the problem. Indeed, Hegel seems to want to paper over an ambiguity in the ought (as hollow formal possibility and as non-formal good purpose) that should in fact have given rise to a different typology of possibilities.

Adorno's "decisive break with Hegel" can then be summarized as follows:

> The seriousness of unwavering negation lies in its refusal to lend itself to sanctioning things as they are. The negation of a negation does not [automatically] undo negation; it [may show], rather, that the negation was not negative enough. Otherwise, dialectic—as it was integrated into Hegel's thought at the cost of its depotentiation—remains indifferent to what was posited as its starting point. What is negated remains negative until it has passed.[89]

Thus, to maintain the good purpose as good and to set it against things as they are, but then, in the moment of its failure, to simply fall back on the categories like those of subjectivity, finitude, impossibility, and so on, is nothing other than to abrogate the responsibility of thinking to *really* negate the negative. The moment that we are made to feel the persistence of the negative—for example, contradiction, senseless suffering—and its refusal to be dissolved in the face of the subject's good purpose is the moment at which the good purpose must be thought *in the objective and subjective forms of its blockage.* Otherwise, insisting on the fulfillment of the good purpose (the reconciliation of the ought and the is) is merely to help oneself to the *category* of realization within *thought,* while leaving everything else intact. That "things are as they must be" in that very instant becomes an apology for the existent. However, a non-depotentiated—or better: repotentiated and repotentialized—dialectic would be one in which a theory of blocked possibility and the real ought would take up "the seriousness of unwavering negation."

Adorno's point is thus that "emphatic cognition," at the moment of its most extreme subjectivity, has to be able to grasp the substantive content of its objective failure. This is just what he calls primary experience. As such, the "now possible, but nevertheless not actual" that characterizes blocked possibility should be reflected somewhere in the metaphysical categories of modality. But there is nowhere within Hegel's typology that such things can go, except into the category of formal possibility. To speak cogently about our historical situation, we have to free these possibilities from the fetters that come from assuming that they can be put only in the category of formal possibility.

This "twilight zone" of non-identity between the Hegelian is and ought is the zone in which Adorno's thought operates. And while it may be true that "essence must appear," he reads Hegel's "must" as marked by a fatal ambiguity. There is a hidden, unrecognized ought in Hegel's "must"—an ought that is part and parcel of every pang of satisfiable yet unsatisfied hunger. This ambiguity is particularly clear in a passage in which Adorno pits a certain "counter-essence" against the orthodox Hegelian view of essence:

> Dialectical thinking counters the suspicion directed towards what Nietzsche called the "hinter-worldly" with the assertion that the concealed essence is a counter-essence [*daß das verborgene Wesen das Unwesen sei*]. Dialectical thinking, irreconcilable with the philosophical tradition, affirms this counter-essence, but not because of its power [over us]. On the contrary, dialectical thinking

criticizes the contradiction it designates in relation to appearances, and, ultimately, the contradiction it designates in relation to the real life of individual
human beings. We have to hold fast to Hegel's dictum that essence must appear.
But it is precisely because essence must appear that it comes into contradiction with appearance. Totality is not an affirmative but rather a critical category.
Dialectical critique seeks to salvage or help to bring about what does not obey
totality, what resists it, or what at first only takes shape as the potential of a not
yet existent individuation.[90]

Normally, the generally negative term *Unwesen* would refer either to a topsy-
turvy, anarchic, or dreadful state of affairs or, with some philosophical pressure,
to something that does not have the status of an essence (*Wesen*), that is, a non-
essence or phantasm. However, interestingly, Adorno here gives the expression
a positive turn, deploying it to mean that which runs counter to and resists
appearances, to that which lies suppressed within them and which philosophical thinking has to interpret and make explicit. Such a "counter-essence," says
Adorno, "must" appear, but it does so at first only in the form of contradiction:
it is *not* the essence that is actualized in the persistent injustices of contemporary society but rather that which remains locked away within it as its own better potential. In other words, it is that which makes the statement true that "no
one ought to go hungry anymore" and therefore gives the lie to actuality qua
totality (here understood as the inevitable actualization of all real possibilities).

The accusation of fallacy therefore turns on the claim that, contra Hegel,
actuality contains such counter-essences or real oughts, blocked real possibilities of redemption. And to the extent that they are still expressed, however
faintly, within experience, the non-identical or the non-conceptual cannot be
tidied away or mediated within the stream of conceptual determinations in
which there can be no remainders or loose ends. The non-identical here is still
eminently "identical" insofar as it is concretely identifiable (conceptualizable)
within experience, but it remains non-identical insofar as it refers to a counter-
essence or blocked real possibility whose substantive content cannot be identi-
fied formally or a priori, because it depends on social experience for it to take
shape. Marx provides one example—but only one—of how this can occur at
the crossroads of metaphysics and social theory. But the point is generalizable:

Thus in identificatory idealist thought, the tendency is to equate actuality and
possibility, and so to eliminate possibility as the subjective element of tension

that corresponds precisely on the subjective side to non-identical being on the objective one. It is this elimination that sanctions the disparagement of possibility. Nowadays, when Hegel's philosophy has long since been forgotten, this tendency has been secularized—or rather, vulgarized. It has become a common bias to claim that utopia is not permitted and that it is therefore not possible.[91]

Thus, the non-identical refers to the substantive content of the subjective experience of that which is objectively possible in the mode of that which actuality denies us rather than in the mode of conceptual identification or total actualization. It is what it is only as blocked possibility. However, Adorno's critique of Hegel is just the beginning of the story. Are there more concrete forms of blocked possibility at work in Adorno's thought? In what sorts of experiences do we come into contact with "what would be different" or, equivalently, with "the difference with respect to what merely exists"?[92] To answer these questions is the task of the following chapter.

CHAPTER 3

ADORNO

Nature–History–Possibility

> The form of actuality excludes the possibility of those actions that
> seem imminent in Marx. Only a liar would act today as though one
> could change the world tomorrow.
>
> —Adorno, as reported by Ralf Dahrendorf[1]

> Negative dialectic penetrates its hardened objects through
> possibility—the possibility of which the objects' actuality has
> cheated them, yet which gazes out of each one.
>
> —Adorno[2]

Between Two Possibilities

As we have seen, an Adornian critique of Hegel's theory of actuality leads towards a reorganization of the Hegelian typology of possibilities. Specifically, Adorno's thought requires us to make room for non-formal blocked possibilities. For Hegel, the totality of existing circumstances is seen as coextensive with and exhaustive of the conditions of future actuality, whereas for Adorno current actuality is by and large not merely a totality of conditions of possibility but also a sum of self-perpetuating conditions of *impossibility* that come together to block possibilities of emancipation. Essentially, blocked possibilities, while inhering in existing actuality in the manner of real possibilities, are nevertheless neither actualized nor immediately actualizable, to the extent that they are systematically kept at bay by existing actuality's prevailing possibilities of self-reproduction. Adornian blocked possibilities may therefore be said, somewhat paradoxically, to bear features of both formal and real possibilities on Hegel's use of these terms. It is precisely this ambiguity that suggests a need for a more fine-grained typology of possibilities.

In this regard, Jay Bernstein aptly remarks that, for Adorno, "lodged somewhere between logical and actual possibility," there is something that is "neither fully actual nor fully non-actual."[3] This is an important insight into Adorno's concept of possibility, and one that merits further development. The trouble is that Adorno nowhere provides a full-fledged or even a detailed sketch of a theory of possibility. Happily, as we have begun to see, his views can be reconstructed on the basis of various remarks but also—and perhaps more productively—by following a recurrent theme in his thought: the nature-history dialectic. The advantage of this approach is twofold: It provides a relatively stable conceptual framework within which Adorno's concept of possibility can be situated, and it allows us to see it at work in different aspects and periods of his thought. In fact, it would be no exaggeration to say that the nature-history dialectic is central to Adorno's thought from the beginning right up until the very end of his career. One could even say that this dialectic provides a kind of template for his philosophical-sociological-aesthetic project and so comes to play the role of a structural motif in his writings: in the relation of myth to reason, society to individual, and practice to theory, as well as in the peculiar transcendence of the artwork vis-à-vis the history of art.

Following a general presentation of the nature-history dialectic, this chapter describes society and art as figures of it. Accordingly, Adorno's concept of society unfolds on the basis of its apparently natural heteronomous command over the individual, along with its attendant though suppressed possibilities of autonomy and radical historical transformation. Art, in contrast, follows the opposite course: the historical dynamism of autonomous art takes the upper hand (at least on the plane of aesthetic semblance) over the real, over existing art and what has come to seem natural in the history of art. Ultimately, we shall see that society and art are not merely distinct instantiations of the nature-history dialectic but together form another version of it, with society as a figure of nature in need of ruthless historical critique, and art as a figure of history that has become a refuge for the precondition and universal objective of that critique: autonomy. Within this movement, the notion of blocked possibility comes to play a central and critical role.

Nature-History

Adorno's 1932 paper "The Idea of Nature-History," published posthumously, is at once challenging and elliptical, presenting the reader with various puzzles and problems of interpretation.[4] In the first instance, the concepts of nature and history he presents are somewhat unusual and synthetic, bringing together elements from Hegel, Marx, Lukács, and Benjamin, in combination with features of Adorno's criticisms of Heidegger and of what has come to be called the myth of the given.

We can perhaps cut to the heart of the matter via Hegel's conception of second nature and the recurrent threat of its degradation into a sort of "spiritual mechanism."[5] This is arguably the most basic historical and theoretical point of reference for understanding Adorno's approach to the dialectic of nature and history.

On Hegel's view, second nature appears most prominently in the form of ethical life (*Sittlichkeit*), the tissue of largely unconscious habits of communal living that takes the form of a system of culture, religion, and laws to which the individual is assimilated and which provides the dynamic basis for self- and community-actualization. However, as Christoph Menke has argued, the self-actualization of spirit in ethical life carries with it a risk of which Hegel is well aware, namely, that of the unconscious reification and replication of pre-given universal forms or the "lapse" of ethical life into a kind of spiritual mechanism: "Because spirit is, by its very concept, the reality of freedom, its self-generation as (second) nature is an act of self-dissimulation or self-inversion: spirit appears to itself *like* or *as* nature; it *inverts* or *perverts* itself into nature."[6] This inversion or perversion of spirit consists essentially in a momentary break in spirit's power of continuous self-actualization. Absolute spirit, or the power to establish the truth of ethical life, can fall into rote behavior and blind obedience, thereby degenerating into mere finite spirit. Instead of engendering and dynamically animating second nature, overcoming its internal contradictions as these become evident, individuals adhere blindly to their precious social and cultural forms and lapse into patterns that resemble those of mechanistic first nature.[7] In this way, possibility and actualization are constrained by the apparent necessity of affirmative being, that is, the sheer authority of the merely extant. For Hegel, of course, spirit cannot help overcoming itself, cannot help giving itself its own salutary potentialities, which appear in the experience of ethical life, although individuals may well misinterpret the latter's content.

Spirit will liberate itself from this predicament simply because it *can,* because that is its power of self-actualization. Thus, succumbing to the familiarity of second nature—allowing it to become a heteronomous force—remains a possible station, but no more than a station, on the way to the ultimate destination of rational self-critique and the social actualization of the forms described in the *Philosophy of Right.* Or so the story goes, according to Hegel. This moment of inversion or perversion forms a good basis for understanding Adorno's use of the term "nature."

On Adorno's view, "nature" refers to anything (a belief, custom, law, commandment, principle, and so on) that purportedly refers us to a necessary, permanent substratum of ultimate and immutable sense informing history. This use of the term is therefore not reducible to the sensuous, material nature studied by natural science; it is a higher-order term that encompasses not only the notion of a constituent domain of matter governed by law but *any* pre-given or allegedly a priori foundation. It is what Antigone refers to as "the unwritten and unfailing statutes given us by the gods. For their life is not of today or yesterday, but for all time, and no one knows when they were first put forth."[8] In 1932, Adorno describes nature as "what has always been, what as fatefully arranged pre-given being underlies history and appears within history; it is what is substantial within history."[9] In other words, "nature" refers to that which passes itself off as *necessary,* even if it is second nature that is really at issue. Nature is the life of spirit in the degraded form of spiritual mechanism. This merely apparent, second-natural necessity pawning itself off as absolutely necessary is, in general, the only form of necessity that is really of interest to Adorno.

In contrast, "history" is described as "a movement that does not play itself out in pure identity, in the pure reproduction of what has always been, but is one in which the new occurs and gains its true character through what appears in it as new."[10] In other words, history, as the emergence of the new, is non-identical with respect to the apparent laws of so-called archaic, eternal nature. It occurs, for example, in the experience that belies the past or defeats expectations, urging us on to self-correction. Thus, interestingly, history does not merely refer to the past but also to the new; and as the new, it is that which "makes history," as it were, by breaking with archaic nature and time-honored concepts that turn out to be contingent—even false—in spite of their venerability. As such, history implies both radical *transience* (the downfall of the ever-same) and *transition* (the emergence of the new), which properly occur in the moment of liberation from nature as ideology. In this way, Adorno echoes

Marx's sardonic comment that classical political economy presents us with the ridiculous portrait of history dressed up as nature, as though "there has been history, but now there is no longer any."[11]

Adorno illustrates the dialectical movement from history to nature through reference to Lukács's concept of second nature. Essentially, the thought here is that the world in which we live is a world of conventions that collectively constitute a second nature, as in Hegel's use of the term. For Lukács and Adorno, however, the focus is decidedly on the fact that this world has been thoroughly alienated from its historical conditions of emergence, and so appears to us as "what has always been" or, alternatively, as embodying natural necessity—for example, in the form of apparently inescapable ancestral injustices and their more modern forms, such as the distinction between those who own the means of production and those who can only sell their labor power. The critical point is that historically produced laws take on the appearance of inescapability by becoming detached from their genesis, thereby coming to act as heteronomous forces. Adorno here insists, in a very Benjaminian way, on the "charnel-house" or "ossuary" of the present, quoting Lukács, who says that second nature, the world of petrified conventions, is "a charnel-house of long-dead interiorities; this second nature could only be brought to life—if this were possible—by the metaphysical act of reawakening the souls which, in an early or ideal existence, created or preserved it; it can never be animated by another interiority."[12] (As Hegel puts it, "A shape of life has grown old and it cannot be rejuvenated.")[13] Through reference to Lukács, then, Adorno stresses that such a second nature is not merely habit qua spiritual mechanism (say, a system of unquestioned, time-honored traditions) but also—and thereby—something *dead* that nevertheless persists and longs for an impossible resurrection.[14]

A few things are worthy of note here. First, there is in Lukács the suggestion of an all-too-necessary moment of progress being impeded by a situation in which petrified forms continue to hold sway. On this basis, picking up on Lukács's mention of the unfulfilled need for a "metaphysical act," Adorno says that we are seemingly faced with a "metaphysical possibility," that is, a possibility that is essentially unavailable to us as long as these forms persist. But he quickly moves to criticize this view, asserting that the becoming-natural of historical forms of ethical life (such as the initially positive emergence of humanistic bourgeois values that ended up serving the economic interests of the few) does not necessarily lead us into an impasse: history can bring about a breakthrough of the new.[15] On a related point, it is worth underscoring that Adorno insists on the riddle- or cipher-character of second nature, which suggests the chance of discovering something new—or at least the promise of something new—within the ossified forms of the old. In this way, he points to the conversion of the first moment of the nature-history dialectic (history becoming nature) into its second moment: the movement from nature to history or from merely apparent necessity to the possibility of the new.

At this point things become somewhat more tortuous, as Adorno's point of reference—Benjamin's book on the German mourning play—is somewhat gestural. However, it is at least clear that for Adorno the return movement of the dialectic, from nature to history, consists in the discovery that "nature itself proves to be transient nature [vergängliche Natur], history."[16] By this statement, Adorno means to draw attention to the fact we can analyze and diagnose enigmatic features of life that appear to guide us in the manner of natural laws, so as to show us that what seems immutable and unequivocal is, in fact, a riddle that calls for its solution, which in turn will lead to its overcoming through determinate, dialectical negation.[17] Thus, the suffering of the world (its vanity, its passions, its pains, and so on), though understood in a very visceral, natural sense, is seen not as a senseless subjection to abstract natural laws but as decipherable according to its historical determinants. What is first taken to be the expression of ineluctable nature is revealed to be contingent and surmountable—hence the emphasis on transience. As Adorno says elsewhere, half-quoting Nietzsche: "Woe says: pass."[18] The horizon of suffering is its overcoming.

All of this sounds fairly straightforwardly dialectical in a sense at least broadly compatible with Hegel's views on second nature and determinate negation. Second nature, once it recollects its historicality or its having become second nature, can liberate itself from the stranglehold of immutability and give rise to a structural transformation of ethical life. Strangely, though, Adorno's presentation of the issues, which relies so heavily on Benjamin, neglects, for whatever reason, several important aspects of the book on the mourning play that support claims he will make later in his career. More specifically, he downplays somewhat the notion of blockage (the persistence of nature, the obstruction of historical potentials) that will later prove to be so important.[19] Why precisely he does so is unclear, but the result is an uncharacteristic air of optimism. In any case, at least two aspects of Benjamin's text are worthy of mention in view of later developments.

First, while Benjamin certainly stresses transience,[20] and does so on the basis of the Baroque period's constant reminders of the ephemeral nature of human existence, he is ultimately more interested in the relation between the mourning play and the effective, historical impasse it illustrates, in the sense that the works analyzed contain no real, immediate, and immanent possibility of transcendence. Thus, mere transience slips into a kind of repetition, impotence, or hopelessness:

> Whereas the Middle Ages present the futility of world events and the transience of the creature as stations on the road to salvation, the German mourning play is taken up entirely with the hopelessness of the earthly condition. Such redemption as it knows resides in the depths of this destiny itself rather than in the fulfillment of a divine plan of salvation. The rejection of the eschatology of the religious dramas is characteristic of the new drama throughout Europe; nevertheless, the rash flight into a nature deprived of grace is specifically German.[21]

Of course, this hopelessness is not an ultimate form—it is historically produced and therefore not immutable—but the moment of transcendence that would redeem it appears out of reach *from within the period itself*. It is this central characteristic that so interests Benjamin.[22] Thus, to the extent that transcendence appears, it is given only negatively, in the spiritual shape of *blocked* or *deferred* transcendence. Thus, we must see the mourning play as the reflection of a struggle to come to terms with the immanence of this vale of tears and so with the constant postponement of transcendence, which is depicted in countless ways—for example, in the Lutheran view that dead souls perhaps sleep until the Day of Judgment.[23] First a world of pain, then an indeterminate but protracted period of insensible waiting: suffering and then nothing until the End of Days. But the point is this: Benjamin is more interested in the mourning play as the unconscious, unintentional representation of this situation of blockage than he is in the period's obsession with the vanity of existence or transience.[24] To put it succinctly, *transience* is only one component of the movement from nature to history, the other of which is *blockage*; and the two come together in a kind of melancholy impotence that Benjamin describes in detail.[25]

A second, related aspect of the treatment of the mourning play that Adorno neglects concerns its difference with respect to ancient tragedy. The key point here is that in ancient tragedy the hero is a hinge figure, according to Benjamin, and the drama plays out a historical crisis point or catastrophe that transforms history. The tragic sacrifice is "at once a first and a final sacrifice."[26] In other words, Janus-faced, "the tragic death has a dual significance:

it invalidates the ancient rights of the Olympians, and it offers up the hero to the unknown god as the first fruits of a new harvest of humanity."[27] We might think here of Orestes and the transformation of the Erinyes in Aeschylus or of the Hegelian reading of Sophocles's *Antigone*. In any event, this process amounts to "the undermining of an ancient body of law in the linguistic constitution of the renewed community."[28] Something is discovered to be awry in the seemingly eternal constancy of divine law, which causes this law to undergo a transformation. It is here that transience takes on its true importance: the so-called natural order is revealed to be historical insofar as its apparent necessity is shown to be shot through with contingency and urgency. "What has always been" suddenly becomes "what can and must be otherwise." Benjamin notably describes this as similar to the legal situation described by the verdict *non liquet* (it is not clear): the judicial declaration that a case has not been proven or cannot be decided, which Benjamin understands emphatically as the acknowledgment of a fateful lacuna—the insufficiency or structural inapplicability of existing laws—that announces a need for transformation, however this actually plays itself out.[29]

We can certainly see how such situations would have a certain appeal for Benjamin and Adorno. The *non liquet* evokes, with some dialectical pressure, the image of a contradiction between law and life that fuels, or *might* fuel, determinate negation. However, crucially, this remedy is not available in the mourning play. Instead of playing out the redemption of the flawed whole, there is just an inexorable movement towards melancholy on the way to death. As Benjamin puts it, "These are not so much plays that cause mourning, as plays through which mournfulness finds satisfaction: plays for the mournful."[30] The era is one in which there is effectively no real possibility of inner-historical redemption, so historical events take on a fateful character. Second nature becomes a spiritual mechanism that succeeds in masquerading as eternal nature or what is taken to be divine creation. It is here that the Benjaminian concept of nature-history reveals what is perhaps its most important aspect:

> [Fate] is not rooted in factual inevitability. The core of the notion of fate is, rather, the conviction that guilt (which in this context always means creaturely guilt [*kreatürliche Schuld*]—in Christian terms, original sin—not moral transgression on the part of the agent), however fleeting its appearance, unleashes causality as the instrument of the irresistibly unfolding fatalities. Fate is the entelechy of events within the field of guilt.[31]

The necessity involved here is not that imposed by nature in the abstract but by both nature and history acting together in a meaningful, though also closed—and so seemingly inescapable, immanent—whole. Necessity is not natural necessity, which would be truly binding, but a quasi-nature (passion, suffering, creatureliness) that is expressive of historical structures and meanings. More specifically, the difficult concept of "creaturely guilt" names the historical context in which we are *created* by the interpretation of humanity as defined, in its apparently natural essence, by original sin, for example. The guilt imposed on us by the doctrine of original sin, or the indebtedness (*Verschuldung, Schuld*) of the individual to such a historical form, is precisely what makes the human being the creature (the *ens creatum*, the *created* being) of historically mediated fate, which in the Baroque period is defined by the vanity of immanence and the postponement of transcendence. In other words, we are the beings we are, believing certain things to be possible or impossible, because of the historical presuppositions that inhabit us and take on the appearance of necessity. In short, fate is the ideological form of a historical but seemingly ineluctable constraint placed on the natural creature of history.

On these points—hopelessness and fate as historical necessity—Adorno has little to say in the paper on nature-history, simply insisting on transience. Later, of course, he would treat these issues on his own terms. In the paper, however, blockage does not come to the fore; only the riddle-like quality of experience is mentioned. In fact, one could be forgiven for thinking that Adorno merely wished to point out that what appears necessary and eternal within society is in fact contingent and ephemeral; but without looking more closely at the context of obstruction (i.e., at what hinders us from seeing the falsity of second nature and acting on it), this notion of transience seems fairly weak. How strong can so-called nature become in its repression of history? It is difficult to say. However, the claim is not so much that in 1932 Adorno was unaware of these aspects of Benjamin's project, for that would be impossible to maintain.[32] Rather, perhaps he is not yet fully clear on the modal structure of this context of obstruction or on the modal content of his own burgeoning project. Or, at the very least, he may have been unsure at this early date about how to position himself with respect to traditional notions of modality, such as Hegel's emphasis on actuality in relation to second nature. In the paper "The Idea of Nature-History," however, Heidegger rather than Hegel is his adversary on the question of modality; and his remarks on the former may shed some light on later developments, especially the priority he ultimately gives to possibility. A quick glance at this reference may help frame this question.

In a remarkably lucid critique of the whole notion of the project of being (*Entwurf des Seins*)—which seems to presage the emphasis that Heidegger himself later put on this notion in the form of the *Geschick des Seins,* the apparent destiny that an interpretation of being imposes on us—Adorno takes aim at the priority accorded to possibility in *Being and Time* (discussed in more detail in the next chapter). A cursory reading might give the impression that Adorno refuses to acknowledge any priority of possibility at all. But what he disputes is the priority of *formal conditions of possibility* over actual, historical content. He thinks, for example, that Heidegger's existentialia (the basic characteristics of existence) delineate a purely formal structure that eliminates the difference between history and being, effectively affirming a tautology, an identity, where there is rather difference. In other words, Heidegger deciphers history not according to the insufficiency and transience of its concrete forms and problems but in terms of an all-too-static system of necessary basic concepts (or pre-given possibilities of being) to which concrete existence must conform and through which transience is defused and recast as necessity. This earns Heidegger an accusation of idealism.[33]

In this way, Adorno declares himself against *idealist* attempts to give possibility priority over actuality, where idealism refers, in general, to doctrines in which existence or empirical multiplicity must conform to essential possibilities of existence or to a subjectively given categorial structure. Such conformity amounts to a tautology insofar as there is or should be no essential difference between possibility and actuality: actuality ought to be the empirical mirror image of possibility's fixed and a priori reality. Adorno thinks that such essential possibilities of existence—such as Heidegger's existentialia—act as idealist first principles to which existence should conform.

There is, however, a clear sense in which, from a *materialist* standpoint, we can attribute to Adorno a certain priority of possibility, and this sense is already suggested—if not yet fully developed—in the nature-history dialectic. Certain aspects of the modal character of the dialectic are discernible in the way Adorno sets up the terms, although he does little to stress this aspect. Thus, nature, taken on its own, is the figure of *seeming necessity*: of what has always been and must always be, unfolding under the iron law of the so-called natural order of things. Conversely, history is the figure of *contingency*, in the specific sense of the promise of the new that belies nature's claim to be necessary being.

History is not *mere* contingency, of course, but rather that specifically historical contingent and subjective experience that illuminates and disrupts "what has always been." In this way, the nature-history dialectic is readily transposable into a dialectic of necessity and contingency. At this point, however, Adorno adds an interesting twist: he says that there is an ineliminable "discontinuity" that marks the relation of nature to history.[34] According to Adorno, there are two aspects to this "discontinuity."[35]

"Discontinuity" first of all means that nature and history, despite their entwinement, are not straightforwardly resolvable into each other. They are not like Hegel's concepts of being and nothing, which, while distinct, also promptly transform into each other because they have the same content. Rather, nature and history are in constant tension with each other. "Discontinuity" therefore means that the two terms do not resolve into identity; we cannot posit a theoretical equivalence between the two—that would be idealism. Moreover, there is no third term that would teleologically guarantee the identity of their identity and non-identity. Instead, they leapfrog over each other in unpredictable ways. At times, what seems natural and fateful can be shown to have been produced historically—a realization that gives rise to the possibility of the new; and likewise, the new, as the expression par excellence of history, may come to congeal into nature—that is, we may end up ascribing necessity to the new that emerges from the criticism of the old necessity (as when one theological order is superseded by another). One might say, with a glance forwards to *Dialectic of Enlightenment*, that nature is already history and history reverts to nature, not because they are dialectically identical but because the one grows out of the insufficiencies of the other.[36]

The second essential aspect of discontinuity is bound up with the possibility of the new and of the becoming-historical of nature. However, Adorno does not use the word "possibility" in this way in the text, except when he refers to the "metaphysical possibility" of redemption. Moreover, as already suggested, he does not dwell on the social mechanisms by which redemption can be effectively reduced to the status of a mere metaphysical possibility: how nature (or creaturely guilt) can come to block the new indefinitely. For the most part, the emergence of the new seems relatively unproblematic in 1932. The idea here seems simply to be that critique can reveal the dislocated interrelation of nature and history, which sparks a doubt with respect to whatever presents itself as natural and thereby already announces the new that will cause the former order to crumble. In this way, somewhat curiously, Adorno sidesteps the problem of blockage, as well as more-developed modal language, although in some ways such language would greatly ease the theoretical burden of explaining the new in relation to the archaic. Instead, he presents us with vaguely defined notions of discontinuity and structural instability, laced with riddles and ciphers, to which he gives the global name "semblance." However, tellingly, in the last moments of the 1932 paper, it is this notion of semblance that he finally describes in modal terms, at least in part:

> The moment of the actuality of semblance, in contrast to its mere image-character, the fact that we perceive semblance as expression wherever we encounter it, the fact that it cannot merely be tossed aside as illusion, but rather expresses something that appears within semblance, but which cannot be described independently of it—this is likewise a mythical moment of semblance [e.g., the spectral presence of something that belies the so-called natural order of things]. To make a final point: the definitive, transcendent motivating force of myth, reconciliation, also inheres in semblance. . . . I am referring to that moment of reconciliation that is present wherever the world appears most as semblance: the promise of reconciliation is most perfectly given where at the same time the world is most firmly immured from "sense" [*Sinn*, i.e., *ultimate* meaning].[37]

The notion of transcendence as the promise of reconciliation is clearly of central importance here. Moreover, what is at stake is the emergence of transcendence from the actuality of semblance, on the basis of reading actuality as a cipher. But a cipher of *what*? That is the question. Of the "real" possibility of transcendence, opposed to the real actuality in which we are mired? That seems insufficient as an answer, for the simple reason that we cannot merely ignore the effectively "more real" possibilities that perpetuate the context of semblance in the form of fate and, therefore, of apparently irresistible, preordained outcomes: those outcomes, today as in the Baroque period analyzed by Benjamin, are far more likely to extend suffering into hopelessness than to abate it. But then what is this transcendence that Adorno names here?

In 1932, Adorno gives us very little to go on in this regard. However, as the *promise* of reconciliation, transcendence at least suggests that actuality contains a hope or a potential that is not compatible with archaic fate and its regime of real possibilities and necessities. Moreover, it seems to be the case that the nature-history dialectic hinges on the critique of what *ought not* to exist: the semblance of necessity. As Adorno would later say, "Dialectic is the ontology of the wrong state of things."[38] Indeed, in many ways the concept of nature-history would be utterly incomprehensible without reference to *what ought not to exist* and, thereby, to the possibility that it might not exist, which is suggested, once again, by the promise of reconciliation. However, what ought not to exist does anyway, which is to say that semblance and transcendence imply the problem of suppressed or blocked possibilities of reconciliation, whose actualization is precisely not guaranteed.[39] But the notion of blocked possibility—which would amount to the *broken* promise of reconciliation—is not yet adequately sketched in "The Idea of Nature-History." In later years, however, these issues become increasingly pressing.

Uselessness and Need

Already in 1932, Adorno suggests, paradoxically at first glance, that although second nature may turn out to be semblance, we have no access to a first nature unmediated by second nature that could serve as a safety net that might save us from the potential invalidation of second nature. Indeed, it is only in the sedimentations of history that something like first nature appears *as* first nature (whatever is at issue: an origin, a first principle, an ancient criterion of truth, or physical nature): "It is second nature that is, in truth, first nature."[40]

Consequently, "nature," often unqualified by "first" or "second" in Adorno's usage, ultimately refers only to the apparent necessity whose inner mediations historical subjects seek to understand and overcome, not by moving backwards towards an unscathed original nature but by moving forwards towards and beyond the contingency of what once seemed necessary. In other words, there is no *redintegratio in statum pristinum* for the simple reason that the solution to the contradictions of second nature can be found only *within and as second nature.*[41] As Adorno would put it in 1968, "There is absolutely nothing between heaven and earth—or rather on earth—that is not mediated by society. . . . This applies even to society's apparently most extreme antithesis, nature and the concept of nature, which is essentially mediated by the need to control nature, and therefore by social need."[42]

In the posthumously published typescript "Theses on Need," written in 1942, Adorno emphasizes this aspect of the nature-history dialectic: the social mediation of nature. This text was first presented in the context of an informal seminar involving Max Horkheimer, Herbert Marcuse, Friedrich Pollock, Ludwig Marcuse, Günther Anders, Bertolt Brecht, Hans Eisler, and others.[43]

The meetings revolved around two central themes: (1) Aldous Huxley's *Brave New World,* which presents the worrying portrait of "frenzied material progress minus emancipation,"[44] that is, social domination perfected through a technologically conditioned will to conformity; and (2) the problematic notion, suggested earlier in 1942 by Henry A. Wallace, that technological advancements could guarantee a ration of milk (and perhaps even of food) to everyone in the world while leaving the foundations of the existing order intact.[45] These concerns prompted Adorno and his colleagues to respond with reflections on human needs. Adorno's contribution to this discussion begins with the strong claim, already touched on in "The Idea of Nature-History," that need, even in its seemingly most natural forms, "is a social category."[46]

Adorno gives the example of hunger, which would seem to be a classic case of a natural category. However, to the extent that hunger can be fully understood only on the basis of its lived reality and concrete possibilities of satisfaction (as Hegel himself admits in the dialectic of ground and conditions), it seems that we cannot simply ignore the social dimension. For Adorno, even physical disgust is not a natural constant, as though eating insects, for example, were *intrinsically* horrible.[47] Rather, the disgusting, the delicious, and everything on the spectrum between them have to be understood through the social and cultural mediations of nature.[48]

It seems clear that Adorno's remarks are motivated by a renewed reference to the nature-history dialectic, with the emphasis on the social articulation of nature. But how closely are the two texts related to each other? In "The Idea of Nature-History" (in spite of Adorno's seeming disinclination to formulate the issue in these terms), nature and history map neatly onto the modally charged notions of necessity and contingency. In "Theses on Need," we are again confronted with an entwinement of nature and history, but what of the modal dimension? What of the possibility of the new? How is the transcendence promised by the nature-history dialectic discernible here, if at all? The "Theses" are particularly interesting on these points.

In the first instance, just as soon as we realize that all our needs, even the most natural, are socially mediated, then the question of how society meets or fails to meet them springs to the fore. In particular, any successful theory of need has to confront the danger

> that domination might come to reside permanently within human beings through a monopolization of their needs. This is no heretical belief that could

be magically conjured away; it is a real tendency of late capitalism. This danger does not consist in the possibility of post-revolutionary barbarity, but in the fact that total society is an impediment to revolution.[49]

We see here a notion of impediment that was only hinted at ten years earlier via references to Lukács and Benjamin. Specifically, at issue is the fact that the promised reconciliation (which here goes by the name of "revolution") may not occur if the tendency towards the totalizing social mediation of needs is not recognized, criticized, and treated. What is noteworthy is both the sense of something being impeded and the impediment itself as figures of modality and, more specifically, of blocked possibility. As for what is impeded, that is, an alternative organization of needs and their satisfaction, what Adorno has in mind two notions.

First, we must diagnose the organization of needs based on current—and questionable—social presuppositions in order to directly address the systematic suffering of the needy, that is, the suffering caused by calculated penury and the class divisions that make such suffering possible: "The question of the immediate satisfaction of need is not to be posed in terms of social and natural, primary and secondary, correct and false; rather, it coincides with the question of the *suffering* of the vast majority of all human beings on the planet."[50] In this context, measures such as Wallace's would be no more than an isolated concession to suffering or no better than a grudging "handout"[51]—measures that will inevitably be diluted by other social mechanisms that perpetuate the current state of affairs. More generally, the trouble, according to Adorno, is that needs are *structured, managed,* and *exacerbated* by the capitalist mode of production. Consequently, the systemic character of the suffering that society allows to persist becomes more difficult to discern: the satisfaction of an isolated alimentary need does nothing to address our increasing inability to recognize the global contingency and remediability of such suffering. The superficial satisfaction of admittedly real needs (a pint of milk a day) inevitably bears a condescending and dubious stamp of official approval from the very powers that create these needs.[52]

However, second, the emancipatory reorganization and social satisfaction of needs is no fantasy. Adorno obviously thinks that it is possible, here and now, not only to provide to all what is most urgently lacking (clean water, food, shelter, medicine, and so on) but also to overcome the whole bourgeois regime of artificial lack and for-profit production that produces need as we currently know it. Although he will say it more clearly in other texts, here he hints that the means to accomplish this already exist. For example, he refers to Marx's denunciation of the "fetters on the forces of production," which implies that bourgeois society, "as practical as it is irrational," organizes production in order to manage needs while simultaneously refusing to meet them.[53] His central point is this: Liberating the concept of need from false classifications and distinctions—such as that between first and second nature—allows us to see that society hinders us from discovering that it might yet be possible to free ourselves from existing relations of production, which pass themselves off as first nature. We would thereby come to see that Wallace's promise of milk for all, were it genuine, would necessitate the thoroughgoing transformation of existing social structures and not just a ration of milk that would leave everything else intact.[54]

Adorno then ends the "Theses on Need" with a direct reference to the actual and the possible, which he relates to what he calls the "useful" and "useless" in the seemingly surprise context of the artwork. (He is taking his cue from *Brave New World,* in which only that which is useful to social stability and the satisfaction of bodily needs is allowed to exist and in which genuine art and culture are seen as damaging to these ends.) He leads off with some rather rare reflections on the form that emancipation will take, including the idea that the classless society will dispel the illusory standard of usefulness in production: "To be useless will then no longer be shameful."[55]

The tension between the useful and the useless is significant. The useful today is that which is entirely dissolved into its social function within the cycle of production and consumption.[56] By contrast, the useless is that which resists its dissolution into such functions. Or to put it differently, the "useless" (on Adorno's emphatic use of the term) is a way of talking about something that is incompatible with capitalist actuality—something that at the same time subsists within it as possibility and promise:

> Within this society, usefulness is the only measure. The cultural moments that refuse this usefulness are characterized by an intention to get beyond existing reality. This is not a reference to art as a traditional cultural good but to art that rescinds the social contract. Art that refuses itself in earnest to praxis can take on a transcendent aspect, in the sense of the classless society. . . . Is there not something more to art [than a claim to universality within class society], namely, the fact that it expresses a possibility of thought, intuition, and living that is not constrained by the universal, but rather points beyond it?[57]

However, for the moment, it is only in the aesthetic realm that the "useless" has any real sway. In the classless society, though, that which is now deemed useless will take the upper hand, just as conformity to existing practices will be transcended by emancipatory possibilities of relating to the world that are now held at bay. Adorno then says:

> If classless society promises the end of art by sublating the tension between the actual and the possible, then at the same time it also promises the beginning of art, the useless, in which we can glimpse a reconciliation with nature because it is no longer in the service of usefulness to the exploiters.[58]

What is the exact nature of this tension between the actual and the possible that would be sublated by and within the classless society? For the moment, an answer can be inferred from what we have just seen: what is possible beyond sadly real possibilities of repression (and the lived actuality they create) would be the actualization of blocked possibilities, here conceived under the banner of the universal satisfaction of needs and the reorganization of society that this would involve.

In this regard, art provides an approach to the issues of the false universality of usefulness and of blocked possibility; for while artworks are certainly commodities (and so "useful" within capitalism), they are not only that. They are special because they are both useful and useless at the same time. As will become clearer below, that uselessness resides in the way genuine, autonomous works of art surpass the totality of what already exists. In more general terms, what is most useless to capitalism is that which structurally opposes it: the *new* or, more specifically, real possibilities discontinuous with extant reality, which art presents as possible in a medium other than society. In this sense, the true "beginning of art" would correspond to the liberation of the radically new in society.

In the terms of "The Idea of Nature-History," art is a figure of the productive discontinuity of nature and history. The new artwork is never a decisive reconciliation of the dialectical tension between nature and history but rather the resurgence of history within nature—a resurgence that may be quickly normalized back to the schema of the "natural," the same old thing. In "Theses on Need," Adorno approaches this issue by a sketch of a real possibility at odds with actuality, the satisfaction of needs that is suspended by the cycle of capitalist production and consumption. What results is the claim that the most pressing need today is precisely a diagnosis of the tension between actuality and possibility or, equivalently, between what exists and what would be different.

In sum, the "Theses on Need" define a double trajectory, which can also be taken as a description of the general stakes and form of Adorno's thought. On the one hand, the distinction between the useful and the useless calls attention to the context of obstruction caused by the determination of needs according to the criterion of what existing society considers useful. This leads us in the direction of the analysis of late capitalist society and its basic presuppositions. On the other hand, the useless points towards the role of art and aesthetic experience in helping us understand our predicament. In both cases, the modal character of Adorno's reflections—especially his increasing emphasis on possibility—will prove to be central. Each of the two aspects of this double trajectory will be treated in turn.

Society, Block

Adorno was, as he once said, "averse" to definitions.[59] In the article "Society (1)," he claims that neither is the concept of society definable according to formal criteria, nor is it a classificatory concept, nor can it be referred to the laws of natural science: "For society is essentially process; its laws of movement say more about it than any invariables cobbled together from it."[60] It is, in other words, a product of historical processes that coalesce into binding objective forms; thus, it exists only in the structural yet also contingent and historical interrelations that subtend both the social whole and the individuals within it. However, this has today taken the extreme outward form of a system of "natural"—that is, apparently necessary—functions that have become ends in themselves, perpetuating a "preponderance of institutions over human beings, the latter coming little by little to be the incapacitated products of the former."[61]

Worse, society has become incomprehensible to traditional theory, a fact that glares as soon as we realize that we have found no way to reverse the contradictory subservience of human beings to the relations of production we have created; they have become a petrified second nature, indifferent to the human needs that animate them. The contradictions are numerous: society is "rational and irrational in one: a system and yet fragmented, blind nature and yet mediated by consciousness."[62] Yet the incomprehensibility of society is not inevitable: "If this conception of social reality as contradictory does not sabotage knowledge of it and abandon it to contingency, then it is because of the possibility of yet conceiving the contradiction in its necessity and, in that way, expanding rationality to encompass it."[63]

It is not difficult to discern here the mark of the nature-history dialectic, expressed in the form of a generated inability to tear away the veneer of sham necessity in order to rationally uncover society's transience and thereby the possibility of change for the better.[64] For Adorno, it is this mask or veneer of necessity—the "natural" character of contingent society—that sociology has had difficulty deciphering. The answer to this apparent incomprehensibility lies in a reorientation of theory: "Sociology today would especially have to undertake to understand the incomprehensible, the advance of human beings into inhumanity."[65] But what is motivating Adorno here, apart from the inhumanity of reified social structures? And how are we to criticize and move beyond them? Pointing out the inhumanity of human relations is after all not a very novel thing to do, while understanding the incomprehensible would seem to be a rather tall order. It may therefore seem unsurprising that Adorno was often criticized for the alternating generality and impenetrability of his claims.

Ralf Dahrendorf, for example, takes what he deprecatingly calls Adorno's "total analysis" to task for its "all or nothing" approach, which ignores concrete opportunities for social improvement in favor of social and philosophical abstractions.[66] Essentially, Dahrendorf criticizes the tendency—evident in Marx and Adorno, among others—to mix sociology with philosophy. To do so is to create a pair of "logical bastards," as he puts it: a philosophy that has "the appearance of empirical validity" and a sociology that has "the force of indubitable truth."[67] So while Dahrendorf, like Adorno, sees social roles as contingent and changeable rather than as the reflection of "an inescapable and inherited fate,"[68] he also thinks that the task of the sociologist is to become an "empirical scientist who seeks only piecemeal knowledge and expects only piecemeal progress."[69] His view is that class conflict should not be taken to be the centerpiece of a grand philosophy of history that predicts or even strives for the establishment of a peaceful, classless society. Rather, we should come to terms with the fact that social antagonism is inevitable, which leaves us with the more modest and achievable task of finding ways to regulate it. The basic aim is to increase social mobility, which will in turn mitigate conflict: "The more upward and downward mobility there is in a society, the less comprehensive and fundamental are class conflicts likely to be."[70] Consequently, there is no need to fret about the possibility or impossibility of a classless society, which in any case is, for Dahrendorf, nothing more than a "Utopian fiction."[71] We would be far better off working on conflict regulation.

Such a pragmatic, problem-solving approach has its appeal, especially in the wake of the failed social experiment of institutional Marxism. After all, should we not be aiming to improve the well-being of individuals rather than continuing to work on obsolete theories? Pleading in favor of the Weberian notion of life chances, social mobility, class-independent access to education, and so on, Dahrendorf's criticism seems trenchant:

> It is one thing when one person eats caviar while someone else eats nothing at all, and quite another when the one eats caviar and the other herring. The question we have to ask is: what conditions still restrict life chances when certain basic presuppositions of such chances are [actually] provided by social structures and developments? Where do the dangers to life chances lie in our society? And where, on that basis, concretely speaking, are we to find the starting points for transformation? Full employment engenders the possibility of choice; and it is perhaps in these choices—and thereby in an enhancement of life chances—that the starting points for transformation consist.[72]

This may seem fair enough from the perspective of improving the lives of real people on the basis of changes that can realistically be made to social conditions. Moreover, it sounds as though Dahrendorf too were interested in blocked possibilities and the attempt to show that an enhancement of life chances is not only theoretically viable but well within our grasp. However, without underestimating or downplaying the suffering of real individuals, Adorno refuses to endorse Dahrendorf's approach. His reaction reveals something important about the possibilities and obstructions that are central to his own view.

Adorno takes up Marx's reflections on poverty to make his point, noting in passing the absurdity of Dahrendorf's suggestion that his—Adorno's—philosophical sociology is unconcerned with proposing concrete improvements to social conditions. But there is an underlying problem that Dahrendorf does not address, stemming from the nature-history dialectic: "The inhumanity at issue is the one that makes human beings in their living fate into objects. A sociology that attempts to express this does not partake of inhumanity."[73] Anticipating what will follow, one could say that the heart of this response lies in the modalities that it implies, in the question of what has "greater" actuality: the brute fact of poverty or the structural relations that make poverty seem necessary to the individual or, in Dahrendorf's case, tributary of conflicts that can be regulated but not eliminated?

Adorno's point is twofold. First, individuals are not merely poor in particular circumstances or due to chance; they are also the *objects* of structurally perpetuated poverty and, as such, the pawns of what can only appear to them as their fate in this life. Or, to put it in the terms of the nature-history dialectic, we have a tendency to take our lot to be natural, whereas it is actually a result of reified human relations; or, alternatively, we are the victims of "creaturely guilt" insofar as we are created as functions of a system for which we are responsible, while at the same time being structurally unable to see in what this responsibility consists or how to discharge it.

So far so good, although we cannot yet say that Adorno has added anything substantial to the debate, as he is quite aware that Dahrendorf rejects the notion of social fate and is well versed in the Marxian understanding of poverty. But there is a second aspect to the reply: Adorno clearly thinks that Dahrendorf falls prey to a related error. Instead of simply mistaking the contingency of poverty for necessity, he treats *conflict* as a basic social reality. As Dahrendorf himself puts it, "The concept of [definitive and complete] conflict resolution [is] a sociologically mistaken ideology according to which complete elimination of conflict is possible and desirable."[74] On the basis of the impossibility of eliminating conflict, he not only thinks that regulation must suffice to treat the evil; he also believes that we have no need for philosophical tenets and niceties but need only refer to existing practices and their attendant real and available possibilities of reform. In this way, he misses the importance of tackling the problem of conflict as rooted in the nature-history dialectic, whose modal interpretation can help us untangle and understand both local and structural problems. Accordingly, Adorno points out the error of passing conflict off as something basic and goes on to underscore the rival potentialities—self-destruction and reconciliation—that should instead be our focus:

> To respond to today's torn, antagonistic society by way of social struggle does not authorize us to posit, in the absolute, conflict itself as a constant of human nature. I find that such anthropological games come at all too high a price. The forms of conflict that are real and actually relevant are precisely those which quite literally threaten to snuff out human life. . . . In view of the destructive potential of contemporary technology—but also in view of a foreseeable, radically peaceful state of affairs—I do not believe that this notion of the inspiring power of conflict has any validity at all.[75]

Now, Adorno does not go so far in his reply to Dahrendorf to speak directly in terms of the nature-history dialectic, but its modal underpinnings are clearly visible in the related dialectic of society and individual. It is this dialectic that leads us not just to a better understanding of his reply to Dahrendorf but to the core of Adorno's social philosophy. We begin with the standpoint of the individual.

If laypeople and sociologists alike fall prey to the error of rigidifying the contingency of suffering or conflict, turning it into a "living fate" or a necessary social reality, then the counterpoint to this reification is the pathos of singular, individual experience—not as a confirmation of atomistic social reality but as caught up in, and therefore reflective of, the structural forms of repression at work within society as it currently exists. For it is the individual, and only the individual, who can register within experience the contradictions and paradoxes of social existence and who can thereby attempt to exorcise them by naming and criticizing them. Naturally, the situation is complex, not least because the individual is the site of a struggle: few individuals are, for the moment at least, *subjects* capable of autonomous thought; in fact, we are all first and foremost the *objects* of effectively a priori, reified social structures (i.e., "nature"), from which we have (with a measure of uncertainty) to be able to free ourselves. It is this problem and its lived forms that make society into something seemingly "incomprehensible"—but once again in the manner of a riddle that calls for a solution. Adorno formulates the problem as follows: "The state of universal mediation and reification of all the relations between human beings sabotages the objective possibility of specific, emphatic experience of the [social] fact—can this world be experienced at all as something living?"[76]

Solving the riddle requires us to understand the rigidified forms of society to which the individual is subject. We therefore move from the individual as the object of social forces to the forces themselves, "society as such,"[77] as constitutive of a blockage that adversely affects individual spontaneity and autonomy. In this regard, Adorno will not merely gesture towards "total society" as a problem, he will spell out in what this total society consists qua repressive whole. His most general claims take aim at the global supremacy of relations of production over the forces of production. But more specifically, one might say that just as Marx began from a simple social contradiction, so too does Adorno. Marx's initial contradiction was: "Workers become all the poorer the more wealth they produce."[78] Adorno's, built upon the failure of the allegedly natural or nature-like necessity of the Marxist solution to this contradiction, is that the dominant relations of production have remained in place in spite of being outstripped, as it were, by the potentials borne within the forces of production.[79] Adorno is, of course, interested in making such potentials theoretically intelligible and so available to praxis, but he can accomplish this only by determining and diagnosing the social processes that have come to thwart such potentials. Such claims are made more specific in various ways. We shall briefly consider four ways in which society blocks autonomy and the possibility of what would be different.

First, the culture industry, which serves up art in its most reified and commodified forms, is a part of this story—including the tendency, exemplified by jazz music, not only to misrepresent non-autonomous art as autonomous but to encourage the defenders of such products to enthusiastically but falsely proclaim their unconventionality and independence from the mainstream.[80] However, the defenders of so-called high art do not necessarily benefit from any protection on this count: all art can be leveled out, packaged, and sold as a commodity that meets a socially pre-defined cultural need.[81]

A second factor is the philosophical tendency, exemplified by Heidegger, to "ontologize the ontic,"[82] to claim that historically produced forms of experience such as anxiety (*Angst*) are primordial—and so, again, "natural."[83] In this way, Heidegger contributes to the reduction of human beings to functions of the social whole: it is only natural that we should be existentially uncomfortable since anxiety is just part of what it is to be a human being. However, this claim is not straightforwardly false. The trick is that the Heideggerian myth of primordiality also *reflects,* in ideological form, the sad truth of such allegedly essential anxiety, which is that it really *is effectively,* albeit *socially,* transcendental. Society makes our anxiety seem natural to the extent that it produces it universally. Thus, Heidegger is not just repeating the old philosophical trope of the a priori, trying in vain to give it a new twist, but unwittingly contributing to and perpetuating the very problem that should be at the forefront of philosophical and sociological research: the problem of an anxiety whose a priori character is socially mediated.

Third, Adorno also blames official social institutions such as social security for barring the way to solidarity: "Those who are by default the possible [individual] objects of such social welfare, and so do not know themselves as subjects standing in solidarity with each other, uncontrollably prohibit the thought of actualized freedom—a thought which, in spite of everything, cannot be magically done away with."[84] Likewise, seemingly unstructured social institutions, such as free time as it is currently understood, fall prey to the same criticism, precisely because, qua social institutions (structured or not), they are part of the total society that blocks freedom. Free time is not a release from relations of production but rather their confirmation to the extent that its function is social: the regeneration of labor power.[85]

To the preceding three elements we can add a fourth emanating from the broader theoretical background to critical theory. As Franz Neumann argues, the end of capitalism may not lie with economic crises. On the contrary, the ruling class could (and does) resort to "political means to prevent this collapse from becoming politically effective."[86] Thus, the transformation of society could be kept in suspense, perhaps indefinitely, by a concentrated political apparatus with the institutional and material means to do so. Yet, from Adorno's point of view, the situation is perhaps worse than Neumann imagines, for reactionary political power and its opposite, dogmatic insistence on revolutionary praxis, complement each other. In fact, the power structures inherent in revolutionary praxis operate along the same lines as reactionary political power. Praxis that has shown itself to be ineffective "is no longer a [legitimate] forum for objections against self-satisfied speculation; it is mostly a pretext used by executive authorities to nip allegedly vain critical thoughts in the bud—namely, those that transformative praxis would require."[87] In this way, dominant political groups and an increasingly superannuated radicalism unwittingly conspire to block theoretical advancement and the transition to more relevant emancipatory practices. They both block transformation by defending their particular versions of the status quo. This is particularly effective because the mortal enemies remain in deadlock, each spellbound, and so trapped, within the horizon of the mutual threat to their reciprocally defined forms of political legitimacy—with each side claiming history as its ally.

What these examples have in common is their contribution to society as "universal block."[88] But this is a peculiar sort of block. We are not merely occasionally hindered from realizing our goals or potentials as human beings, as though, all else being equal, happiness were generally within our grasp. The block is rather more insidious. It leads us to believe we have achieved something: access to culture, truth, fairness, or political legitimacy. Yet such achievements are, for Adorno, little more than palliatives or, worse, screens that prevent us from fully experiencing and correctly conceiving our predicament. In other words, the block in question is universal not only because it is present at different levels of experience and society; it is also universal in the sense that it blocks awareness of the block itself.

This type of universal block can be brought further into focus through Adorno's frequent use of the term "technological veil," which dates back to the early 1940s and his collaboration with Horkheimer on what became *Dialectic of Enlightenment.*[89] In the 1964 lecture course *Philosophical Elements of a Theory of Society,* he gives a clear explanation of the term:

> The expression takes over from the so-called "veil of money" [*Geldschleier*], which once cloaked social relations, but which subsequently disintegrated due to currency intervention and ever-recurring periods of inflation. This had an effect on mass consciousness insofar as the masses finally stopped believing that money was a [separate] thing unto itself and that it possessed intrinsic value. By "technological veil," I mean that various compulsions and necessities, which are [in fact] a consequence of social relations, are rather taken to be the result of technological advancement as such—for example, all those phenomena which have to do with the standardization not only of consumer goods, but also of the contents of consciousness. But in this way, we completely disregard, for example, that technological advancement for its part was shaped in a wholly one-sided and particular manner, namely, by the dominant profit motive and in view of reducing production costs. Accordingly, anything that had to do with decentralization, individualization, or qualitative diversity was suppressed and, if I may say so, artificially hindered by the profit-motive compulsion.[90]

The precise historical origin of the term "veil of money" is somewhat obscure, but in the context of classical political economy its meaning is clear: money is veil-like insofar as it is considered separate from or at most a facilitator of real economic activity—primarily exchange. Consequently, to understand the underlying economic forces on which money itself had no real effect, one had to "lift the veil" to see what was actually going on. The wrongness of this view, as Adorno points out, became increasingly evident in recurring periods of inflation and in the consequences of currency manipulation. At this point, the veil disintegrated although the myth of the free-market context of which it was a part has evidently persisted.

The technological veil renews the obsolete metaphor, emphasizing that technological advancement (which includes technical refinements to the process of production as well as legal and social reforms that leave the mode of production intact) may seem on the surface to be beneficial to civilization, but in fact obscures the profit motive and class interests that animate it and that fetter the forces of production more generally. In this way, mere technological advancement is mistaken for social progress, and structural injustices are thereby mistaken for civilization. Human needs are exclusively mediated by and dependent on market-driven forces, which do not serve need (let alone its elimination) but rather what is deemed useful in the sense of serving the perpetuation of existing social relations and the profit motive. Nothing significant diverges from the pattern of conforming to these relations and of giving ever-freer rein to this motive. This leads to greater uniformity, both in the marketplace and in consciousness, which, not knowing any better, accepts technological advancement as a force for human betterment. We might therefore happily accept the government's "pint of milk," thinking that we have made some real social progress. But to the extent that reality does not offer us possibilities of social progress that are independent of market-driven technological advancement, consciousness may be fooled into thinking that they cannot exist, that "what would be different"—a society in which all material needs would be met—cannot exist.

More generally, the technological veil is a key concept in the dialectic of nature and history. It converges on the idea that what presents itself as really given is, in fact, a social function that serves to mask the historical character (the genealogy and contingency) of that givenness. Often this takes the form of a suppression of social potentialities (e.g., the relations of production are said to adequately harness the forces of production, whereas they hinder them). Technological advancement comes to be an end in itself, disconnected from its real potential for social progress. Evident efficiencies come to obscure the possibility of alternative social forms—and indeed of a different way of relating to technology itself. And this situation is taken to be "just the way things are." (We shall return to the question of progress in the next chapter.)

Thus, Adorno suggests that the purpose of the technological veil is to perpetuate the "myth of the positive" or of the given as a natural reality: "Reality becomes its own ideology through the spell cast by its faithful reduplication. This is how the technological veil and the myth of the positive is woven."[91] In other words, what society really produces can, by sheer repetition and constant reinforcement, become the reified criterion of what society is and can be, to the extent that that is *all* that society produces. Moreover, the Hegelian identity of actuality and real possibility seems to confer metaphysical legitimacy on this view. After all, induction gives us nothing further to go on, and there is no axiom from which true society could be deduced. The only hope here, if we can spot it, resides in the dictum *consuetudo quasi altera natura effici:* habit or custom produces a sort of second nature.[92] The nature in question is precisely a product of habits and customs and may therefore be *refashioned*. But there is a particularly negative consequence that too often attaches to this second nature: the less the particular diverges from the whole (i.e., the more qualitative diversity falls prey to the profit motive), the more the whole appears to exhaust possibility in the pseudo-diversity of what is immediately given. A veil flutters quietly at the horizon of the given, but the given is what fills the landscape, as far as the eye can see. This raises the pressing question of what, precisely, is veiled.

As Adorno makes clear, capitalist society veils the true social relations that determine value. On this point, he agrees with Marx, who says that the commodity or money form "veils" the social character of labor.[93] In this way, Marx inherits the concept of the money veil and imbues it with critical intent. This provides Adorno with a point of departure: it is not merely that real social relations are veiled by technology (or, previously, the money form). It is that the veiling of these social relations is also a veiling of their transformability.

Adorno's point is thereby more general than Marx's, though also dependent on it: "[The] excision of possibility . . . makes second nature into all that is actual and thereby also turns it into a substitute for the possible—hence, the semblance of the natural arises."[94] Thus, while the veil prevents us from seeing that things are not as natural and inevitable as they seem, the accusation of semblance is simultaneously an admission—tacit or otherwise—of the possibility of things being otherwise. The semblance of nature and necessity is related to possibility through its suppression of it. Hence the rigorous presentation of what is really going on beneath the surface of apparent necessity is, from another angle, also the presentation of "knowledge" (if only "in itself" or implicitly) that things could be organized differently—and more justly. This returns us to the concept of possibility and, thereby, to the odd metaphysics of modality that underpins Adorno's thought.

In particular, the veil's primary function is to make the possible seem impossible:

> It is undeniable that with the increasing satisfaction of material needs, despite their deformation by the apparatus, the possibility of a life without deprivation has become incomparably more concrete. Even in the poorest countries no one need go hungry any longer. The veil before the consciousness of what is possible

has become more transparent; but this is also expressed by the panic sown everywhere by forms of social enlightenment that are not accounted for within the official system of communication.

But it is not merely capitalism that is responsible for veiling the consciousness of what is possible. Adorno adds:

> What Marx and Engels, who desired a human organization of society, denounced as utopia, claiming that it merely sabotaged such an organization, became a tangible possibility. Today, criticism of utopia has degenerated into an ideological commonplace, while the triumph of technical productivity deludes us into believing that utopia, which is irreconcilable with the relations of production, has nevertheless been actualized. But the contradictions in their new, international form—I am thinking of the arms race between East and West— make the possible at the same time impossible.[95]

Several important ideas are advanced in these lines. First and foremost, Adorno makes it absolutely clear that it is *the possible* that is veiled or shrouded from consciousness by society. But, here as elsewhere, this is a rather special notion of the possible. It is not reducible to that which society might produce on the basis of its usual mechanisms of development. At issue are possibilities that are *incompatible* with existing techniques of social production and reproduction (i.e., the "official system of communication," by which Adorno means the communication of existing knowledge and the circulation of familiar opinions). Moreover, the reference to Marx and Engels shows that Adorno includes them in his indictment of repressive social structures because their criticisms of social utopias imply a reduction of the possible to what is immediately contained within existing actuality as they defined it: the unstoppable teleological development of society towards communism. In this way, just as the veil of technology sets up the real (the given, the existent) as being exhaustive of the whole, so orthodox Marxism also sins against the possible by declaring that which does not coincide with that specific vision of emancipation to be utopian, unreal, and so beneath serious consideration.

Thus, for conservatives, reformists, and revolutionaries alike, the possible is systematically reduced to that which lies *on this side of the veil,* that which reality produces or will forthwith produce in its progression towards either continued exploitation, piecemeal and inadequate reform, or the realization of the orthodox view of emancipation—depending on which standpoint one takes up on this side of the veil. That said, Marx and Engels are a special case. Adorno's view is not that they were plain wrong. His view is that we have wrongly turned their critique of nineteenth-century social utopias against a *utopian outlook now become defensible*. In other words, theory and practice have not kept up with actuality; and today, actuality no longer justifies the cavalier dismissal of utopianism: the means exist here and now to put an end to global hunger. To put it more generally, and to bring out the modal character of the claim, what we have to analyze and overcome is the tendency to view the possible as being impossible—of mistaking real, albeit socially blocked, possibility for formal possibility. In this way, Adorno implicitly juxtaposes officially sanctioned possibilities, whether these stem from state-authorized dialectical materialism or from capitalism, with those possibilities ruled out by such hegemonic perspectives. He thereby explicitly lays claim to possibilities that suffer from a falsely imposed yet objectively real impossibility: the impossible possibility that is nevertheless possible because its impossibility is an effect of ideology. The term "utopia" designates this modal paradox in his writings.

Adorno further stresses this concept of utopia and the sorts of possibilities he has in mind in the 1968 reply to Dahrendorf:

> Even utopia is subject to a historical dynamic. . . . The forces of production, the material forces of production, have been developed to such a point today that in a rationally organized society material need would no longer be necessary. That such a state of affairs, extending around the world on a global scale, can be brought about is something that would have been condemned as crassly utopian in the nineteenth century. Something of this condemnation still resonates in [Dahrendorf's] example of the caviar and the herring. Objective possibilities have proliferated without end, to the point where criticism aimed at the concept of utopia—criticism that was based on the persistence of scarcity—has been stripped of all actual relevance.[96]

Recalling that, on the basis of his sociological theory of conflict and as a matter of pragmatic expediency, Dahrendorf had suggested that hunger could be sated by caviar or herring and that it would be preferable to aim for a situation in which some have caviar and others herring than either to engage in philosophical speculation or to persist in a situation where some have caviar and others have nothing at all. Adorno's rejoinder is that the very distinction between caviar and herring eaters, which Dahrendorf is quite happy to main-tain, is itself a piece of socially perpetuated injustice that has nothing to do with the objective possibilities of the forces of production but only with inequalities taken to be basic and insurmountable. That is, Dahrendorf remains on this side of the veil: he cannot see beyond the "realism" of his piecemeal reforms. Worse, that very realism brings him to implicitly judge the elimination of the social distinction between caviar and herring eaters to be "less" possible—perhaps even practically impossible—than merely improving access to herring within universal conditions of social injustice. As Adorno elsewhere puts it, "In the case of Dahrendorf, there is an overtone of fresh and cheerful conviction: if only you change little things here and there, then perhaps everything will be better. I cannot accept this presupposition."[97] In fact, we should perhaps go one step further and say that Dahrendorf's approach, based on the notion of regulating social conflicts rather than eliminating them, has woven into its fab-ric the notions of natural antagonism and inevitable conflict (recalling Kant, perhaps), precisely in Adorno's sense of second nature ideologically imitating first nature.[98] It may well be "crassly utopian" to think that *all* conflict could be eliminated from human society once and for all, but Adorno's point is that the unreality of *that* fantasy in no way excludes the legitimately utopian elimina-tion of the *systemic* conflicts emanating from the preponderance of capitalist relations of production over human relations, needs, and productive forces. Against this possibility, any insistence on the natural or inevitable character of antagonism can only be counter-productive.

It is perhaps worth emphasizing the reasons why Adorno chooses to re-claim, even insist upon, the concept of utopia, which usually connotes straight-forwards impossibility. Essentially, the explanation begins with the fact, already mentioned, that the technological veil makes the possible out to be impossible and, in so doing, establishes a dual system of social potentialities. Adorno calls attention to this in various ways, not least in the form of criticizing the "natu-ralness" of those possibilities of piecemeal reform that sometimes bubble up in society but that are in fact inherited from the usual, conflict-ridden pos-sibilities of self-preservation that capitalist society perpetuates. As a result, it is society understood as a system of such possibilities of existence that must be examined, diagnosed, and criticized. As such, sociology cannot limit itself to an analysis of mere social givens: we ought not to "rob sociology of that moment of anticipation which essentially belongs to it."[99] The object of such anticipation is, of course, the possibility of what would be different.

Society is something non-identical, as Adorno sometimes says; it is at odds with itself in such a way that the sociological concepts and categories that seek to describe it can come up short when naming the inhumanity that characterizes that most human of endeavors: living together. However—and this is key—this conceptual, theoretical shortfall does not concern society as the sum of existing practices and institutions, as though something positive, some given reality or characteristic, had been overlooked. Rather, it is something *negative* that has been overlooked—namely, those social potentials that are shunted into structurally managed latency while others are pushed to the fore because they are compatible with the reality of the profit motive, national narratives, ideological agendas, and so on. As he puts it in conversation with Arnold Gehlen, who pushes him to say more about this negative potential:

> Of course I don't know in positive terms what this potential is, but on the basis of all possible partial insights—including scientific insights—I do know that the processes that fuel conformism, and to which human beings are subjected today, end up crippling them to an indescribable extent.[100]

For Adorno, then, if the potential is negative, it does not follow that it is indeterminate. It lies in undoing the reification of the social apparatus and thereby its superiority over human beings in whose service these institutions ought to exist. Indeed, Adorno sometimes stresses the insanity of this situation, in which, for example, technology makes everything possible except that in the name of which it exists, that is, the creation of conditions that support the unrestricted flourishing of human life: "The fact that the extended arm of mankind can reach distant, empty planets but is incapable of establishing a permanent peace on earth makes visible the absurd goal towards which the social dialectic is moving."[101]

Thus, on the one hand, on *this* side of the technological veil, we have the "disproportionate superiority of the given" and of the "real" existing practices and possibilities that have become familiar and natural, but that now, in the era of nuclear arms and global warming, also include the possibility of total self-destruction.[102] (Indeed, there is perhaps no better example of socially mediated natural potentialities than the possibility of self-destruction through unchained natural processes.) On the other hand, on the *other* side of the technological veil, there is what Adorno calls a "better potential," which, though currently hindered, remains in play in the sense that consciousness, in spite of everything, still "adumbrates the possibility of the real autonomy of individuals in this life, refused us by the latter's [current] arrangement and shunted into mere ideology."[103]

It is this autonomy—which Adorno elsewhere calls maturity (*Mündigkeit*), the expression of socially charged, critical, spontaneous, primary experience—that offers an effective starting point for social change.[104] For Adorno, autonomy is not just a question of "freedom of thought" (where this expression denotes not sovereign opinion but the real possibility of liberating oneself from heteronomous forces and ideological screens); it is also centrally a question of giving a voice to the socially objectified subject, which means according pride of place to individual experience (qua primary experience) as the site of repression and so of the struggles and contradictions that are to be named and exorcised (and renamed and re-exorcised, as necessary).

From this standpoint, we can see that the dialectical interrelation of society and individual for which Adorno is calling under the banner of autonomy is structurally identical to the nature-history dialectic, now enriched by the notion of blocked possibility. Where in the one case we have nature understood as the apparently ancestral necessity of what are actually just contingent realities, in the other case we have society as a force of repression that has forgotten its origins in human relations; and where in the one case we have history, or the promise of the new, in the other case we have the individual who, anachronistically as it were, steps out of time with heteronomous practices by experiencing society as the repression of redemptive possibilities. Likewise, just as was the case with the nature-history dialectic, individual and society are discontinuous: they no more tend towards a pre-defined τέλος than nature and history. They merely leapfrog over each other, with the risk of the new becoming the archaic once again and the archaic bearing within it the germ of its overcoming in the form of repressed possibility.

To put it in other terms, the Adornian dialectic of individual and society is guided by that for which society in its repressive function has no use: the revolutionary, the incompatible, or the non-identical. Art is an important social expression of such uselessness.

Art, the More

The uselessness of art is grudgingly tolerated by society because artworks are bound up with it through their commodity character. Like any commodity,

they are produced and consumed, and so respond to the demand that everything conform to the principle of exchange and capitalist relations of production. They are useful insofar as they contribute through the commodity form
to the perpetuation of this social arrangement. To that extent, art does not escape the net of existing society. But its commodity character is haunted by uselessness: "Artworks fall helplessly mute before the question 'What's it all for?'
and before the reproach that they are actually pointless."[105] Or more exactly,
Adorno will say that art's social function and lack of function go together.[106]
While artworks are indeed commodities, they are ambiguous or paradoxical
absolute commodities, invoking—though never quite actualizing—an absolu-
tion or release from the false totality of what is socially useful.[107] This "double
character" of art works in its—and our—favor, allowing us to glimpse within
it the possibility of emancipation from the nature-like bonds of capitalist relations of production.[108]

But to really grasp art's critical dimension—and thereby how it refers to
emancipatory potentials—we have to dig a little deeper into its double character, which extends to the question of what art has become and can yet become
at this juncture of its historical evolution. Traditionally, this would involve the
question of how to define art. However, art does not currently lend itself to
simple definitions. Like society, it cannot be reduced to any pre-established list
of objective or subjective criteria: "On no account does an artwork require an
a priori order in which it is received, protected, and accepted. . . . The dubi-
ousness of the ideal of a closed society applies equally to that of the closed
artwork."[109]

The openness of art, which it shares with society, is, at its best, the possibility of its autonomous self-overcoming. Art actualizes this possibility insofar as
it becomes whatever it *can become* in determinate moments of liberation from
the reality of what already exists. Only in this way does it become what it is. In
other words, this is how art becomes *itself,* rather than by displaying certain set
characteristics or adhering to some pre-ordained idea.[110] It is, of course, indebted
to society, not just in the ways already mentioned but intrinsically, in terms of
the concrete inheritance it receives from the history of art: genres, media, conventions, techniques, materials, prior works, and so on. But it does not accept
what it receives as an incontrovertible givenness ("an *a priori* order"). On the
contrary, art's autonomy should be understood negatively, in the form of a claim
as to the essential *insufficiency* of what already exists. This means that artists
cannot simply produce copies of what already exists (be it of nature or of other

artworks) and expect the results to be called art, nor can they produce works merely through the mythical power of genius or explicit artistic intentions (both of which Adorno criticizes severely). Rather, artists and artworks depend upon the discovery of *emergent opportunities* in what has come before. They thereby tap into potentialities that are historically determined and objective (i.e., related to the tradition) yet also hidden (i.e., not pre-given but discovered within and articulated out of the given) and excessive (i.e., not reproductions of what already exists, which is shown to be insufficient). It is in watching artistic production accomplish the task of discovering such "intentionless" and emergent potentialities that we come to an understanding of art's non-closed "laws of movement."[111] Put dialectically, art's autonomy, tied to the articulation of emergent potentialities, involves a kind of determinate negation whereby the real (i.e., the given, the extant) is overtaken by something that is unheard of and not yet real but that both arises within the real and goes beyond it.

Consequently, autonomous art's only "definition" consists in the way that it articulates and actualizes possibilities foreign to what has hitherto counted as art, but that are nevertheless developed out of its history: "It can do this because through the ages, by means of its form, art has not just come to the assistance of persistent reality by giving form to its features, but has also turned against the merely existent and persistent."[112]

So while art has certainly served to reinforce the status quo (e.g., socialist realism,[113] the art market's importance, or decorative uses), it has nevertheless also shown itself to be a constellation of elements that evolves by reconfiguring what already exists in relation to possibilities beyond those sanctioned by the status quo. The possibilities at issue here are thus not neutral with respect to existing art. They instead necessitate the retroactive transformation of the entire field of what is considered art. This is what the history of modern art shows so well, although Adorno thinks it is true of all great art.

This is all part of art's double character. Another way to present its inherent ambiguity is to say that art offers us a rare perspective on both sides of an ideological veil. On the one hand, on this side of the veil, new art is often considered a "monstrous impossibility,"[114] at least according to the cultural conservatism that inevitably rears its head when new art emerges (as in the cases of Baudelaire, Duchamp, and the Second Viennese School). On the other hand, such monstrosities prove that what was hitherto seemingly "impossible" was, in fact, possible and even salutary: "Artworks must emerge as if the impossible were for them possible."[115]

Nevertheless, historically speaking, the existence of such a veil implies that the emergence of the new is no protection against reification. Advanced art is also prone to cultural assimilation, for example, in the form of integration into a canon of staid cultural values. In fact, the flip side of the radically new is that art has inevitably to define itself against what has already been "naturalized" by being incorporated into the domain of existing art and "tamed" possibilities: "Works are usually critical in the era in which they appear; later they are neutralized."[116]

To summarize, three essential moments can be discerned here: (1) the disruption of the status quo of existing art; (2) a glimpse of autonomy through the actualization of unfamiliar possibilities; and (3) the recuperation of these possibilities by the status quo. From this vantage point, we can easily see how the nature-history dialectic informs art and artistic production. First, with regard to nature, neutralization means that the dynamism of artistic production falls prey to the sweeping inclusiveness of society. No sooner does the new emerge than we become inured to its effects: it becomes "natural." Prostitutes and urinals are no longer shocking, dissonance is no longer surprising, and we have all but forgotten the initial novelty of techniques such as montage. In this sense, the new is merely the surprise reality that has not yet capitulated to the uniform totality of existing things: "Modern tendencies, in which irrupting shock-laden contents demolish the law of form, are predestined to make peace with the world, which gives a cozy reception to unsublimated material as soon as the thorn is removed."[117] Worse, this cozy reception—in the form of canonization—often implies imbuing works with the dubious authority of cultural icons. They are granted a veneer of necessity, which the canon shares with the society it serves: "The more inexorably the world, ever the same, is ruled throughout by the universal, the more easily the rudiments of the particular are mistaken for immediacy and confused with concretion, whereas their contingency is recast in the form of abstract necessity."[118]

This puts the emphasis on the artwork's ideological aspect, the moment at which it converges with the status quo: the moment of history becoming nature in the nature-history dialectic. Here too, as previously discussed, nature (the apparent necessity and bindingness of cultural norms and so-called icons) is the result of the petrifaction of history, not an archaic source of truth. Yet it is just as true to say that art emerges only in a moment of liberation from nature, the real. Art is ideological and anti-ideological at once.

Of central and critical importance here is the moment of rupture and transcendence, by which the real is at once superseded and expanded. Art is, as already mentioned, the production and actualization of discontinuous possibilities—of what Adorno calls the "more." This is the other moment of the nature-history dialectic: the becoming historical of nature. This moment's modal structure perhaps requires a closer look.

The more can be approached in various ways, but it is perhaps important first to stress what it is not. The transcendent gesture of autonomous art is not actualized in the trivial creation of a novel, incongruous object, a merely posited $n+1$. It is given in the concrete, continual demonstration of a fundamental idea: reality as it exists at a given point in time does not have the final say on what it is or on how it should evolve. Yet this weakness of the real can be addressed only by looking into its "proportions" and specifying, in each case, what is out of joint within them. Art is thereby the real's double and thus is already more than the real:

> What is non-actual and non-existent in art is not free of the existent. It is not arbitrarily posited, not invented, as is commonly thought; rather, it is constructed from the proportions between existing things, proportions that are themselves defined by the latter's incompleteness, pressing need, and contradictoriness, as well as its potentialities.[119]

This returns us once again to Adorno's curious notion of possibility, of which the artistic more is another incarnation. It is composed of two moments that bring together what we have just seen.

First, possibility in the relevant sense is circumscribed by a "negative canon," as it were, which Adorno describes as "a set of prohibitions against that which the modern disavows in experience and technique; and such determinate negation is virtually a canon of what might be left to do."[120] This is essentially a prohibition against anything like aesthetic paradigms or guidelines that tell us how to proceed or how to produce art based on past accomplishments.

Second, to avoid the absurd consequence that "anything goes so long as it's different," which the concept of a negative canon might suggest, this canon is in turn circumscribed: a central determination of genuine art is therefore, for Adorno, "what falls due" (das Fällige), in the sense of that which shows itself to have been what the situation objectively demanded yet without reference to any positive canon.[121] Indeed, we often realize what "fell due" only retrospectively, in the (perhaps astonishing) persuasiveness of the gesture.

Adorno mentions a number of examples. Montage showed us the untruth of organic unity.[122] Cubism allowed art "for the first time [to document] that life no longer lives."[123] Klee first brought out the relationship between painting and music through painterly *écriture*.[124] Schoenberg fully actualized dissonance and thereby, in that very gesture, abolished the difference between consonance and dissonance.[125] And so on. None of these accomplishments could properly be said to have been a stage in the teleological unfolding of the metaphysical essence of art, yet each was a justified, non-arbitrary moment of originality, the renewal of art's definition and form.

Moreover, the recognition of this fact is a form of autonomy shared by the artwork and the subject capable of following the dynamic at work. Artworks interpellate social subjects by demanding an autonomy that responds and corresponds to that of the artwork, an autonomy of apprehension that reflects the work's liberation from reality. We may or may not be up to the task. But this very uncertainty is what is at issue: the question of the possibility or impossibility of autonomy is the question of art. Thus, art is again the reflection of society, but, to the extent that it is both autonomous and demands autonomy, it also lets us catch a glimpse of a *transformed* society in which autonomy would be the rule rather than the exception. In this way, art's substantive content is utopia itself: "Every artwork is utopia insofar as through its form it anticipates what would finally be itself, and this converges with the demand for the abrogation of the spell of self-identity cast by the subject."[126]

Mirror, Mirror

We are now in a position to say that art is another re-enactment of the dialectic of nature and history, which, in its non-teleological, discontinuous, leapfrogging movement, calls for a subjectivity strong enough to grasp heterogeneous possibility and articulate its form instead of capitulating to the inertial perpetuation of the ever-same. And, as we have seen, this applies to social critique as well—so much so, in fact, that art and society are inextricably bound together (for now, at any rate).

Art, for its part, translates the nature-history dialectic into a socially useless object or performance, which nevertheless preserves the possibility that what is today considered useless—namely, socially prevalent autonomy—may one day animate society: "Relating negatively towards the immediacy inherent in artistic production, the artist unconsciously obeys a social universal: in

every successful correction, watching over the artist's shoulder is a whole subject [*Gesamtsubjekt*] that has not yet succeeded."[127] Such a "whole" subjectivity would not be one that is metaphysically complete, corresponding to some
pre-defined essence of humanity. Rather, it would be a subjectivity not riven by
contingent but persistent, systemic contradictions and antagonisms, and one
that society makes available to all: a subjectivity finally come of age.[128]

Yet art's determinate negations only *hint* at the possibility of whole subjectivity, and, to that extent, it is powerless. This is another facet of its uselessness.
Worse, making art is not automatically a sign of autonomy; on the contrary,
unless the link between art and society is made and developed through the notion of heterogeneous possibilities, art remains complicit with the status quo,
no matter how autonomous it may seem: "Admittedly, through its refusal of society, which is equivalent to sublimation through the law of form, autonomous
art also makes itself a vehicle of ideology: the society at which it shudders is left
in the distance, undisturbed."[129] This is, once again, history reverting to nature.
Art cannot avoid this fate to the extent that it is mere semblance, and so not
socially transformative in and of itself. But its semblance is nevertheless related
to real emancipation; that is the peculiarity of its mimesis. So "even radical art
is a lie insofar as it fails to create the possible that it produces as semblance," yet,
at the same time, "artworks draw credit from a praxis that has yet to begin and
no one knows whether anything backs their letters of credit."[130] The paradox of
art is that it is a "wondrous thing" (a social παράδοξον) that is both a piece of
reality and its nemesis, both autonomous and impotent, both a perspective on
emancipatory possibilities and merely their semblance.

The difference between art and society is that the former recognizes the
right to exist of "what would be different" while the latter does not. Alternatively, art is "freedom, which under the spell of necessity did not—and may not
ever—come to pass."[131] This possible non-actualizability of freedom is again
a symptom of blocked possibility and the reality of dealing with the discontinuous relation of nature to history, and vice versa. But the path that we have
followed to this point provides a unique outlook on this central problem of
Adorno's thought.

For the nature-history dialectic is not just a story of forgetting and remembrance, heteronomy and autonomy, or paralysis and liberation—although it is
certainly all these things as well. It is also a dialectic that can be discerned in
the relation of society to art, with each acting as the other's reflection, each
mimicking the other like different but coordinated twin actualities.

On the one hand, there is society, with its principle of exchange and rule of the useful—a false whole that reveals its insufficiency through its persistent inner contradictions. Taking up these contradictions, a critical theory of society serves to undo the natural character of the "socially necessary illusion" of completeness and of the unreality of any alternative to existing reality.[132] On the other hand, there is the work of art, which shows us repeatedly and insistently that reality is always less than what it contains, that unheard-of possibilities continually emerge from art's historical unfolding. The task of aesthetic theory, in this regard, is to follow the artwork's laws of movement and form and, in this way, to make an appeal for the development of a subjectivity whose active autonomy is able to redeem and realize the powerless, socially useless autonomy that art mimetically enacts.

Thereby, art and society are mirror images of each other, with the powerless autonomy of art mocking the authoritarian hegemony of society; and conversely, with the powerful conformism of society constantly working to assimilate the (for the moment) heterogeneity of art. The two together form yet another figure of the nature-history dialectic, this time writ large.[133] Society is a figure of nature in its denial of transience and transcendence; and art is a figure of history—the new—that is powerless to resist its inevitable naturalization. But just as ideology makes the possible seem impossible, so do artworks accomplish the reverse: it makes the impossible possible. Society and art each turn in a way that opposes the one to the other, but with each one emulating the other symmetrically. The plane of symmetry that binds them together is the concept of what would be different. A veil separates and unites the real possibilities proper to the perpetuation of the status quo and those equally real, yet blocked, possibilities of the different.

Woe Says: Pass—An Adornian "Ought"

Taking a step back from art and society, it should now be clear that Adorno's critique of reality as a self-enclosed, self-reproducing totality has a number of implications. If the world is not reducible to whatever happens to be the case, nor a sum of immutable social realities, nor even self-enclosed, self-manifesting actuality in the Hegelian sense, the reason is that "what is, is more than it is,"[134] in the sense of being marked by a type of possibility that, metaphysically speaking, corresponds to neither mere formal nor real possibility (as Hegel defines these terms). To phrase it differently, Adorno claims that there is a kind of "middle" possibility that lies between the possibilities that actuality sanctions and those that are abstract, formal, or absurd.[135]

Of course, Adorno's view suggests more than a mere modification of modal terminology. It is not mere blocked possibility that matters, no more than making room for it in a table of modal concepts. What really matters, for Adorno, is *transformatively charged* blocked possibilities, those emancipatory possibilities that ought not to be suppressed. Such blocked possibilities should be distinguished from other types of unactualized possibilities. For example, as one might well imagine, merely unheard-of possibilities will not do: the so-called artist who creates an incongruous object has not thereby created an artwork. Likewise, some possibilities should rightly remain out of reach: for example, Adorno speaks of a contemporary "potential for absolute horror" (whether in the form of repetitions of Auschwitz, nuclear war, or some other waking nightmare).[136] How then does Adorno help us move from the modal concept of blocked possibility to the "ought" to which the latter must correspond if it is to gain substance and purchase on reality? One might even question how we are able to detect such possibilities from within self-reproducing actuality or be led to wonder whether the Adornian ought is purely negative, a general imperative against absolute horror? After all, Adorno sometimes expresses himself in this way.[137]

We already have good reasons to think that the Adornian ought is more than a negative imperative, while still not imposing any positive prescriptive content on us; however, it may be worthwhile to spell this out more explicitly. Of central importance in this regard is shared, socially conditioned suffering.[138] The urgency, so the normativity, of unactualized possibility is felt and made real by its systemic nature: that *I* (as an individual) suffer may or may not be relevant or treatable, but when suffering is *shared* because society *universally* and *systematically* produces it in us, then it may well point the way to an unexpressed possibility of liberation. Moreover, it is not just shared suffering in general that matters but especially *contingent* and *socially remediable* forms of suffering that are falsely presented as being necessary and natural, in the sense of the nature-history dialectic. It is from this very concrete perspective, and contrary to Hegel's general view, that we can assert that some oughts are not mere formal possibilities: they are *real*.

The imperative of suppressed possibility is, as Adorno puts it, "Woe says: pass" (*Weh spricht: vergeh*).[139] It is the imperative of a suffering that *ought not to be*, however unable the individual sufferer may be to name the suffering adequately. More specifically, as the German *vergehen* (to pass, wear off, fade) suggests, it is an imperative of transience and transition from a painful actuality to another actuality that has eliminated the prior actuality's condition: a particular kind of transition from essence to existence that operates on the basis of the "ought" of possibility rather than remaining on the level of the "is" of what happens to be real. It is here that the nature-history dialectic begins its work of revealing necessity to be contingency; and likewise, it is here that the "ontology of the wrong state of things" reveals its driving force: "The lived moment tells cognition that suffering ought not to be, that things ought to be different."[140]

In other words, the inevitability or necessity of some forms of suffering can be unmasked as semblance, which opens the way to transcendence. These levels are often presented together to put their entwinement on display:

> Putting an end to suffering, or its mitigation up to a point—a point that can neither be set in advance by theory, nor have any limit imposed upon it—is not a matter for the individual who suffers but solely for the species, to which the individual continues to belong even in becoming detached from it subjectively and, objectively, in being thrust into the solitude of a helpless object. All activities of the species refer to the continuation of its physical existence, even when this is misrecognized and these activities become organizationally independent, carrying out their business only "along the way."[141]

Of course, the species cannot act socially qua species to mitigate or put an end to suffering, but there is nevertheless the possibility of collective action through social organization, whose ultimate principle, shared with the species, is self-preservation or life. It is in this context, which is lived out historically, that the ongoing mitigation of suffering takes on the force of an imperative tied both to what ought not to be and to its dialectical counterpart, the "real ought" that is contingently but continuously blocked by our current social arrangement and its semblance of necessity. The experience of suffering therefore takes on the form of a contradiction: for example, society as a means of self- and species preservation currently takes the form of relations of production that hinder the forces of production that make putting an end to senseless suffering "immediately possible."[142]

Adorno is calling attention to the utter stupidity of this contradiction, not merely pointing it out. It is first of all stupid because we put our self-preservation at risk through actions that misguidedly aim for self-preservation in too narrow a sense (e.g., ethnic conflicts, nationalisms, our dependency on fossil fuels). But it is also stupid because the means to put an end to many socially contingent forms of suffering are within our grasp. In fact, like the good-bad Hegelian that he is, Adorno gives us the contradiction in its determinate form: self-preservation can be carried out for the good of some or for the good of all, but our current social arrangement privileges only some, while making the goal of actualizing the good of all seem impossible. But to state the contradiction in this determinate form is already to gesture towards its overcoming: putting an end to socially unnecessary suffering is, in fact, emphatically possible.

What all of this amounts to is a description of the shift from "is" to "ought" via what "ought not to be." From the experience of lived suffering, theory can help us determine its causes and, in some cases, lead us to an awareness of its social contingency and remediability. Here this takes the form of a social contradiction: a real possibility of emancipation rendered impossible by a contingent social arrangement. From this standpoint, the reality of the blocked possibility becomes evident and the is of suffering becomes the ought of its elimination: "Woe says: pass."

Hegel conceptually demands the banishment of the ought from the domain of real possibility or, what amounts to the same, the assimilation of real possibility to real actuality, because for him real possibility is just—and only—the complete surrender of (existing) actuality to (emergent) actuality. More specifically, recall that in Hegel's thought, the category of formal possibility comprises the "unreal" possibilities of the merely possible (e.g., the sultan may become the pope or the moon may fall to earth).[143] However, along with absurd possibilities, it is also in this category that Hegel places those possibilities that merely ought to be but that are too impotent to become actual. In other words, according to Hegel, what merely ought to be is not a true (real) possibility at all but an illusion—not the real essence or in-itself of something not yet actual but in truth a straightforward impossibility, for otherwise it would be effective within actuality. As Hegel puts it, "Possibility [in the form of the ought] is contradiction, or it is *impossibility*."[144] In this way, actuality stands higher than possibility, which it either *contains* and actualizes or *condemns* as an irrational ought.

From an Adornian perspective, part of the trouble here is that this view can only create a strong bias in favor of existing actuality, in the sense that real possibility is reduced, without remainder, to the necessity of what actuality really produces: "things are as they must be."[145] Adorno also suggests that German philosophy, from at least Leibniz on, has tended to offer explicit justifications

of suffering, whether in the context of a theodicy or otherwise (and philosophy has probably always been related to consolation, even in its most technical
forms).[146] The point is not to assert that *all* suffering is remediable or to say that
the "better potential" of society is somewhere *else* than in existing actuality. As
Adorno puts it, "The choice of a standpoint outside the sway of really existing
society is as fictitious as only the construction of abstract utopias can be."[147]
But neither can utopia—understood as a better future, the possible, or the different—be blithely *ruled out* on the basis of what existing conditions produce
under the sign of necessity. If utopia is more than fantasy, it must find some
middle ground between pure fiction and existing actuality. This is the space of
the Adornian ought.

The root of the matter, to put it succinctly, is that there are two kinds of
ought that need to be distinguished: the ought of formal possibility—the fantastic wish that Hegel rightly ridicules—and the real possibility that society and
philosophy shunt into the category of formal possibility in order to maintain
an illusion of totality, that is, completeness with regard to the possible (since
for Hegel all real possibilities are consumed in the self-production of actuality).[148] As we have seen now through numerous illustrations, this distinction
appears most clearly when a socially necessary illusion blocks emancipatory
transformation, which is then written off as a vain fantasy just because actuality
does not produce the transformation. On this point, Adorno has the following
to say (special attention should be paid to the juxtaposition of the two uses of
the modal verb *sollen*):

> [The conformist tendency to deny the possibility of what ought to be] stems
> from the fact that people are only capable of dealing with the contradiction be-
> tween the obvious possibility of fulfillment and its equally obvious impossibility
> by identifying with the impossibility, by appropriating it. To use [Anna] Freud's
> terminology, they "identify with the aggressor" and say that something *cannot*
> be [*nicht sein* soll], when they know full well that it *ought* to be [*daß es gerade
> ja sein* sollte], though it is withheld from them through a bewitchment of the
> world.[149]

To some people (e.g., Hegel or Dahrendorf), the refusal of what merely ought
to be and its apparent metaphysical legitimacy may seem readily comprehen-
sible. On this view, the refusal of what ought to be is just real actuality manifesting itself as an absolute rational norm by which possibilities can be judged.

In other words, if real possibility is reduced to what is always already contained within real actuality, then whatever does not fit the norm will inevitably appear to be impossible. But there is an untenable presupposition at work in the apparent innocence of the simple distinction between formal and real possibilities—namely, that the mere reproduction of actuality (if that is what actuality produces) is necessary, just because real actuality is always the expression of what is really possible, understood as an actual and complete circle of conditions that formerly existed.

It is precisely this presupposition that Adorno implicitly rejects. For him, the distinction between the "mere" ought and what "really" ought to be, but *nevertheless is not,* is a critical one. It is this emphatic ought—the real ought that complements real possibility—that has no place in many traditional theories of possibility, least of all Hegel's. Adorno says, "Negative dialectic penetrates its hardened objects through possibility—the possibility of which the objects' actuality has cheated them, yet which gazes out of each one."[150] For Hegel, such a notion of "doubly negative" possibility—a non-being of which we would be "cheated" or "deprived"—is utterly unphilosophical or sheer nonsense. Adorno's response is to point out that the intelligibility of a legitimate ought does not exclude it from the sensible realm and, a fortiori, from actuality: "The concept of the intelligible realm would be the concept of that which is not, yet which is not merely 'not.'"[151]

A few more examples will bring out the alternative view of modality that Adorno has in mind, in addition to demonstrating the importance of blocked possibility for understanding Adorno's thought. First, the well-known and apparently contradictory final lines of the introduction to *Negative Dialectic,* where Adorno writes:

> [Utopia], the consciousness of possibility, clings to both the concrete and the undisfigured. Utopia is blocked by what is possible, never by what is immediately actual; that is why what is possible seems abstract in the midst of what exists. Inextinguishable color comes from non-being. Thought, a piece of existence, serves non-being, which thought reaches, however negatively.[152]

The apparent contradiction lies in the way utopia, which is supposed to be the consciousness of possibility, is also *blocked* by possibility. However, if we admit the possibility of what would be different or the real, emphatic ought that is at issue here, then the contradiction disappears. The passage can then be relatively straightforwardly understood as follows: Utopia "is blocked by what is possible"—that is, by familiar but limiting real possibilities—"never by what is immediately actual," which is contingent but which nevertheless holds sway, as though it were necessary. As such, "what is possible"—the *real ought*—"seems abstract in the midst of what exists."[153] In other words, the real possibilities of the existing order are seen as total and exhaustive only because we are accustomed to regarding self-reproducing actuality as an absolute norm. But if we refuse this prejudice and admit the category of blocked possibility, then actuality opens itself up to the different and thereby frees itself from the tyranny of the ever-same.

A similar problem of interpretation arises at the end of Lecture 17 of *An Introduction to Dialectic*:

> It is also part and parcel of the historical dialectic that, under certain circum-
> stances, precisely what appears anachronistic possesses greater living actuality
> than that which lays claim to greater living actuality today, at least superficially,
> namely, in terms of what functions best within existing structures.[154]

This passage, like the previous one, at first seems convoluted and perhaps even confused. But the appearance of confusion is dispelled as soon as we see that there is a double modal structure in play, hinging on the special kind of "anachronism" that for Marx describes a society that has fallen "beneath the level of history."[155] "Living actuality" is not reducible to what merely *appears* to have actuality and relevance, the administered world and its inherent, self-reproducing real possibilities. Rather, it refers first and foremost to the "greater living actuality" of an *other* actuality, of an other future, that is blocked by ideological and metaphysical prejudices. Actuality here again expresses an emphatic ought that is suppressed by what so-called real actuality makes possible. "Anachronism" names this difference or this gap: the time of actuality and its self-reproduction versus the time of blocked possibility and of an other future.

Other examples include Adorno's critique of popular psychology, which standardizes normal and abnormal behavior and thus reduces human possibilities to schemata, thereby sacrificing the process of dialectical experience to "ready-made enlightenment,"[156] that is, reductive or even illusory "real," pre-delineated possibilities of health and illness. A more substantial example is the running critique of crass institutional Marxism in Adorno's writings, a critique that takes aim at the metaphysical prejudice to which Marxism's emphasis on determinate praxis often blinded it: the prejudice according to which a specific future will emerge teleologically and naturally from the economically determined possibilities of the present (e.g., the apparently necessitarian character of the *Communist Manifesto*'s "grave-digger" argument).[157] At root, this prejudice is just the economic manifestation of what is taken to be the metaphysical nature of actuality, which Hegel's theory of possibility especially defines and defends.

Adorno, however, offers us an implicit philosophy of possibility that challenges the prevailing view. The possible is to be measured not merely positively in terms of what already exists but also negatively, in terms of the *difference* from actuality that actuality itself emphatically suggests in the form of an ought that is not reducible to formal possibility. Perhaps the simplest example we have seen in Adorno's writings is the demand "that no one ought to go hungry anymore." The technical means to eliminate hunger are available here and now, but at the same time the current relations of production seem to support the conformist's all too "abstract impossibility" of actually realizing this aim.[158]

Thus, the "real context of delusion" that Adorno seeks everywhere to undo is for him nothing other than this reality's global tendency to treat as impossible all unsanctioned real possibilities of emancipation.[159] Metaphysically, the fault lies with a critique of the ought that treats systematically unactualized possibilities of emancipation as vain, formal possibilities. But the social and metaphysical aspects go hand in hand. For Adorno, if a socially legitimate ought remains unactualized, it is on account of ideologies that depend—implicitly or explicitly, in whole or in part—on the claim that actuality is a totality exhaustive of possibility and complete in itself. Of course, Adorno accepts the claim that actuality is productive of possibility and that it is, in this way, self-productive. He is not a fantasist. But the Hegelian ought cuts away too much; consequently, only those possibilities that become actual are considered real. Yet among those that do not become real are some whose unreality is in fact the sign of a sham totality. There is, of course, a gap separating Hegel's view from the purely ideological affirmation that the reproduction of existing conditions is right and good because that is in fact what actuality produces. However, bizarrely, it is made smaller by his relegation of the ought to the status of mere formal possibility. Against this relegation, Adorno effectively pleads for an intermediate category unrecognized by Hegel: a real ought that is reducible neither to the pre-sanctioned real possibilities of the status quo nor to the fantastic unreal possibilities of our imagination gone wild. In this way, he also lays claim to a future for dialectical thinking.

However, this future is not assured. Adorno's greatest adversary, Martin Heidegger, also provides us with an elaborate model of blocked possibility—and one that runs directly counter to Adorno's. Which of these views is capable of withstanding the challenge of its rival?

CHAPTER 4

ADORNO AND HEIDEGGER

Possibility Read Backwards and Forwards

> There are two Ends that Men propose in writing Satyr, one of
> them less Noble than the other, as regarding nothing further than
> the personal Satisfaction, and Pleasure of the Writer, but without
> any View towards *Personal Malice*; the other is a *Publick Spirit*
> prompting Men of *Genius* and Virtue, to mend the World as far as
> they are able. And as both these Ends are innocent, so the latter is
> highly commendable. With Regard to the former, I demand whether
> I have not as good a Title to laugh, as Men have to be ridiculous,
> and to expose Vice, as another hath to be vicious.
>
> —Swift[1]

The Priority of Possibility in Heidegger

How does Heidegger's concept of possibility serve as an inevitable point of reference for understanding Adorno's view? To answer this question, we should begin with Heidegger's most important published statement on the issue. Simply put, *Being and Time* is a book about possibility. Moreover, it is a book about the priority of possibility over actuality. For this reason, it is also already about the end of metaphysics insofar as the latter defends the inverse priority.

Despite appearances, the project of fundamental ontology is not primarily about the way in which human beings relate to their lived possibilities.[2] It would be more true to say that the portions of the book published by Heidegger in 1927 supply the existential framework to make it possible to think the end of metaphysics and, on that basis, the beginning of another way of relating to beings and ourselves, which Heidegger later calls "the other beginning" (*der andere Anfang*). True, this aspect of the project is developed only in the years and decades following the publication of *Being and Time*. It is, however, announced in § 6, where it is a question of "destroying the history of ontology." Already in this preliminary formulation of the task, which would take on much greater breadth later on, Heidegger makes it clear what he is after: a possibility of thinking and experiencing being that has been covered over by the metaphysical tradition. What is at issue is *the recovery of a positive, albeit blocked, possibility of thinking being* and not, for example, a mere discrediting of metaphysics.[3]

For Heidegger, the question of metaphysics and the question of the ontological constitution of *Dasein* (the kind of being that characterizes human beings) should not be seen as separate. Indeed, what we learn from existence is that actuality is downstream from possibility. Whereas the metaphysical question par excellence—"what is a being in its being?"—seems naturally to ask us to begin from present or actual beings (e.g., in external nature or divine creation), Heidegger thinks that this is already a fundamental distortion of how beings come to appear to us at all, that is, on the basis of the disclosedness (*Erschlossenheit*) of *Dasein* in relation to its possibilities of existence. The analysis of *Dasein* is thereby the first step in a provisional demonstration of the primordial *non-actuality* of being itself or of being understood on the basis of possibility rather than actuality. In other words, the way in which possibility informs the ontological constitution of *Dasein* in fact provides the key to understanding why metaphysical thinking, with its priority of actuality over possibility, can and must be undone. However, given that *Being and Time* was left incomplete and that Heidegger focused increasingly on metaphysical thinking and the alternative to it, the question of possibility understood as an existentiale of *Dasein* in no way exhausts the question. On the contrary, it only encourages us to look more closely at how possibility was subsequently treated. Nevertheless, the concept of possibility in *Being and Time* is a necessary starting point for this endeavor.

That *Dasein* is a being *of* possibility and not merely a present-at-hand being is announced at the outset of the book: "*Dasein* always understands itself in terms of its existence—in terms of a possibility of itself: to be itself or not itself. *Dasein* has either chosen these possibilities itself, or got itself into them, or grown up in them already."[4] The same idea is brought up in more formal, existential terms at the beginning of Division One: "The 'essence' of this being lies in its 'to-be' [*Zu-sein*]."[5] One might say that it is one of *Dasein*'s most essential ontological characteristics that, whatever else it may be, it can only *be* by *becoming*, by thrusting itself in front of itself into the unfolding of what it has (yet) to be. Much of Division One is therefore dedicated to showing how this is so on a number of different levels, such as the apparent presence-at-hand of real things, dealings with other human beings, and the so-called reality of the world. On every level, possibility is shown to be more primordial than any actuality. These issues can be initially approached in reference to the problem of inner-worldly things.

As is well known to readers of *Being and Time*, Heidegger shows that "equipment" or things that seem present-at-hand in one respect—banal things that are accessible and available for use—depend on the "in-order-to" (*Um-zu*) and "for-the-sake-of" (*Um-willen*) relations that center on *Dasein's* possibilities. What a thing *is* in its availability within the world has to be approached through what it *can do* or *be*.[6] Consequently, the hammer *as* hammer in its accessibility and use is unthinkable outside this relation to *Dasein's* possibilities. For it to *be* a hammer, it must be *possible* for me to hammer with it (however well or badly and whether or not the thing in question corresponds to any allegedly archetypal image of a hammer). To the extent that it is *for* something at all, a thing has to take its place within a network of possibilities that relate it to us and to other things. And even if something is "good for nothing," then that very uselessness would still be relative to possibilities *Dasein* has determined to be more relevant. These possibilities are most fundamentally those of *Dasein's* "to-be," its projects, and its future. More generally, there are hammers only to the extent that we can and do sometimes hammer.

Thus, *Dasein* is not a being like others. It is the being for the sake of which there are possibilities and inner-worldly beings.[7] To exist is therefore to relate to possibilities: to inherit them, invent them, communicate them, transform them, and actualize them. To exist is already to be that which is not yet and therefore to be to some degree always already "elsewhere" at all times. *Being and Time's* first task is, in this regard, to spell out the necessary presuppositions and consequences of this notion of existence. It aims to show that to the extent that "*the essence of Dasein lies in its existence*,"[8] then the existence at issue is not the mere presence of something flatly real but rather the ek-sistence of a being always already "outside of itself"[9]—of a being that is constantly not yet what it is and for the sake of which things come to be within the horizon of what they *can be*.

Bearing this in mind, it should come as no surprise that Heidegger sets about dismantling nearly every priority of actuality or reality that the history of metaphysics has ever defended. To be perpetually and necessarily *elsewhere* than in the moment of the sheer presence of things is precisely not to be actual or real in any primary sense. The corresponding critique of the primacy of actuality is pursued in a number of ways in *Being and Time,* all centered on the "outside of itself" that is the kernel of *Dasein*'s existence and temporality.

One example is presented in § 43 of *Being and Time.* The general point of this paragraph is to complete the portrait of *Dasein* as a being of possibility by evaluating and relativizing the notion of reality, *Realität,* understood as referring to given or merely subsistent things, present-at-hand nature, and so on. (It will be a question of actuality, *Wirklichkeit,* in a moment.) As already mentioned in relation to the seeming presence-at-hand of everyday things, reality is not fundamental; on the contrary, Heidegger offers something like a "refutation of realism" in these passages. Yet the point is not to say that reality "does not exist" but rather that it is a philosophical abstraction derived from a lack of understanding of being-in-the-world, that is, the embeddedness of beings in the web of possibilities in which each thing is taken up in relation to *Dasein.* The problem with the "realist" view is that we take "*Dasein* [to be] *present-at-hand as real,* like any other being. In this way *being in general* acquires the meaning of *reality.* . . . Ultimately, [this] shunts the general problematic of being off course."[10]

The refutation of this false reduction of being to reality takes place in several steps, but the central point is that realism begins its explanations with the assumption of givenness, whereas it is precisely the givenness of beings that is at issue.[11] In this sense, realism begins its work too late in the day, after the disclosure of beings has already "happened." Thus, it is not that there is nothing "real" in experience—on the contrary; but the concept of reality makes sense only *post festum.*

Against this view, Heidegger asks that we look back at the analysis of *Dasein*'s being-in-the-world and appreciate that things are what they are only in relation to the existential infrastructure of *Dasein*'s possibilities:

> If the term "reality" means the being of beings present-at-hand within-the-world (*res*)—and nothing else is meant thereby—then when it comes to analyzing this mode of being, this signifies that inner-worldly beings are ontologically conceivable only when the phenomenon of within-the-world-ness has been clarified. But inner-worldliness is based upon the phenomenon of the *world,*

which, for its part, as an essential item in the structure of being-in-the-world, belongs to the basic constitution of *Dasein*.[12]

This applies to all things, even those things that belong to so-called external nature. In all cases, Heidegger maintains the same line, to the effect that the very accessibility of discrete real objects of whatever kind presupposes their prior—albeit generally forgotten—embeddedness in the world of *Dasein*'s possibilities, as well as their dependence on the totality of existentialia that was laid out in the book's earlier chapters and that Heidegger encapsulates in the concept of care (*Sorge*). Consequently, "among the modes of being of inner-worldly beings, reality has no priority."[13]

What holds for banal things holds a fortiori for *Dasein*, which is, properly speaking, not a thing at all but that "for the sake of which" things are the things they are. Thus, reality proves to be an entirely inappropriate category for dealing with existence.[14] For *Dasein* exists rather than subsists—it is always *more* than merely *real*: it is defined by its *potentiality-for-being*, or the structural openness to the possibilities that constitute it in its becoming.[15]

If *Dasein* is no "substance," the reason is that it has no pre-determined essence or potentiality that would be proper to its form and towards which it moves in order to accomplish itself. It has a potentiality-for-being that builds its actuality out of its openness to possibility rather than presupposes an end—understood as a τέλος—that structures it in advance. Contrary to the standard Aristotelian view, the end of *Dasein* is that for the sake of which it is ahead of itself, not in the form of some actuality towards which it moves, but in the form of its pure potentiality-for-being. Once again, there is no priority of actuality. *Dasein* as being-ahead-of-itself means, first of all, that it is that which it is not yet—in a very special sense of "not yet."

The critique of reality has therefore to be supplemented by an explanation of the specific way in which *Dasein* is always already ahead of itself without being a substance of any kind. This broader explanation is clearly intended to shatter once and for all the priority of actuality over possibility. Not only is *Dasein* not merely *real* (not a *res*, not merely subsistent in its brute givenness); it is not primarily *actual* either. To the contrary,

[*Dasein*] is primarily being-possible [*primär Möglichsein*]. *Dasein* is in every case what it can be, and in the way in which it is its possibility. . . . The being-possible that *Dasein* is existentially in every case, is to be sharply distinguished both from empty logical possibility and from the contingency of something present-at-hand, in the sense that with the present-at-hand this or that can "come to pass." As a modal category of presence-at-hand, possibility signifies what is *not yet* actual and what is *not at any time* necessary. It characterizes what is *merely* possible. Ontologically, it is on a lower level than actuality and necessity. Possibility as an existentiale, on the other hand, is the most primordial and ultimate positive ontological characteristic of *Dasein*.[16]

In this passage, Heidegger takes issue directly with the determination of possibility as a modality subordinate to actuality and necessity. As a basic determination of *Dasein*, however, it is bound up with the presence of beings in the world as their condition, as we already saw: only by virtue of what a thing can be or do for the sake of *Dasein* is a thing what it is. What remains to be seen is how *Dasein*'s possibility—"its most primordial and ultimate characteristic"—differs from other notions of possibility, building on the indications that Heidegger provides in the last quotation. How does *Dasein* "stand outside" actuality, so to speak?

Whereas *reality* as factual givenness is generally opposable to absence or unreality, *actuality* is generally opposable to possibility or potentiality. In *Being and Time*, how this latter opposition is structured in metaphysical thinking is turned around such that *Dasein*'s peculiar "not yet"—that it is primarily a being-possible—establishes one of the central conditions of what appears to us in the form of actuality. The peculiarity of this "not yet" is presented mainly in § 48, where it is distinguished from other kinds of possibility. The concept of death—or, properly speaking, being-towards-death—is central to this distinction. However, Heidegger's aim is not to insist on death as such but to characterize the "outside-itself" of *Dasein*—its ek-sistence—as temporality. Being, in this way, will be said to "happen" only in the modal dislocations of time that *Dasein* expresses existentially. In the meantime, being-towards-death provides the basis on which Heidegger defines *Dasein* as a whole—not as total actuality (as in Hegel) but as the totality of its possibilities.

Heidegger proceeds methodically, progressively eliminating defective ways of characterizing *Dasein*'s "not yet" in order to finally arrive at its core determination. Does *Dasein*'s "not yet" refer to something outstanding, like looking forwards to placing the last piece of a jigsaw puzzle or making the last outstanding payment that would discharge a debt? The trouble with this view is that it is at once far too vague (amounting to the mere thought that "something's missing") and too tied to ready-to-hand things (a puzzle piece, a sum of money) that are thought in their possible or necessary togetherness or whole-ness. *Dasein* is not such a whole. Its "not yet" is not a missing part or element of any presumed whole.[17]

Likewise, Heidegger rules out the progressive appearance of a given ob-ject in perception as a model for existential possibility, such as the last quar-ter of a waxing gibbous moon. Here the "not yet" corresponds to the "not yet perceived." The moon itself is *there*, but its waxing is, at the same time, the provisional inaccessibility of an object in its givenness and phenomenological horizonality. But the waxing moon presents us with a purely perceptual "not yet," which, though related to *Dasein's* possible perspectives on it, does not pro-vide an adequate model for understanding *Dasein's* peculiar "not yet." This lat-ter possibility cannot be actualized by any change of perspective, the passage of time, or in general the eventual appearance of some thing whose actuality is, for the moment and contingently, not quite fully revealed.

Heidegger finally comes to the Aristotelian model of the unripe fruit pro-gressing towards ripeness, δύναμις progressing towards ἐντελέχεια.[18] The ad-vantage of this paradigm is that it belongs intrinsically to the fruit to be unripe, to *be* this "not yet" whose non-actuality corresponds to it essentially. Here, pos-sibility is neither something outstanding nor a possible perspective on some being. It is taken to be proper to being itself: "The 'not yet' has already been included in the very being of the fruit, not as some random characteristic, but as something constitutive. In corresponding fashion, as long as any *Dasein* is, it too *is always already its 'not yet.'*"[19] However, this too falls short of *Dasein's* "not yet" to the extent that there is no fully actualized form towards which *Da-sein* proceeds in the unfolding of a determinate potentiality. The end towards which *Dasein* moves is not a τέλος that guides actualization. In fact, *Dasein* has no existential need for "full" actuality at all, at least to the extent that the term implies the *culmination* and *fulfillment* of its potentiality-for-being: "For the most part, *Dasein* ends in unfulfillment, or else by having disintegrated and been used up."[20] In other words, *Dasein's* potentiality-for-being *cannot be actualized at all,* at least not if actuality implies the complete actualization of a pre-given form. The fact that *Dasein* is "primarily being-possible" is not oppos-able to actuality in the way that δύναμις is generally opposable to ἐντελέχεια. *Dasein's* "not yet" corresponds only to the "ahead-of-itself" of existence, quite independently of any reality or fulfilling actuality. In this respect, Heidegger also says that being-towards-death is less about death in any normal sense of the term than it is a way of talking about the metaphysically counter-intuitive priority of possibility over actuality.[21]

It is this priority, first made evident in *Dasein*'s existence, that opens the door to a more wide-ranging critique of metaphysical thinking. Indeed, Heidegger's continuing attacks on the priority of actuality culminate in the notion of beyng (*Seyn*) that he discerns beyond any metaphysical conception of being (*Sein*): "Being is not and therefore does not become a [real or actual] being—this can be most pointedly expressed by saying that beyng is possibility."[22]

In *Being and Time,* this view, however implicit or underdeveloped, is nevertheless discernible, for example, in the claim that "what is essential in [the phenomenological approach] does not lie in how *effective* it as a philosophical 'movement.' Higher than actuality stands *possibility*. We can understand phenomenology only by seizing upon it as possibility."[23] On the surface, the claim is clearly methodological: A phenomenological ontology is capable of more than what Husserlian phenomenology had hitherto been capable.[24] However, given what we have just seen, it seems clear that the standing of possibility in relation to actuality cannot easily be limited to a merely methodological reflection. The methodological claim would be just one instantiation of a motto that holds more generally and extends into the very foundations of fundamental ontology. As Heidegger puts it in a 1927 lecture course, "Within the ontological sphere, the possible is higher than everything actual"—to which he adds that this "peculiar relationship is relevant to philosophy in all its aspects."[25]

However, in spite of the obvious importance of possibility in *Being and Time,* it would have been quite difficult, if not impossible, for its first readers to appreciate the breadth of the critique of actuality that Heidegger begins there. *Being and Time,* "astonishing torso" that it is,[26] does not give us the means. Moreover, Heidegger himself soon bemoaned misunderstandings of the book along existentialist, scientific, and foundationalist lines, to which the notion of fundamental ontology unintentionally contributed.[27] Only beginning with the texts and posthumous manuscripts of the 1930s—and stretching forwards to the end of Heidegger's career—is the critique of actuality (and of modalities more generally) developed and presented in more substantial terms. It is on the basis of these texts that the notion of possibility as "higher" than actuality can really be understood, most notably in terms of the "other beginning."

For a number of reasons that have already started to become clear, it would be difficult to underestimate the interest of the critique of actuality for understanding Heidegger's thought. Indeed, the core of what is arguably Heidegger's most fundamental philosophical thought—that the Greek beginning of Western thinking was not the only possible beginning—must be understood in terms of a serious challenge to actuality and modality traditionally conceived. This challenge ultimately comes in the form of a revised notion of possibility (and, concomitantly, of necessity and actuality), although for the time it remains submerged within the "first," Greek beginning. At issue is an "other" beginning that is more true to the original impetus, if not the historical results, of Western thought.

The relation of the first to the other beginning can no doubt be characterized in different ways—for instance, as a tension in the history of being that calls for a transition from the ancient "guiding question" of metaphysics (τί τὸ ὄν; i.e., the question of the being of beings) to the "basic question" (the question of the truth of beyng itself).[28] But when Heidegger writes of these entangled beginnings, he frequently does so in the vestments of modal language (although, as we shall see, he rejects the whole notion of "modalities" as fraught with unresolvable problems and ambiguities). The interplay of these two beginnings comes, for example, in the form of "the necessity of the *other* beginning,"[29] which is a call to "[dislodge] what is conceptually grasped [in metaphysics] into its impossibility,"[30] or in the claim that "*Da-sein* signifies the ground of the possibility of future human being."[31] (Heidegger here and elsewhere spells *Da-sein* with a hyphen in order to stress its here/there structure and the fact that *Dasein* is always ahead-of-itself in possibility.) There are many such modally charged statements in Heidegger's works. To grasp their common thread and understand the real nature and import of Heidegger's project with regard to a transformed future free of metaphysical errors and prejudices, we must first see that the possibility of which Heidegger speaks is unlike any other. It is unheard of and systematically repressed but also fundamental to thinking. It represents neither the uninterrupted continuation and confirmation of real actuality nor the simple critical development of pre-existing concepts and views. Heidegger aims at an overthrow of metaphysical actuality and, to this end, a revolution more revolutionary than any hitherto.[32] As the foregoing no doubt suggests, this involves a very particular conception of possibility. If the possibility of the other beginning requires a revolution and the collapse of habitual actuality and its attendant possibilities, then the reason is that existing actuality, structured by metaphysical thinking, *impedes* the accomplishment of this more primordial possibility.

The deep-running attack on metaphysical modality in the name of a deeper and more essential blocked possibility traverses Heidegger's writings and is easy enough to spot once we know what to look for. Of course, the near-total dominance of metaphysical thinking in the last two and a half millennia poses certain problems, among which is the fact that there is absolutely no guarantee that what is "essentially" possible (or what is "most inceptual") will ever come to pass. In this regard, the fragility of thinking and the preparatory nature of philosophical experience still under the sway of metaphysics are common themes, often coupled with a tinge of gloom: "Metaphysics might possibly remain in the last stage of its history in such a way that the other thinking cannot come to light at all—and yet nevertheless *is*."[33] Here again, amid the doubt, what is striking in this passage is the configuration of something that Heidegger holds to be distinctly possible and in some sense hidden within the history of metaphysics—namely, the "other thinking," that is, the thinking of the event of beyng. Yet that other thinking is also *inhibited,* possibly to the point of its perpetual neutralization and repression. On the one hand, such a possibility is clearly real, on Heidegger's view, insofar as "real" possibility is to be distinguished from merely logical or formal possibilities; on the other hand, insofar as it is structurally inhibited by metaphysical thinking, it remains unreal, in the specific sense that the conditions of its actualization are by and large unavailable. Such is the nature of blocked possibility.

This structural blockage is described in various ways in Heidegger's writings. For example, technology for him constitutes an all-encompassing, exclusive perspective on beings. But the historical configuration of beings in and through technology and what he calls enframing (*Gestell*) is not just the modern approach to beings. It also serves to conceal the fact that technological enframing is merely one way of revealing beings to us and that it suppresses a more "inceptual" possibility of revealing that is entirely different, incompatible with enframing and with the modalities that are in play within this historical destiny. For Heidegger, this incompatibility extends to *any* interpretation of being in terms of beings that are ultimately understood as given, present beings, whether these are taken to be produced by nature, God, or the knowing subject.

More generally, metaphysical thinking (the interpretation of being in terms of beings understood as unconcealed, present beings) hinders us from considering the alternative to it—the other beginning. But the blockage is not so total that the transition between the first and the other beginnings is fantastic or impossible. In fact, the danger that metaphysics represents also indirectly transmits to us specific knowledge both of the shortcomings of erroneous interpretations of being and of the nature and shape of the other beginning. This danger appears first of all in the importance accorded to actuality in the metaphysical tradition, which skews possibility and necessity in relation to an actuality too narrowly conceived as the mere unconcealedness (givenness, createdness, etc.) of beings along with all their interrelations and properties.

Heidegger's attack on metaphysical conceptions of modality once again takes as its first target the traditional priority of actuality over possibility. As he puts it in § 158 of the *Contributions to Philosophy*: "The provenance and dominance of the 'modalities' are *even more* dubious than the interpretation of beings in terms of ἰδέα,"[34] which for Heidegger stands at the origin of the first, Greek beginning. But to understand this provenance, he then adds, "What is important is the priority of 'actuality' (cf. *existentia* as what pre-eminently stands in distinction to *essentia*): actuality as ἐνέργεια, with possibility and necessity as its two horns, so to speak."[35]

The problem here (as was the case in *Being and Time*, though in a slightly different way) lies first and foremost with the way in which the metaphysical tradition has, almost without exception, defined possibility and necessity *in terms of* actuality, which acts as a central point of reference and criterion for these "modalities." One version of this priority of actuality, stemming from Aristotle, is that to any possibility there must correspond an existing active or passive power of actualization. Another view is that possibility—or at least what is later frequently called real possibility—can be defined in terms of what is at least *sometimes* actual, while necessity corresponds to what is *always* actual.[36] In this way, actuality holds first rank in the metaphysical order of things, not only by virtue of its intrinsic priority—which is largely conceded as soon as being is understood in terms of presence—but also in the relative extensions of its subordinate terms: possibility and necessity constitute the *total* spectrum of actuality, running from the sometimes-actual to the always-actual. They guarantee, as it were, that actuality *exhausts* all being, up to and including that which *is not* in the form of the non-being of the possible (the not-yet-actual). This interpretation corresponds to what some have called the "principle of plenitude."[37] According to this notion, *everything*, even that which *is not yet* (e.g., that which is *in potentia*), is reduced to the order of actuality, like points on a scale running from remote possibility through common potentialities up to fullest actuality, or from δύναμις to ἐνέργεια or ἐντελέχεια. As Heidegger puts it, metaphysically speaking the word "being" (entity, *Seiendes*) does *not* just name the actual (and certainly not if this is taken as the present-at-hand and the latter merely as the object of knowledge), not just the actual of whatever kind, but at the same time the possible, the necessary, the contingent, and everything that stands in beyng in any way whatever, including whatever is "null and void" and nothingness.[38]

Things only went from bad to worse, according to Heidegger, when we later began to interpret the present actuality of beings in terms of things created through an act of divine will; in terms of representable, thinkable, subject-related objects; or in terms of emanations of the will to power. For example, in the writings on Nietzsche we find the following summary objection: "The priority of the actual furthers the forgetting of being. Through this priority, the essential relation to being is buried—namely, the relation that is to be sought in rightly conceived thinking."[39]

Clearly, Heidegger intends to turn the tables on metaphysics and the privilege it accords to actuality. He will thus go on to say that what has, since Aristotle, been taken to be the absolute priority of actuality (or presence) is, in fact, the ominous sign of an unopposed withdrawal of beyng. In each of the key phases or destinies of metaphysical thinking, there lingers a version of the fateful presupposition that the real being of beings lies in their enduring presence, their effectivity, or (ultimately) their actuality, whether in the form of the ἰδέα, ἐνέργεια, ἐντελέχεια, *actualitas, deus,* the absolute subject, and so forth. And in the context of this history (the history of the first beginning), modal concepts are so many tools for naming the different levels of the participation of beings in the fundamental standard of revealed presence and actuality, whatever its specific nature.

Against this view, then, Heidegger calls on us—and on those philosophical and poetic visionaries he calls "the future ones"[40]—to dismantle this tradition from within as a way of discovering its most intimate ground of possibility, denied to metaphysical thinking because of its obsession with presence and actuality. And in seizing on this innermost possibility, we are supposed to see that "there is no problem of 'modalities' at all; rather, under the *illusion* of empty metaphysical astuteness, this problem only conceals the origin of the inceptual explication of being, and hinders the primordial question of being."[41]

In sum, the other beginning resonates in the history of the first beginning as its innermost possibility, since the other beginning is, as it were, the truth *behind* the being of revealed beings proper to the first beginning; but it resonates only as a blocked possibility—a possibility that remains "real," but only in the form of a future that is incompatible with the actuality (of nature, of God, of the knowing subject) that is so prized in the history of the first beginning. According to Heidegger, this blockage is due to the fact that beings and *Dasein* itself cover over and dissemble the ground of their own possibility, turning it into a repressed and therefore hidden ground (*Ab-grund*).[42]

Critical Approaches to Heidegger

There is more than one way to skin a cat. In his novel *Old Masters,* Thomas Bernhard has the central character, Reger, embark on a particularly humorous invective, which is related through the recollections of the narrator:

> Heidegger, in a manner of speaking, was a philosophical marriage fraudster . . . who succeeded in getting a whole generation of German philosophers to stand on their heads. Heidegger is a revolting episode in the history of German philosophy, Reger said yesterday, an episode in which all philosophical Germans participated and *still participate.* To this day Heidegger has still not been entirely exposed for what he is; true, the Heidegger cow has become thinner but the Heidegger cow is still being milked. . . . Heidegger has so reduced everything great that it has become *German-compatible,* you understand: *German-compatible,* Reger said. Heidegger is the *petit bourgeois* of German philosophy, the man who has placed on German philosophy his kitschy night-cap, that kitschy black night-cap which Heidegger always wore, on all occasions. Heidegger is the carpet-slipper and night-cap philosopher of the Germans, nothing else.[43]

The passage continues at this pitch for almost five pages. Bernhard was, of course, a master of satire and an unrelenting critic of ideology and nationalism. In this case, the novel's insight is very simple: Every great work of art or philosophy, every achievement of human spirit is flawed. "If we study them intensively," Reger says, "we sooner or later discover an awkwardness, or indeed, even in the very greatest and the most important creations, a flaw, [and] if we are uncompromising *a serious flaw.*"[44] *Not* noticing this flaw, this defect present in every work, is the point of departure for fetishism: To treat the work as simply the work of an "old master," for example, and to admire it as duty requires, is to fetishize and dehumanize the work, to project on it an aura of greatness or uniqueness and to assume its authority as given without putting it to the test of critique. There are great works but not flawless and irreproachable ones—and those works that *deliberately* invoke a grandeur that covers over their inevitable defects are the ones that most readily "crumble for us," says Reger, "leaving only a flat taste, in fact most of the time a very bad taste, in our mouths."[45]

Bernhard's notion of a "serious flaw" should not be understood as a mere imperfection (as though perfection were an option) but as the error of uniqueness itself, to which Heidegger succumbs. However, the idea that Heidegger falsely lays claim to some sort of uniqueness does not come from Bernhard. It comes from Heidegger, who did not shy away from viewing his thought as channeling the unique—as an attempt to bring about a turning in the history of being and to finally do justice to the unique origin of thinking that gave rise to the first, Greek beginning. For him, the one and only mission of his thought is to move us into the realm of "the primordially-unique" (*das Ursprünglich-Einzige*),[46] which the history of metaphysics left behind in its ascension.[47]

To strip him of this aura of uniqueness would be to liberate thought from the mythical and ritualistic domination of the belief in an origin that we are called on to repeat or retrieve (*wiederholen*), as Heidegger puts it. For Adorno, however, the potential to be released from within history lies not in an imagined origin but in a future that the notion of the "primordially-unique" itself blocks. In other words, for Adorno, that which metaphysical thinking blocks is, unbeknownst to Heidegger, also a block. The task of criticism is thus to demolish this blockage or, what amounts to the same thing, to liberate the salutary possibilities that the fascination with the false uniqueness of the mythical beyng-origin prevents us from grasping and articulating.

However, even if Bernhard's lampooning of Heidegger suggests such an act of defetishization and criticism, it does not on its own push us towards a redeemed future, except perhaps to the extent that the defect that marks the great work can also be understood as an *insufficiency* indicating that there is perhaps still something to say, still something left to do. We might say that Bernhard's criticisms come with an implicit additional task, which Adorno in particular tries to develop. The serious flaw is, in this way, the negative sign of excess possibilities that the merely *real* (given reality, existing works) has not mastered.

In this light, Bernhard's satirical attack on Heidegger can and should be complemented by a more thorough and detailed philosophical critique of what this claim to uniqueness prevents us from seeing: possibilities other than those promised by the belief in a repetition of the origin of thinking. The question therefore remains open as to what the satire specifically asks of us, what orients it and motivates it, other than the deflation of one of the twentieth century's most influential—though also problematic—thinkers. What end does it serve? Bernhard himself may have had no other aim than to carry out a demolition of Heidegger as one representative among many others of the nationalistic Germanness that he so despised and lambasted.

Of course, Bernhard represents only one way to excoriate Heidegger— specifically, the satirical way. But before coming to Adorno's complementary approach, another line of attack should be considered: Emmanuel Faye's all-encompassing—and self-discrediting—assault on Heidegger's Nazism.[48] As is by now well known, Faye has spent years attempting to prove that Heidegger's thought is "nothing more than the theory for which Nazism is the realization," as Peter Gordon aptly summarizes it,[49] and therefore devoid of philosophical value.

For the sake of clarity, it should perhaps be stated at the outset that no one today has any right to claim ignorance or irrelevance about Heidegger's political commitment. Such responses are inadmissible. Moreover, the publication of the so-called *Black Notebooks* has revealed Heidegger's anti-Semitism,[50] as well as the explicit binding together of his thought of the "other beginning" with the National Socialist revolution that he thought would reveal to the German people their destiny. One passage stands out in particular:

> The preformation of a planetary state of affairs can be glimpsed in total systems of every kind.
>
> In human affairs the same old thing is attained and overcome only by the same old thing. But it is part of overcoming that within the same old thing something *wholly* different may at the same time be in the process of unfolding its essence.
>
> In this way—thinking prodigiously—within the essence of that of which "National Socialism" had only a vague sense, there lay the possibility of standing up to this [planetary] state of affairs. [But] what called for prodigious thinking was instead destroyed through terrible intrigues. [Yet] for a brief moment, a few people were thinking of the possible.[51]

It is quite beyond the scope of this chapter to delve into the full extent of the imbrication of Heidegger's thought and National Socialism, or what he elsewhere calls his "essential affirmation" of the impetus driving German fascist revolutionary ideas.[52] However, it is nevertheless possible to underscore a few key points.[53] Heidegger at one time clearly thought that the National Socialist movement could bring about the transition to the other beginning: "In the years 1930 to 1934, I took National Socialism to be the possibility of a transition to an other beginning, and interpreted it in this light."[54] However, the potential and power of the movement was misunderstood: German fascism was not the endgame Heidegger thought it was.[55] Nevertheless, even if National Socialism was not up to the task, the essence and force it incarnated can and must be reaffirmed because of its "basis in thinking" (denkerischen *Gründen*).[56]

Much of this is grist for Faye's mill, and one might well—and quite legitimately—wonder whether there is anything worth retaining from this philosophical-political morass. Unfortunately, there are many rather astonishing claims in Faye's work that undermine the quite legitimate need to criticize Heidegger.

With regard to the *Gesamtausgabe,* the so-called complete edition of Heidegger's writings, Faye stakes out a radical position: "In its very content, [the *Gesamtausgabe*] disseminates within philosophy the explicit and remorseless legitimation of the guiding principles of the Nazi movement."[57] And while some critics, including Adorno, might rightly wish to emphasize the ties that bind Heidegger to German fascism, Faye takes the claim to authorize not only criticisms of the edition itself and of Heidegger's thinking, which are sometimes justified, but also a generalized defense of philosophy itself against its destruction at Heidegger's hands and, correspondingly, the removal of Heidegger's works from the philosophy section of libraries:

> In order to preserve the future of philosophical thought, it is . . . indispensable for us to inquire into the true nature of Heidegger's *Gesamtausgabe,* a collection of texts that are racist, eugenic, and radically deleterious to existence and human reason. Such works cannot continue to be placed in the philosophy section of libraries; their place is rather in the historical archives of Nazism and Hitlerism.[58]

Of course, this would be a little less problematic if Faye had indeed seized on these works' true, entirely non-philosophical, entirely fascistic or partisan nature, but his judgment depends, fatally, upon a philosophical ideal whose implementation is not only disputable but provides the reader with what could be a textbook example of a *petitio principii.*

Faye's central claim is that Heidegger's "intention" was "to lead astray, lay waste, and radically destroy philosophy" and that he "never belonged to philosophy in the deeper sense of the term."[59] But this is so, according to Faye, because philosophy is to be understood in a quite specific way, to which Heidegger admittedly does not subscribe:

> I . . . have long concentrated my research on humanist thought. . . . The vocation of philosophy is to serve the evolution of man. It is totally incompatible with a doctrine that, claiming to promote a particular people, language, and "race" by dominating to the point of annihilation everything that is different from them, destroys the very being of man, both in his individual existence and in his universality.[60]

Elsewhere, Faye adds to the "vocation of philosophy" that its "heart and soul" lies in the "moral attitude" and "moral obligation to respect the human being."[61]

Now, while it is one thing—a quite important thing, in fact—to recommend that we submit Heidegger's anti-humanism and its historical implications to questioning, it is quite another thing to wield a one-sided and quite specific conception of philosophy against Heidegger, claiming for it a status and primacy that is neither argued for nor evidenced in the diversity of practices that make up the history of philosophy.[62] Faye is entitled to pursue whatever research he likes and to defend his views, but he cannot lay claim to the universality of these views as the premise for an argument that then goes on to "show" that Heidegger cannot be a philosopher because he does not endorse these same views. More specifically, he cannot say that true philosophy is necessarily humanist on his narrow understanding of the term—which is clearly untenable as a general definition—and then use that to disqualify Heidegger's anti-humanism without begging the question of philosophy's humanist essence.

To this and other errors of reasoning, we might add a number errors of interpretation—association fallacies, really—that seek to disqualify Heideggerian concepts not on the basis of their philosophical illegitimacy or incoherence but on the basis of an alleged association with something distasteful or reprehensible. There is little point in going into these in detail, but their general form helps show how Faye's position is self-discrediting. For example, at one point he sees a *Kruckenkreuz* and swastikas in an utterly banal line diagram of four interrelated terms. Swastikas can in no way be said to be a part of the diagram. Faye then adds, without any trace of an argument in support of his claim, that the same hidden swastikas should be seen in the later concept of the fourfold (*Geviert*).[63] In another example of the same fallacious guilt by tenuous association, Faye claims that the concept of "clearing" (*Lichtung*), which evokes a certain illumination or lightening, is to be understood as a reference to the torches of the Nuremburg rally of 1935.[64] Such associations—the latter of which Faye even characterizes as "obvious fact"[65]—are of course highly problematic and somewhat risible, especially in a context in which no philosophical engagement with the concepts in play is undertaken because, according to Faye, Heidegger cannot, *by definition,* be a philosopher.

Suffice it to say that whatever the merits of Faye's reading may be, there is nothing philosophically helpful about these claims.

On the one hand, then, we have Bernhard's Juvenalian approach to criticizing Heidegger, which is both amusing and suggestive but which should perhaps be completed by a more explicit philosophical critique, at least if we wish to understand just why the satire is so amusing and even satisfying. On the other hand, we have Faye's scorched-earth reading of Heidegger that does nothing to advance our attempts to come to terms with—and perhaps move productively beyond—some of the legitimate philosophical questions that Heidegger puts to us, not least because Faye flatly denies that any such legitimate philosophical questions exist.

What we discover in reading Adorno on Heidegger is the necessary philosophical complement to these views; and while his reading is not without its problems, it is nevertheless a historically and philosophically informed critique, albeit one that has generally been dismissed by Heideggerians because he is said not to have read him in a serious manner. Whatever the shortcomings of Adorno's reading, it is not philosophically sterile.

For one thing, in the present context, the confrontation of Adorno and Heidegger provides us with an important opportunity to assess, side by side, two of the greatest challenges to the long-standing traditional priority of actuality over possibility. But while Heidegger and Adorno both challenge this priority, they do so in very different ways. To take the measure of their differences on this issue is to understand what is philosophically at stake in Adorno's insistent and persistent offensives against Heidegger. Moreover, this difference of perspective, far from being a local dispute in the history of philosophy, is a crystallization of problems that we must face up to in thinking about the future of critical, autonomous thinking.

A Way Forwards

In Adorno's reading of Heidegger, we can readily find elements of both Bernhard's satirical and Faye's anti-fascist approaches. But it also steers between their respective limitations and offers us something in the end quite different: a dismantling and integration of Heidegger's thought into the context of the dialectic of nature and history. In this regard, Adorno accomplishes what—for different reasons—Bernhard and Faye cannot: he acknowledges Heidegger's place in the history of philosophy, not as an "old master" but as a negative moment that must be deciphered and overcome. This explains why Adorno's criticisms are so insistent and frequent: he recognizes that there is no way around Heidegger in the philosophical, materialist, and dialectical overcoming of the prejudices and pitfalls of metaphysical thinking. Of course, the more substantial philosophical critique remains bound up with its satirical and anti-fascist dimensions, so to understand its content, it is important to untwine it somewhat from these other aspects, not to marginalize them but to see them in their right light.

In purely practical-historical terms, we can readily understand the intellectual motivation of Adorno's critique of Heidegger, which took on considerable breadth in *The Jargon of Authenticity* and *Negative Dialectic*. Given Heidegger's towering influence, which continued to develop in post-war Europe, Adorno saw an increasingly pressing need to counter what he saw as the non-autonomous, non-critical, proto-fascist behavior of jargoneers parroting Heidegger and passing that mimicry off as philosophy. Adorno was clearly determined to champion a critical, anti-fascist, and historically essential alternative to such "Heideggerism."[66] However, this attitude had a long history that went well beyond the attack on Heidegger's cult following. Long before the post-war attempt to save German and European intellectual life from the looming threat of a Heideggerian hegemony, Adorno—beginning soon after the publication of *Being and Time* in 1927—saw Heidegger's thought as radically compromised. In this regard, commentators frequently mention Adorno's remark that "Heidegger's thought is fascist to its innermost cells."[67]

With regard to the anti-fascist aspects of the critique, Adorno was well aware of Heidegger's involvement with National Socialism and refers to it in various ways in his writings.[68] As someone who was intimately familiar with the workings of the German university system in 1933, he was aware of Heidegger's Nazi Party affiliation as rector of Freiburg University and of the existence of the "Profession of Loyalty of University and College Professors to Adolf Hitler and to the National Socialist State," of which Heidegger was a signatory.[69] In later writings, in relation to Heidegger's fascism, he refers to Karl Löwith's 1953 *Heidegger: Thinker in a Destitute Age* and to Guido Schneeberger's 1962 collection of documents relating to the period of Heidegger's Nazi Party affiliation and the academic-political anti-Semitism of the period.[70] Furthermore, the first sentence of the section of *Negative Dialectic* devoted to ontology mentions that "the political past" was no deterrent to Heidegger's influence, implying that it should have been.[71] Elsewhere, he refers to Heidegger as a member of the "old guard" (*der alte Kämpfer Heidegger*) and to his "monopoly" on "Blubo" (*Blut und Boden*, blood and soil) doctrines, no doubt aware that Heidegger held himself to be above the fray, including those he considered to be political hacks.[72] (The *Black Notebooks* bear this out in no uncertain terms.) In a similar vein, he comments on the proximity between the community of Heideggerians and the Nazi notion of the *Volk*, in which the faithful find a sense of urgent metaphysical relief (referring to the Winterhilfswerk, the Nazi relief organization), and notes the way that Heideggerian language—a "language of violence" similar to Hitler's—became more prominent as people began to avoid explicitly National Socialist vocabulary.[73] In the same vein, he says that Heidegger's philosophy equates "being and *Führer*."[74] In addition, Adorno mentions notions evocative of anti-Semitism, especially the concept of "never-dwelling-anywhere" in connection with the image of the Wandering Jew,[75] noting that "in the philosophy of 1927, the rootless intellectual wears the yellow badge of the subverter."[76] (The Jew as "subverter" of the dominant order is a common theme of historical and contemporary anti-Semitism.)

In these and many other ways, the anti-fascist dimension of Adorno's critique comes to the fore and may in some ways seem close to Faye's critique, which certainly underscores similar elements. The difference between the two, however, lies in the fact that Adorno braids together anti-fascist *and* philosophical lines of attack, whereas Faye refuses to accord any philosophical value whatever to Heidegger's thought. The question then arises: What is it about Heidegger that obliges Adorno—and us—to take him seriously as a philosopher, in spite of his involvement with National Socialism?

A similar question arises in relation to the Bernhardian dimension of Adorno's critique (to speak anachronistically). Like Bernhard, Adorno seems at times to revel in accusations that hover suggestively between the amusing and the serious. In these highly satirical moments, Adorno strikes at the heart of Heideggerian gravitas in an attempt to remind us of the dynamic and historically configurable character of thinking. He regularly points out moments in which he thinks Heidegger "flops" (in clown parlance), taking himself somewhat too seriously, believing he has captured the phenomena in their innermost truth. In this vein, we find Adorno referring to Heideggerian terminology as an "administrative," "bureaucratic" language because the existentialia of *Being and Time,* for example, form a network of conceptual functions that officiously pre-determine existence.[77] Their enumeration, he says, resembles a kind of overzealous "stocktaking," and their punctilious application is like "riding an administrative hobbyhorse as though it were Pegasus"—an "apocalyptic hobbyhorse"—into the ground.[78] Likewise, Adorno compares the terminological practices of fundamental ontology to the behavior of obsessive compulsives who must continually wash their hands to keep from getting them dirty, because things are less "pure" than the terminological rigor would suggest.[79] Furthermore, in its specific quality as jargon, Heideggerian terminology is said to encourage "bleating with the herd."[80] Heidegger's general mode of expression is called "agrarian" and is said to have an "artisanal" character modeled on "trusty folk art" because it positions itself as more genuine than the calculative character of a colder, technical, more modern approach to language.[81] Similarly, it is said to have the character of "homely murmuring," or just "drivel," falling to the level of mere "clattering" when it refers to overcoming, once and for all, the tension between familiar ways of thinking and what thinking has to make an effort to think.[82] In addition, Adorno sometimes employs sarcasm to make his point: "During the Hitler regime, Heidegger turned down a professorship in Berlin—one can only empathize with him."[83] Coming from someone who in 1933 lost his right to teach in Germany, one can easily understand how Adorno meant this remark.

Perhaps the most satirical attacks on Heidegger are to be found in the transcripts of lectures on philosophical terminology, from 1962 to 1963, which, along with *Ontology and Dialectic,* provided Adorno with a testing ground for ideas that he would later express, sometimes more soberly, in *The Jargon of Authenticity* and *Negative Dialectic.* However, no matter how satirical these passages are, the philosophical thrust of Adorno's critique is also plainly audible.

Adorno lays it on quite thick, deriding Heidegger's appeal to "simple, rustic life,"[84] and he mocks the kitschy, sentimental character of Heidegger's provincial justification for twice refusing a professorship in Berlin (in 1929 and 1933). To this end, he quotes extensively from "Why Do I Stay in the Provinces?,"[85] building up to a somewhat colorful rejection of Heidegger's thought:

> The comic effect of this blood and soil ideology, of which I've given you a good
> taste, consists not least of all in the fact that what it delivers, or what arises out of
> its emphatic claim—namely, that what is at issue is being itself—is so poor and
> so meager, that one might almost say that it reeks of poverty. One has the feel-
> ing that if the absolute is nothing but the air wafting around a wretched fireside
> bench, then one might be better off having nothing to do with it.[86]

However, for Adorno, it is neither simply a question of mockery or even of
underscoring, as he does, Heidegger's political and philosophical complicity
in National Socialism. Adorno's aim is not to ridicule Heidegger—or at least
it does not end there. The philosophical heart of the matter, here as elsewhere,
turns on what he variously calls Heidegger's "archaism," his "superstitious belief
in a first principle," or even his "drilling compulsion."[87] The trouble, essentially,
lies with the priority accorded to what comes *first* in thinking, even—or especially—when that "first thing" is something forgotten or hidden behind something that also lays claim to firstness. This is precisely the nub of Heidegger's
critique of the history of metaphysics, as we saw earlier: The "other beginning"
is based on the claim that metaphysical first principles do not, in fact, constitute the true foundation of thinking at all. The traditional ground of thinking
must give way to an anti-ground, a ground that moves away from or out from
under the deficiencies of other grounds: an *Abgrund,* to use Heidegger's own
term. Against this view, Adorno diagnoses what he takes to be a philosophical
error: the false belief that

> whatever genetically or logically comes first must, for that very reason, have
> a claim to higher dignity or higher truth. I don't think that I'm guilty of an all
> too skeptical positivism by drawing attention to the fact that this view strongly
> resonates with unresolved mythological thinking, e.g., the belief that the old
> gods are the true gods, that what came first must have been better—as in the
> myths of the golden age—that human beings once possessed some truth that
> they then came to lose, whether through some fault of their own or through
> some metaphysical fate.[88]

Adorno stakes out a counter-claim to this view: What is most true (in the sense
of the ground of thinking) is not hidden somewhere in the past or at the origin
of thought but in the inner-historical mediations and riddles that give thought
something to think. More specifically, the problem is not so much that Hei-

degger criticizes metaphysics or tries to orient us towards some better way of being in relation to the world and ourselves, or even that Heidegger refers to rustic life as a way of criticizing certain tendencies of modernity. Adorno will even admit that there is a "glint of reconciliation" in Heidegger towards which a certain legitimate yearning is directed.[89] In fact, he considers his own references to his apparently idyllic childhood trips to the town of Amorbach to participate in something similar. But Adorno sees the difference between his view and Heidegger's to lie in the fact that he does not transform Amorbach into an ideal to which we must return.[90] The point is that the truth lies not in a return to an archaic or mythological past—be it a ground beyond or beneath all metaphysical grounds—but in transforming the world on the basis of what society denies us in the name of the social continuum rather than human well-being. Heidegger's error is therefore that in spite of his recurrent emphasis on the future, the "not yet," and so on, the content of these terms is bequeathed to us from an idealized other beginning that has been concealed from us since the dawn of thinking. A yearning for difference and transformation is one thing, whereas yearning for the true first thing is quite another. To substitute the latter for the former is to "counterfeit" the truth: "The counterfeiting begins only with an inversion of this yearning, such that it is *backwards-facing,* caught up in something unattainable and irretrievable."[91]

These are issues to which we shall return in more detail, but to frame the problem as clearly as is possible at this stage, we can summarize Adorno's point as follows: By adhering to such a primordial, lost ideal that has to be recovered, we bind our hands and put ourselves on a historical course that has extremely limited possible outcomes. That is, the success or failure of history is measured against this ideal rather than against the dynamic creation and actualization of possibilities of betterment within history. For Adorno, however, betterment is historically open and subject to unforeseeable reconfigurations; it is not bound, as it is for Heidegger, to a singular, unique potential that we have hitherto failed to actualize. Rather, we should free ourselves from this backwards-facing stance and orient ourselves towards the future that our social situation prevents us from seeing, that is promised to us by the elimination of socially unnecessary suffering, even at the cost of the ideological suffering that will no doubt result from throwing the presuppositions of historical existence into question.

It should now be clear that neither the satirical nor the anti-fascist currents in Adorno's critique of Heidegger nor even both together provide us with a full picture of his view. So while it is obvious that Adorno was trying to steer a generation of philosophers and students away from Heidegger and from what he saw as an intellectual—and indeed political—hazard, there is something else at work in the critique, visible when the volume of the invective is turned down slightly and temporarily in favor of an examination of their contrasting philosophical approaches. Simply put, a direct satirical or political assault on Heidegger cannot be the end of the story. Heidegger is a target for Adorno not because he gets things *utterly* wrong—can a dialectical thinker really claim that thought has misunderstood itself *irredeemably?*— but because he gets everything *backwards*.[92] In other words, there is not just an account to settle but something *to put right* in this whole story. As Adorno states in a letter to Benjamin, it may yet be possible to imagine "a Heidegger put right side up."[93]

Heidegger is therefore not just a whipping boy for metaphysical presumptuousness but a significant figure in the struggle over the future of redemptive thinking. In this struggle, he represents the historical manifestation of a danger that thought must take seriously and face up to dialectically and immanently. Thus, to situate what Adorno says here within the present context, we might say that if Heidegger get things backwards, the reason is that his thought represents a reversion to myth—hence the negative aspect of the critique. Our task, as readers of this polemic, should be to note this and attempt to understand how myth, however misguidedly or wrongly, also speaks for the non-identical or the incommensurable—hence the productive thrust of the critique. The satirical dimension of Adorno's reading thereby points in two directions, the damning and the redemptive, as indeed it must if it is to instantiate the dialectical thinking that he proffers as the antidote to Heideggerism. It is a question of "determinate negation," to use a Hegelian expression. Were this not the case, were Adorno aiming at merely dismissing Heidegger, as Faye attempts, then the critique would be nothing more than a protracted expression of alleged philosophical good taste in which the reader would be asked to choose sides—while also being told in no uncertain terms which side to choose. While it is easy enough to place oneself on the right side of history by condemning Heidegger, such a critique does not attain the fullest expression of the "Publick Spirit" that Swift (in the chapter epigraph) suggests satire should be; at best, it would be a mere sortie from a safe but immured position.

Instead of reconstructing Adorno's official position as he himself presents it in *Jargon of Authenticity* and *Negative Dialectic*—which the reader could well accomplish alone—the aim of what follows is to approach the issues somewhat obliquely, from a standpoint that Adorno himself does not foreground, the reversal of the traditional priority of actuality over possibility.

As we have seen, Adorno and Heidegger both challenge real actuality as a criterion of truth and legitimacy. As far as Heidegger is concerned, his thought is an attempt to dislodge an unusual and suppressed notion of being from the history of metaphysics. This involves, among other things, a critique of being as presence, as being tied to positive reality or to the eminence, fullness, and unassailable necessity of a particular being's actuality (e.g., God or the knowing subject). He believes that we have to turn around and "destroy" these presuppositions to liberate thinking from metaphysical constraints and to open it up for the "other beginning" in which actuality and its avatars, such as technology, would no longer have the upper hand over *Dasein* and its ownmost possibilities of existence.

While Adorno is similarly concerned about the suppression of certain historically essential possibilities by a self-perpetuating actuality that has become an unquestioned and nearly unquestionable second nature, he does not ask us to return to an origin of any kind. On the contrary, his interest lies with historically determinate "utopian" possibilities that follow the development of capitalist society like its shadow. At issue are real possibilities that suffer from an ideologically informed allegation of impossibility: impossible possibilities that are nevertheless possible because their impossibility is an effect of the veil of ideology and technology. (Of the examples mentioned in other chapters, the most emphatic one is the descriptive-prescriptive claim that "no one ought to go hungry anymore.") In this way, Adorno and Heidegger offer very different yet related challenges to existing actuality and the sum of philosophical prejudices that inform it (going back to Hegel, naturally, but involving many of the defining claims of traditional metaphysics).

We are now in a position to evaluate these two very different claims, for clearly they are profoundly opposed to each other in diverse ways but also in one absolutely central point of contention—namely, in their respective approaches to the salutary possibilities that, through our own doing, lie out of reach, as with Tantalus who finds himself denied food and drink. To redeem Tantalus, as it were, Heidegger asks us first to look back in view of a retrieval, whereas Adorno asks us to look forwards dialectically from the standpoint of historical specificity.

We shall consider two figures of difference in order to take the measure of the dialectical intertwining of Adorno's and Heidegger's contributions to the history of philosophy. The first involves the task of philosophical interpretation; the second is their approaches to questions of progress and technology. Both stand in relation to the possibility of redeeming the past in a future that would be different from what we have known hitherto.

Cat Burglary and Interpretation

Adorno's critique of Heidegger essentially spanned the entirety of his forty-year academic career. His earliest reactions to Heidegger's thought are largely unknown.[94] Things begin to take on definite shape starting from his *Habilitationsschrift* (the postdoctoral thesis required to become a teacher and professor) on Kierkegaard, which he began working on in 1929 and which showed the beginnings of a critique of Heidegger.[95] More-developed critiques are put forwards starting with his inaugural address of 1931, "The Actuality of Philosophy," and "The Idea of Nature-History" from 1932. In the mid-1930s Adorno worked a great deal on Husserl and phenomenology, which he had already explored in his doctoral dissertation of 1924.[96] This research eventually gave rise in 1956 to *Zur Metakritik der Erkenntnistheorie* (*Against Epistemology: A Metacritique*) in which a few references to Heidegger are found.[97]

Adorno returned to Heidegger with increased intensity and focus at the beginning of the 1960s. In 1960–1961, he presented the lecture course *Ontology and Dialectic*, which laid out the main criticisms. In the spring of 1961, he gave a series of three lectures at the Collège de France based on material from that course.[98] The 1962 lecture course *Philosophical Terminology* adds to the portrait.[99] Furthermore, in 1963 he presented "Parataxis: On the Philosophical Interpretation of Hölderlin's Late Poetry" at the annual meeting of the Hölderlin Society, a text in which he once again took Heidegger to task. That paper was not included in the published proceedings of the meeting as would normally have been the case. It first appeared in print in 1964 and then again in 1965 in the third volume of *Notes to Literature*.[100] This period culminated in *The Jargon of Authenticity* (1964) and *Negative Dialectic* (1966), in which the central criticisms are definitively formulated.

Dozens of other references to Heidegger—some cursory, others more substantial—are found in other writings and in Adorno's correspondence. Adorno had in his library a first edition of *Being and Time*, which he heavily underscored and annotated, as well as other books by Heidegger. It is clear from various remarks that he knew Heidegger's thought quite well, especially *Being and*

Time, although he also notes important later developments, such as the less frequent references to *Dasein* in writings after *Being and Time*, the introduction of the archaism *Seyn* (beyng), and the typographical crossing out of the word "being."[101] Additionally, his student and later colleague Karl Heinz Haag wrote his postdoctoral thesis partly on Heidegger and presumably collaborated with Adorno to some extent and contributed to his understanding of Heidegger.[102]

With this background in mind, we can now turn in detail to the first public critique of Heidegger, which comes in 1931 in Adorno's inaugural address "The Actuality of Philosophy." There are at least two levels of engagement in the text, which shows signs of an attentive reading of *Being and Time*, as well as knowledge of unpublished pronouncements from Freiburg. In the main line of argument, Adorno sets about providing philosophy with a task, at a time in history when the actual relevance—or living actuality (*Aktualität*)—of its traditional methods had become questionable.[103] If philosophy is to remain actual, he says, it will not be in any long-awaited, ultimate correspondence of reason to the whole of actuality (*Wirklichkeit*), but only in the rational reconstruction of what, within actuality, prompts reason to react "polemically," that is, not in a faithful *reproduction* but rather in a *refusal* of existing actuality qua totality. In this regard, reason has to begin with an acknowledgment of the failure of metaphysical foundationalism and set to work on these ruined foundations rather than continue the urge to create or discover ever more unshakable ones. Adorno writes: "A philosophy that today pretends [to be able to grasp total actuality] serves only to veil actuality and eternalize its present state."[104] What is striking here is the veiling effect from which actuality suffers if we seek to know it as *total* actuality, as though all possibilities—of knowing and of the knowable—were somehow pre-given and available to a form of reason that would finally establish its foundations and circumscribe the actuality it seeks to know. One might say that it is precisely the *search* for a true totality consisting of the identity of reason and actuality or of essence and existence that constitutes the veil preventing us from seeing what philosophy and actuality might yet become. To put the same thought the other way around, philosophy's repeated failure to grasp actuality as a totality, qua failure, provides us with our only hope for a better philosophy and a better actuality. More specifically, this hope depends on tearing the veil of totality away from existing actuality, in order to uncover possibilities shrouded by the veil.

As for what vision of total actuality Adorno takes as his target, he does not leave us waiting very long: in the next lines, he announces that, among other tendencies, it is primarily the "question of being as such" and the idea of catching it in the net of fundamental concepts—Heidegger's existentialia—that he intends to criticize.[105]

Adorno has two concerns here. First, he is trying to save philosophy from what he calls its "liquidation," either at the hands of the sciences or scientistic philosophy (neo-Kantianism, phenomenology, and what is now called analytic philosophy) or by a lapse into poetry.[106] Second, he takes Heidegger to task for trying to conserve the "archaic dignity" of being, whereas philosophy should begin by admitting its own refusal to recognize the collapse of all claims to grasp the totality of the actual.[107] The trouble with Heidegger, then, is that fundamental ontology persists in the belief that it can fully and adequately grasp the meaning of being as such. More specifically, as Adorno would later say, he "ontologizes the ontic"[108] and so fails to treat history as the guarantor of philosophical insight, instead putting his trust in an abstract ontological historicality (*Geschichtlichkeit*) that is supposed to lead us back to the primordial meaning of being.[109]

Thus, while it is true that Heidegger stresses *Dasein*'s everydayness, its facticity, and its concrete "mineness," these aspects are to be understood merely as the opening gambit in an attempt to refound thinking on its forgotten origins. To phrase the historical problem otherwise, and as Heidegger announced as early as 1930, "history begins only when beings themselves are expressly drawn up into their unconcealment and conserved in it, only when this conservation is conceived on the basis of questioning regarding beings as such."[110] History, in other words, only begins with what philosophy later tries to make explicit: the posing and answering of the basic, all-encompassing question of what it is to be a being. However, metaphysics—which formally determines the *kind* of history in which we find ourselves—makes the fatal mistake of answering this question in terms of beings rather than in terms of the pre-metaphysical disclosure of beings; and so the task of philosophy or thinking (as opposed to traditional metaphysics) is to reverse this movement. *Genuine* thinking, if it is to think being independently of the bias in favor of beings, must penetrate beyond mere history, into the forgotten "first possibility" of metaphysical questioning, on the basis of which it may yet be possible to provoke an other beginning.

Adorno is quite astute on this point. Already in 1931, he not only notices the call to retrieve a forgotten origin but also understands what this entails qua retrieval: a contemporary refounding of thought on new, uncharted ground. So while he would have had no direct textual evidence of the Heideggerian idea of a transition to the other beginning—which in any case was only fully articulated later in the 1930s and mostly in unpublished manuscripts to which Adorno would have had no access—he nevertheless puts the search for an archaic origin together with the notion of a new beginning: "Only an essentially undialectical philosophy, one which aims at ahistorical truth, could even imagine that the old problems could simply be put to one side by forgetting them and starting fresh from the beginning." It is thereby at the "deception of the beginning" that Adorno takes aim.[111]

There are really two interrelated points here. First, as already noted, Heidegger shunts thinking into the past in order to go forwards. (We shall return to this point in a moment.) Second, this tendency to search for the redemptive possibility of the new in an *origin* leads to a neglect of pressing, properly historical riddles or to a reduction of the historical to its alleged existential structure. This latter point represents an ontologization of the ontic, according to Adorno, because the particularity of historical problems and suffering is transformed into a question of incontestably essential concepts. The Heideggerian concept of falling (*Verfallen*), for example, gives the impression of providing an analysis of ideological façades, whereas in fact it simply freezes the façades in place. We are, of course, *prone* to ideological error—and to error in general—but this proneness is, for Adorno, accompanied by the possibility of its dialectical overcoming in its specific historical manifestations. It is this future-oriented moment, this horizon of liberation from the past, that should guide us, *not the proneness as such* and certainly not in the form of a permanent ontological structure. For Heidegger, however, falling, anxiety, and other existential forms of suffering are "eternalized" and so without solution. How could a fundamental trait of human existence admit of a solution? Heidegger admits this explicitly: "We would . . . misunderstand the ontologico-existential structure of falling if we were to ascribe to it the sense of a bad and deplorable ontical property of which, perhaps, more advanced stages of human culture might be able to rid themselves."[112]

It is this eternalization of the negative aspects of *Dasein*—which include anxiety, idle talk, and ambiguity—that so irritates Adorno and provokes him to propose an alternative to Heidegger. However, while his general approach is clear enough, we would be wrong to conceive of these alternatives as *abstractly* opposed to one another. For example, at one point in "The Actuality of Philosophy" Adorno somewhat curiously borrows a simile from Heidegger, to invert it and appropriate it but also to show how they are both responding to the same situation, the threat of the liquidation of philosophy by science or scientistic thinking:[113]

> One of the most influential academic philosophers of the present [i.e., Heidegger] is said to have answered the question of the relationship between philosophy and sociology somewhat like this: while the philosopher is like an architect who develops and executes the building plan of a house, the sociologist is like the cat burglar who climbs the walls from outside and takes what he can grab. I would be inclined to acknowledge the comparison and to interpret positively the function he gave sociology for philosophy. For the house, this big house, has long since decayed in its foundations and threatens, [if it should collapse,] not only to kill all those inside, but to cause the loss of all things stored within it, much of which is irreplaceable. If the cat burglar steals these things, these singular, indeed often half-forgotten things, he does a good deed, insofar as he saves them.[114]

Interestingly, Heidegger's version of the cat burglar simile can be found in a source to which Adorno could not have had firsthand access: the 1929–1930 lecture course *The Fundamental Concepts of Metaphysics*. From whom he came to know about it is a mystery, although notes and transcripts of Heidegger's lectures were widely circulated among students.[115] In any event, it at least shows that he was attentive to more than what he had read in *Being and Time*. The passage in question deals with the relation of the sciences to ontology. Heidegger argues that the discovery of "new facts" is not what explains the historical transformation of scientific disciplines.[116] "Originality," he says, "consists in nothing other than decisively seeing and thinking once again and at the right moment that which is essential, that which has always already and repeatedly been seen and thought before."[117] In other words, the individual sciences depend upon opening up individual domains of beings according to their essences and their deployment through the existential disclosedness of *Dasein*. In short, the individual sciences depend upon ontology. In this context, he says,

> Fundamentally and primarily, it is our approach to the [fundamental question that guides a given science] and our way of seeing that is transformed [when a science undergoes an apparently radical "new" development]—and in accordance with this the facts [are transformed]. This transformation of seeing and questioning is always the decisive thing in science. The greatness and vitality of

a science is revealed in the power of its capacity for such a transformation. Yet this transformation of seeing and questioning is misunderstood when it is taken as a change of standpoint or as a shift in the sociological conditions of a science. It is true that this is the sort of thing which mainly or exclusively interests many people in science today—its psychologically or sociologically conditioned character—but this is just a façade. Sociology of this kind relates to actual science and its philosophical comprehension in the same way in which a cat burglar relates to the architect or, to take a less elevated example, to a conscientious craftsman.[118]

We have here two opposed perspectives on how to view philosophical insight and the possibility of originality, with the cat burglar serving as the figure by which they can be distinguished. Are the plans and the resulting building what is important: the meaning of being, the history of the first beginning, and the possibility of an other beginning? Or is it the cat burglar and his Benjaminian attempt to "save the phenomena," the "half-forgotten things" of an actuality on the point of ruin, that may yet allegorically indicate how to arrive at a better future?

In this respect, it is not so much the perspective on the individual scientific disciplines that is important. What is critical are Adorno's and Heidegger's different takes on the *future,* or on the possibility of a future that would break with the past and offer something new and better for thinking and for actuality. This is really the core of the philosophical critique of Heidegger, the main characteristic that pits them against each other: Whence do we derive this future? It would seem clear that Heidegger is devoted to a *primordial, never yet actualized* possibility, which is prior to the rule of actuality in the history of metaphysics, although its traces lie hidden within the latter. Adorno, however, while similarly denouncing existing actuality, asks that we dynamically liberate new possibilities from a reality in the process of collapse.

Heidegger, for his part, could not be more clear about his position, as later rhetorically stated in "The End of Philosophy and the Task of Thinking," for example:

Is the end of philosophy in the sense of its expansion into the various sciences also thereby the complete actualization of all the possibilities by which thinking became philosophy? Or is there, apart from this *final* possibility (the dissolution of philosophy into the technicized sciences), a *first* possibility from which thinking had indeed to proceed, but which philosophy could not experience and undertake as its own?[119]

Adorno, of course, thinks that such a "first" possibility is the expression of archaic, mythological thinking, but he does not reject the notion that philosophy should rid itself of the ideal of the complete actualization of existing possibilities because existing possibilities are precisely those that are already in circulation and, for the most part, belong to the "building plans" of capitalism. On the contrary, he condemns reality's hold on possibility on the basis of what he characterizes as a materialist conception of the task of philosophy, which he calls *Deutung*, indicative interpretation.[120]

With this, we reach the second level of engagement with Heidegger in "The Actuality of Philosophy." Essentially, Adorno proposes indicative interpretation as the philosophical alternative to scientific research (*Forschung*), certain incarnations of which threaten to liquidate philosophy. What he does not say explicitly, however, is that indicative interpretation is, in fact, a *provocation* in the form of a direct alternative to what Heidegger proposes in *Being and Time*—namely, the need for an interpretation (*Auslegung, Interpretation*[121]) of *Dasein* that is likewise opposed to mere scientific research. While Heidegger defends his notion of interpretation against a too narrowly defined scientific form of research, Adorno seeks to correct Heidegger by proposing another kind of interpretation as an alternative to Heidegger's own versions of interpretation. The distinction is between (1) making explicit essential structures of the primordial disclosure of beings (Heidegger's *Interpretation* and *Auslegung*) and (2) pointing to liberating possibilities that emerge from a clarification of the historical forces that would otherwise determine actuality in a blind, fate-like manner (Adorno's *Deutung*). To distinguish between the concepts in play, we use the terms "interpretation" and "formal interpretation" for the Heideggerian *Auslegung* and *Interpretation*, respectively, and "indicative interpretation" for the Adornian *Deutung*. All of these terms are, on some level, opposed to "research," *Forschung*.

Heidegger uses the concept of "research" in a number of ways in *Being and Time*, also to characterize his own work. He even says that research is a basic mode of being of *Dasein*.[122] However, in § 3 of *Being and Time*, a more specific meaning is given to the term, quite in line with the discussion of the individual scientific disciplines in *The Fundamental Concepts of Metaphysics*, cited previously. Heidegger essentially says that, for the most part, we operate on the tacit assumption that every individual scientific discipline has its proper domain, which has somehow been made available to it through a pre-scientific sharing out of beings. The question is how this occurs. Heidegger's answer involves a primordial interpretation of beings (ultimately focusing on the disclosure of beings that makes them "available" to experience and the positive sciences), which may then be made the object of more formal interpretation, starting with metaphysical rather than ready-made scientific concepts.[123] To approach the question in this manner is to inquire into the meaning of being and embark on the elaboration of a fundamental ontology.[124]

The key to fundamental ontology, then, is to understand the spontaneous existential interpretation of beings that renders them available to us as the beings they are, that is, in and through their attendant possibilities. Interpretation arranges beings in relation to each other and to *Dasein* for the first time in terms of *Dasein*'s potentiality-for-being. In other words, interpretation grasps what something ready-to-hand can be or become or do *as* the thing it is: To be aware that I *can* do this or that with something is to have interpreted it, to have spontaneously and implicitly (for the most part) laid it out *as* what it is in relation to my potentiality-for-being.[125] This allows for a sharing out of beings into different categories, including pre- or proto-scientific categories. Fundamental ontology is, in its turn, the systematic, formal interpretation of this more spontaneous interpretation, along with other aspects of disclosedness. Specifically, to make the spontaneous, disclosive interpretation of beings explicit in rigorous philosophical discourse and in all its ramifications is to answer the question of the meaning of being, which scientific research bears within itself as an unacknowledged presupposition. In this way, Heidegger opposes interpretation and its formal ontological counterpart to scientific research.

Adorno, unquestionably with these distinctions in mind, first sets about ruling out any such search for "ultimate meaning" and then proposes "indicative interpretation" as a better way forwards, warning us against confusing them.[126] Interestingly, while he is more willing than Heidegger to cooperate with the individual sciences—especially sociology—he nevertheless describes them in a manner not dissimilar to what is said in *Being and Time*: "The individual sciences accept their results, at least their final and deepest results, as solid and stable in themselves."[127] For Adorno, such "positivism," such an acceptance of facts, cannot stand on its own, nor does the scientific way of proceeding in any way liquidate philosophy. Thus, the central issue lies with the alternative to scientific research.

But what most worries Adorno about the Heideggerian concept of meaning are its implications regarding actuality: "It is just not the task of philosophy to present such a meaning positively, to portray actuality as 'meaningful' and thereby justify it."[128] As previously noted, this is so because Adorno refuses to accept that there is such a thing as total actuality (be it *Dasein*'s being-a-whole, in spite of being based on a critique of actuality) that a system of reason (be it a fundamental ontology) could grasp in a network of incontestable basic concepts (be they existentialia); and any attempt to do so will sooner or later end up reifying volatile aspects of actuality that could yet be transformed for the better. It is in this regard that Adorno suggests that philosophy should adopt another approach, that of indicative interpretation, which takes up actuality in all its fate-like, often incomprehensible givenness: "The text which philosophy has to read is incomplete, contradictory, fragmentary, and much in it may be delivered up to blind demons; in fact perhaps the reading of it is our task precisely so that we, by reading, can better learn to recognize the blind demonic forces and to banish them."[129]

What are these blind demonic forces? They are the forces that structure actuality behind the back of the living individual, though not in the manner of existential structures. Rather, they are the historical forces that appear to us in and as the givenness and apparent immutability of reality, especially in the form of socially unnecessary suffering that gets passed off as necessary. They are the forms that the dialectic of nature and history take on when history coalesces into a reified second nature that may not make much sense to us but in the face of which we are reassuringly told that "that's just the way things are." Often such demonic forces (demonic because fate-like, or like the playing out of some incontestable divine will) take the form of contradiction, such as the starting point of Marx's analysis of labor under capitalism: "Workers become all the poorer the more wealth they produce."[130]

However, such fate-like contradictions are not insurmountable. They are "riddles,"[131] says Adorno, and it is the role of interpretation not merely to solve them but in solving them to *dissolve* them, to make them disappear, which means essentially two things: first, to effect the return movement from nature to history, to establish that what seems to be immutable nature is, in fact, historically informed and generated—and therefore changeable (e.g., it is not a fact of nature that we must sell our labor power in order to survive); and second, to simultaneously liberate new possibilities for transformation, to indicate real possibilities that do not perpetuate actuality and its apparently natural current form but rather transform it thoroughly and, with some luck, for the better. Marx's diagnosis of the contradiction of the worker's plight is, in this way, nothing other than an act of unriddling interpretation, in Adorno's sense, indicating the way forwards to an actuality no longer in thrall to its blind demons.

Now, it is true that Adorno does not much refer to the concept of possibility in his presentation of actuality and indicative interpretation, at least not conspicuously, but it is obvious from his criticisms of the way philosophy and ideology tend to see actuality that his central interest is to discover a way *out* of this painful, contradictory, fate-like existence, whose conditions of possibility Heidegger renders perennial by treating it as a fixed network of existentialia. Against Heidegger, then, the discussion of the "actuality" of philosophy clearly aims to renew the project of the actualization of philosophy in the Marxian sense, and Adorno's language is modally charged in this sense. As Adorno puts it, rewriting Marx's eleventh thesis on Feuerbach to emphasize the role theory must continue to play in animating praxis:

> The indicative interpretation of a given actuality and its sublation are connected to each other—not, of course, in the sense that actuality is sublated in the concept, but that out of the construction of a figure of the actual the demand for real transformation always follows promptly. The transformative gesture of the riddle-process—not its mere resolution as such—provides the archetype of solutions available only to materialist praxis.[132]

Marx had of course written that "the philosophers have only *interpreted* [interpretiert] the world in various ways; the point, however, is to *transform* it."[133] But whereas he thereby stresses the difference between interpretation and transformation, Adorno emphasizes that we really require *indicative interpretation* (*Deutung*) to articulate any "demand for [the] real transformation" of actuality. This is all the more true in that "it was perhaps an inadequate interpretation that promised the transition from theory to practice"; that is, Marxism's unilinear transition from interpretation to transformation did not work out as planned.[134] In this light, Adornian indicative interpretation represents a more potent dialectical unity of Marx's interpretation and transformation. It is the general process or the drawing board on which unheard-of, radically transformative possibilities come to expression. Ultimately, the actuality of philosophy has to do with the *form* of *what* Marx was doing and with *how* he was doing it rather than the content, which succumbed to dogmatism. For Adorno, doctrine (not to mention dogma) is always less important than the process by which its legitimate content first comes to be formulated.

Interestingly, in his own discussion of Marx's eleventh thesis, Heidegger too stresses interpretation. However, in contrast to Adorno, his commentary takes us in precisely the opposite direction, back to the disclosive interpretation that transformation presupposes rather than forwards towards the solution to historical riddles:

> [It is a question] to what extent one can, in general, speak of a *transformation* of society. The question concerning the demand for the transformation of the world leads us back to Marx's much-cited [eleventh thesis on Feuerbach]. . . .
>
> By referring to this thesis *and* by following it, one overlooks the fact that transforming the world presupposes a change in our *representation of the world* and that such a representation of the world can only be obtained if the world is adequately *interpreted*.
>
> In other words, Marx bases himself on a quite specific interpretation of the world so as to demand its "transformation," but in so doing the thesis shows itself to be unfounded. It gives the impression that a stand is being taken against philosophy, whereas in its second part it implicitly presupposes a demand for philosophy.[135]

It is clear what Heidegger is implying: one cannot transform the world without understanding the world in the way it is constituted, that is, according to the existentialia of *Being and Time* in the first instance. To this, Adorno's response is clear:

> Heidegger comes very close to the idea of indicative interpretation, but it is corrupted—or so it appears to me—because it is committed to the distinction between the ontic and the ontological, while the ontological structure turns out to be something other than what we might truly think of as "meaningful." Basically, it is nothing more than a manifold of universal concepts into which specific phenomena fit. And it is this process of "fitting in" that philosophical, indicative interpretation is meant to transcend.[136]

Progress and Relapse

It is no doubt obvious by now that thinking Heidegger and Adorno together gives rise to legitimate philosophical problems, whatever the degree of tension individual readers may wish to ascribe to this pairing.[137] Indeed, it is difficult to imagine that Adorno himself would have spent forty years formulating criticisms of Heidegger had there not been philosophical—as well as social and political—issues to attend to, and even though he clearly believed that there was no possibility of convergence between the two positions.[138] The aim of immanent critique, after all, is to put thought into motion, not to remain at the level of abstract opposition.

In addition to the question of philosophical interpretation, the problems of technology and progress suggest themselves as important topics for understanding discontinuous, future possibilities as the locus of contestation that binds Heidegger and Adorno together. Their views may even appear to intersect on several key points. This appearance will have to be dispelled.

What points of intersection can be discerned in Heidegger's and Adorno's writings? Based on what we have seen thus far, they both clearly formulate concepts of blocked possibility, which share the same general structure: Actuality as it is currently conceived does not exhaust real possibility on a traditional, metaphysical reading of this term. On the contrary, both Heidegger and Adorno think that experience expresses a kind of emphatic possibility whose reality, while not illusory, is nevertheless not recognized within social and metaphysical regimes of real possibility, for the simple reason that the possibilities at issue are both essential and kept constantly in abeyance or even suppressed and effaced by actuality in its historical and metaphysical articulations. History is therefore to be understood as structured by forces that present themselves as foundational (e.g., the metaphysical thinking of being in terms of beings) or as natural (e.g., ancestral social injustices) but that, in fact, serve only to conceal their contingency and, on that basis, the possibility of thinking, experience, and the world being organized otherwise and for the better.

In "The Question concerning Technology," Heidegger describes how a certain ordering, calculative approach to beings is inherited by thought and experience, in such a way that there appears to be no alternative to it. It is as though we were condemned to live out a certain inescapable destiny:

> The essence of modern technology starts the human being upon the way of that revealing through which the actual everywhere, more or less distinctly, becomes

a standing-reserve [i.e., a subsistent totality of available beings]. "To start upon a way" means "to send" in our ordinary language. We shall call that sending-that-gathers [i.e., a way of thinking that lays out beings in a certain way] that first starts the human being upon a way of revealing, *destiny*. It is from out of this destiny that the essence of all history is determined.[139]

What is the nature of this ordering, calculative destiny? Primarily, it is the way that beings present themselves to us today qua beings, which encompasses our understanding of beings and of nature more generally, but in such a way that the only possibilities that matter are those that pertain to potential uses and energies that human beings can control and regulate. The essence of modern technology therefore has nothing directly to do with machines or mechanization, nor is it a question of the simple domination of nature understood as the way in which nature is put under the yoke of human will. It is instead a question of how beings are understood and, more specifically, of how their possibilities are construed, for example, in terms of what nature *can* yield, *can* produce: it is a way of understanding beings on the basis of the elaboration and controllability of the possibilities of beings. Technological revealing therefore has to do with how beings are present to us within experience and thought, for example, as available for use or as sources of energy.[140] Further, as mentioned previously, Heidegger describes "the way in which the actual reveals itself as standing-reserve" as the "enframing" (*Gestell*).[141]

However, at present the central point has less to do with this characterization of the essence of modern technology than with the way in which it has become a seemingly inescapable destiny for us: "As a destiny, [enframing] banishes human beings into that kind of revealing that is an ordering. And where this ordering holds sway, it drives out every other possibility of revealing. . . . [Moreover, the] challenging enframing . . . conceals revealing itself and with it that wherein unconcealment, i.e., truth, eventuates [*ereignet*]."[142] (One might speak here of a Heideggerian "technological veil.")

The concept of destiny first appears, then, as the playing out of something inevitable; this is, after all, the core of the concept of destiny. However, the inevitability at issue is not fully necessary. To put it modally, since the problem is essentially modal in its structure, necessity is what is at issue, but a kind of necessity that is conditioned and constructed by the historical unfolding of the essence of modern technology. True, we are confronted by the necessity of this modern unfolding of actuality, but the necessity in play is a merely *contingent* necessity, as it were—what Hegel would have called a *relative* necessity. In other words, due to the essence of modern technology, actuality appears to us as a to- tality of technologically effectual or actual beings that constitute an all-encom- passing actuality within which possibility is reduced to what we *can do* with the ordered and orderable beings at our disposal. This is just what real actuality is in the modern age, according to Heidegger. Yet, once the constructed character of this necessity is made clear, we come to see that another approach is possible. The relativity of the destiny in whose current we find ourselves thereby also shows itself to be the possibility of recovering from the illusion of the necessity of this way of experiencing the being of beings.[143]

The key to undoing this destiny, for Heidegger, lies first with seeing it *as* a destiny, *as* something that has been visited upon us and thereby blocks all other possibilities of understanding beings, but especially being understood as *Lichtung* or ἀλήθεια, the clearing or unconcealment that is proper to being and that is prior to all metaphysical interpretations of beings. It is therefore not this destiny's apparent inevitability that is at issue as much as its exclusiv- ity—the fact that it eclipses the truth of being: "Enframing blocks [*verstellt,* disorders and obstructs] the shining-forth and holding-sway of truth."[144] Hence we must come to see the essence of modern technology as a "danger" that affects the human being's essence, the relation to being as such, rather than as a mere technological approach to beings. And taking the measure of that danger is what holds out to us the promise of another way of experi- encing being. This is how Heidegger interprets the "danger" that Hölderlin speaks of in "Patmos": "But where danger threatens / That which saves from it also grows."[145]

Accordingly, the essence of modern technology is to be understood as "emi- nently ambiguous": it blocks the "event of revealing" as such, but qua block it preserves (in the mode of suppression) the possibility of another kind of reveal- ing.[146] Heidegger expresses this ambiguity in many ways. Ultimately, however, it is on the basis of the primordial ambiguity of being itself that this tension arises. Being itself "is a sending" into history, here understood as the essence of modern technology. This essence, as a fundamental mode of revealing, is pre- cisely an example of the play of concealment and unconcealment that is proper to the truth of being, although this aspect remains hidden. Being is given both in the sending itself and in what is sent. It is both the saving power and the dan- ger: "In the unfolding essence of the danger there lies *concealed,* therefore, the possibility of a turning, in which the forgetting proper to the unfolding essence of being inflects itself in such a way that precisely by *this* turning the truth of the unfolding essence of being returns specifically to beings."[147]

Thus, the ambiguity of being itself points to the hidden possibility of avoiding the completion of the destiny of modern technology as the actualization of the more obvious, technological "possibility that it could be denied to the human being to return a more primordial revealing and hence to experience the appeal of a more inceptual truth."[148] Two possibilities, then: one proper to the completion of the possibilities proper to enframing qua destiny; and another possibility of returning to the origin of thinking, which lies with the truth of being.

We should understand from this arrangement of modal concepts that Heidegger's "other" possibility, which he elsewhere calls the "other beginning," is singular. That is, it is the unique possibility to which we could return that would not leave us bound to some metaphysical mode of revealing and so to the false understanding of being in terms of beings—which here is presented as enframing, along with its attendant possibilities of ordering. Heidegger describes this modal structure explicitly:

> The essence of technology lies in enframing. Its sway is proper to destining.
> Since a destiny at any given time starts human beings on a way of revealing, the
> human being, while on this path, is continually on the brink of the possibility
> of pursuing and pushing forward only that which is revealed in ordering, and
> of deriving all standards on this basis. Thereby, *the other possibility is blocked,*
> [namely,] that the human being might be admitted more and sooner and ever
> more inceptually to the essence of that which is unconcealed and to its uncon-
> cealment, in order that he might experience as his essence his needed belonging
> to revealing.[149]

With this, the path that Heidegger is recommending becomes clear: we must go back to the origin of thinking itself, back to being as self-concealing unconcealment. The answer to the danger of enframing is therefore not to be found within history but within that which conditions and opens up history to us as destiny—within that which is first or earliest, older than any metaphysical understanding of being. The answer lies with returning to the ground prior to all grounds hitherto known, an *Abgrund,* an ἀρχή against all ἀρχαί:[150]

> All unfolding essences, not only modern technology, keeps itself everywhere

concealed to the last. Nevertheless, it remains, with respect to its holding sway, that which precedes all: the earliest. The Greek thinkers already knew of this when they said: that which is earlier with regard to the arising that holds sway becomes manifest to human beings only later. That which is inceptually early shows itself to human beings only ultimately. Therefore, in the realm of thinking, a painstaking effort to think through still more inceptually what was inceptually thought is not the absurd wish to revive what is past, but rather the sober readiness to be astounded before the coming of what is early.[151]

In simpler language, Heidegger says something similar in "Hegel and the Greeks": "Freed also from the determination of 'being' as actuality," the first, Greek beginning "shows itself to our thinking . . . as a 'not yet.' But this is the 'not yet' of the unthought—not a 'not yet' that does not satisfy us, but rather a 'not yet' to which *we* are not sufficient, and which *we* fail to satisfy."[152] In this way, the essential "not yet" of *Dasein* finds its counterpart in the history of being.

This means that releasing ourselves from the false necessity of enframing—and from metaphysics more generally—requires the concept not merely of blocked possibility (real possibility as suppressed by actuality) but of *one particular and, indeed, unique possibility:* the transition to the other beginning via the return to an origin even more original than the Greek origin of metaphysical thinking. The possibility of a future that would break with the false necessity of actuality as a totality of ordered beings and relations of making available is determined in advance by the structure of the truth of being. In other words, the redemptive future envisaged by Heidegger, "freed also from the determination of 'being' as actuality" is a structurally *unactualized past possibility.* In the face of such a past possibility, history is helpless, except to the extent that it might yet come to reactivate it and conform to it: "So long as we do not, through thinking, experience what is, we can never belong to what will be."[153]

For reasons that were sketched previously, Adorno wants nothing to do with the postulation of such a lost origin, which he takes to be nothing more than "archaism." We cannot free ourselves from metaphysical thinking by drilling even further down into the ground from which we want to escape. Crucially, however, Adorno does not wish to do away with the notion of blocked possibility or with the priority of such possibilities over existing actuality. Structurally speaking, like Heidegger, he issues a challenge to metaphysical theories of modality in the name of emphatic oughts, real possibilities whose reality is denied by existing actuality and the real possibilities in circulation within it and that serve to perpetuate it. In this way, the philosophical core of the conflict between Heidegger and Adorno can be represented as turning on the issue of how to articulate such blocked possibilities, in such a way that we can take the measure of their differences—and of Adorno's unrelenting criticisms. As already mentioned, however, it would be unhelpful to simply enumerate Adorno's views. The point is to approach the site of the contestation somewhat obliquely and thematically, so as to represent the elements of the opposition more substantially.

Adorno's essay "Progress" provides fertile ground for understanding the motivations of his critique of Heidegger, not least because it poses the question of the insufficiency of technological advancement for thinking what is at stake in the promise of progress. In this regard, he sees something essential at work "behind" the veil of purely technological progress. The question is whether, in the context of Adorno's understanding of historical progress, he can escape Heidegger's charge of technological behavior that leads us away from the possibility of the other beginning. Is indicative interpretation simply calculative, merely historical-technological? To answer this question adequately, the word "progress" is no doubt in need of some clarification, not least because it is essentially the opposite of what Heidegger wants to bring about. However, for Adorno too certain varieties of progress are highly problematic, although he accepts "what it promises" at root—"an answer to the doubt and the hope that things will finally get better, that people will at last be able to breathe a sigh of relief."[154]

Before examining the notion of progress in further detail, it may be remarked that Adorno seems to share some of the general features of Heidegger's view of technology and the transition to a better future. For both, this transition cannot be reduced to mere technological advancement: "The fetishization of progress," says Adorno, "reinforces its particularity, its restrictedness to techniques."[155] Indeed, there is no guarantee that technological progress will not lead to catastrophe. Not only did "insecticide [point] toward the death camps from the outset,"[156] as Adorno puts it, but there is no universal history in the normal sense of the term—no linear improvement across time—that will automatically save us from the increasing potential for harm that also stems from technological advancement. The opposite would be rather more true: "No universal history leads from savagery to humanity, but there is one leading from the slingshot to the megaton bomb."[157] Furthermore, like Heidegger, Adorno thinks that we are curiously wont to subvert the possibility of a better world by allowing ourselves to become trapped in a historically specific way of seeing things, such that the very sense of "better world" becomes confused and entangled with the categories of thought that need to be overcome. Neither believes in an unambiguous actuality qua self-sustaining and self-sufficient totality. Rather, actuality is rent, divided between the possibility of its self-perpetuation, including a claim to being a totality, and the realization that it is only a pseudo-totality, constructed out of the suppression of real possibilities of transformation that would not merely herald the shift to a new epoch but also an entirely new way of viewing nature and history that would put an end to ancestral errors of thinking and experience.

That, however, is where the similarities end. Already, it should be clear that Heidegger is not particularly worried about catastrophes that occur within history: true history "does not consist in the happenings and deeds of the world."[158] He is more concerned with the abandonment of beings by being and the loss of the possibility of the other beginning. Admittedly, this abandonment and loss are the ultimate source of historical catastrophes, according to him, but this is precisely why he thinks we must return to the source rather than attempt to manage historical events piecemeal. (This was no doubt more clear to him after the Freiburg rectorate.) To do the latter is to engage in mere historical calculation. From the source we will finally be able to draw the forces required to begin anew and aright.

For Adorno, however, Heidegger's call to return to the forgotten unique origin of thinking and experience promises a transition to a better world while simultaneously blocking it to the extent that it insists on a unique principle—be it an anti-ground opposed to metaphysical thinking—that is absolutely not required for there to be real progress. Instead, Heidegger's other beginning runs directly *counter* to Adornian progress. As Heidegger himself puts it, "When philosophy attends to its essence, it makes no progress at all. It remains where it is in order constantly to think the Same. Progressing, that is, progressing forwards from this place, is a mistake that follows thinking as the shadow that thinking itself casts."[159]

Indeed, instead of progress (*Fortschritt*, literally a stepping forth or forwards), Heidegger explicitly advocates the opposite: what he calls "the step back" (*der Schritt zurück*):

The step back goes from what is unthought [namely, the difference between being and beings], into what is to be thought [namely, being itself]. . . . The step back therefore moves out of metaphysics into the essence of metaphysics. . . . Viewed from the present and drawn from our insight into the present, the step back out of metaphysics into the essence of metaphysics is the step out of technology and the technological description and interpretation of the age, into the *essence* of modern technology, which is to be thought first of all.[160]

For Adorno, however, true progress is a stepping forth, not *out* of history into historicality, or *away* from technology into its essence, but *onward* into a future belonging to unheard-of possibilities that have to be construed within history through indicative interpretation. As Adorno says explicitly, Heidegger must spurn progress because progress, rightly conceived, means moving forwards out of archaism:

[The denial of progress] represents the inconsolable return of the same [i.e., yet another "first"] as the message of being, which must be hearkened to and respected, although being itself, which has had this message put into its mouth, is a cryptogram of myth, the liberation from which would be a moment of freedom. . . . The attitude of those [like Heidegger] who defame the concept of progress as insipid and positivistic is usually positivistic itself. They explain the way of the world, which repeatedly thwarted progress and which was also always progress, as evidence that the world does not tolerate progress and that whoever does not renounce it commits sacrilege.[161]

With regard to Adorno's alternative, we have already seen how his concept of indicative interpretation serves as an archetype for solutions to historical riddles. In many ways, his concept of progress is the counterpart to it on the level of history and humanity; it is what indicative interpretation opens onto, what it promises. It derives directly from his double refusal of (1) any singular essence of progress (e.g., universal history or technology) that could or should unfold immanently within history, according to what has existed hitherto, and (2) any purely transcendent promise of progress that could never be fulfilled in this life. It is thus neither purely immanent nor purely transcendent. It is, as we saw in the previous chapter, the movement of the dialectic of nature and history, in which the immanence of second nature blocks—while also calling for—the discontinuous transcendence of its historical configurations.

From this standpoint, we can say that progress, on Adorno's view, takes root in blockage, in the experience of what ought to be in spite of the non-actuality of this ought. Progress is first announced in this experience and makes no sense outside it. Thus, while it may seem uncontroversial that progress should (as cited above) provide "an answer to the doubt and the hope that things will finally get better, that people will at last be able to breathe a sigh of relief," the curious thing is that "one cannot say exactly how people should think about progress because the crisis of the situation is precisely that while everyone feels the crisis, the word that would bring resolution [*das lösende Wort*] is lacking."[162]

It should perhaps be underscored that if a moment of resolution is unavailable, the reason is not that the technical means are unavailable. It is precisely because they *are* available that we generally fail to understand why progress does not occur. Progress and technical advancement are not the same. Once again, the question of material needs is paramount: "Material need, which long seemed to mock progress, has been potentially eliminated; thanks to the present state of the technical forces of production no one on the planet need suffer deprivation anymore."[163] The crisis is not merely that material needs are not met; it is that, in spite of the real possibility of their elimination, this possibility goes unactualized: need *has "actually" been* eliminated, but only *in potentia*. In other words, this *blocked potentiality is the crisis*. And the generalized inability to say why or act on the crisis adequately is its consequence. Progress, were it to come about, would therefore not consist merely in eliminating need (although that is indeed the aim) but in eliminating the blockage of second nature, the recurrent refusal to question the presuppositions and practices of the world in which we live. Specifically, it lies in the refusal to reorganize the relations of production to unfetter the forces of production. But the explanation should not be reified either; it is valid only as long as the terms of the crisis remain the same. If or when they change, whatever the reason, the possibility of progress will have to be reinvented. Adorno refers to the concept of humanity to make his point (alluding to Benjamin along the way). Progress is not progress towards a pre-delineated human essence: It "would be the very production of humanity in the first place. . . . If humanity were a totality that no longer held within it any limiting principle, then it would also be free of the coercion that subjects all its members to such a principle and thereby would no longer be a totality: no forced unity."[164]

We have here the nub of the philosophical difference between Adorno and Heidegger. Progress cannot be measured by reference to a pre-existing essence of any kind, as can Heidegger's transition to the other beginning (i.e., either we succeed in making the transition to the other beginning, or we fail and continue to think metaphysically). The future of humanity would in that case consist in conforming to its essence, which was somehow already given, situated somewhere at the lost origin of experience. Rather, the only content we can give to the concept of humanity is that it "excludes absolutely nothing," that it is not animated by any "limiting principle," no "first" or pre-given essence. There is nothing "inceptually early" to guide us.[165] Consequently, "regressing into sacred primordiality" is quite literally the opposite of progress.[166]

The basic form of such limiting principles is what Adorno calls the principle of totality or identity: the imperative that everything held within a totality (say, society) should be identical (or conform) to whatever alleged essence or ground constitutes that totality as totality. Whether as lord or vassal, whether as pious monk or melancholic, whether as capitalist or worker, we should submit to the whole whose principle of inclusion metes out roles for each and every individual. Every particular must exemplify the universal. And what if some existing thing should not be identical with the essence by which it should measure itself? "So much the worse for the facts," as Hegel is said to have said. Against this view, Adorno retorts: "The more identity is posited by imperious spirit, the more injustice is done to the non-identical. The injustice is passed on through resistance to the non-identical."[167]

The point is this: to say that it is necessary for everything within actuality to conform to its alleged principle, to ask that we renounce non-identity (socially speaking: to ask that we renounce reflection on the systemic nature of senseless suffering, which is written off as natural and so necessary), is both to lay out a (limited) plan for progress and to arrest all progress. The boss says to the worker: be satisfied with your station in life, or else work harder and become the boss—and thereby claims that progress is possible. Or Heidegger says to the history of metaphysics: all philosophy hitherto has interpreted being in terms of beings, whereas what we need to think is the truth of beyng—and then passes that off as the unique possibility of fundamental and revolutionary transformation. The only difference would be, for Heidegger, that it is an essential possibility of existence that it might *miss* actualizing its essence: this is what Heidegger calls inauthenticity or, in another mode, the "danger." Yet such advice, insofar as it is merely a restatement of the principle of the whole, prevents the whole itself from truly evolving. Non-conformity is met, at best, with a renewed invitation to conform to the pre-given principle of the whole—or else the advocates of the non-identical are rendered impotent or annihilated.

In such a regime, whether or not the principle itself undergoes some change (e.g., metaphysical being becomes anti-metaphysical beyng) hardly matters if the structure remains informed by the principle of identity, the demand that existence conform to some fixed essence.

And yet, the experience of non-identity can sometimes be seen as expressive of a possibility other than that of renewed or enforced conformity—as a real ought that the particular suggests through its non-identity. Indeed, such an ought is the possibility of freedom—or, better, of liberation.[168] The heart of the Adornian concept of progress is described by the discovery of such oughts by means of indicative interpretation and the practical demand for their actualization within history. Without such a structure of dominant and blocked real possibilities, no progress could ever come about:

> For eons the question of progress made no sense. The question only arose after the dynamic became free, from which the idea of freedom could then be extrapolated. . . . Progress means to step out of the magic spell [of identity], even out of the spell of progress that is itself nature, in that humanity becomes aware of its own inbred [second] nature and brings to a halt the domination it exacts upon nature and through which domination by nature continues. In this way, it could be said that progress occurs where it ends.[169]

To apply this to society, one might say that the real possibility of real progress came about only, for example, when what the forces of production were *in fact capable* of actualizing (such as eliminating material need) was *suppressed* by the relations of production. In this case, progress would consist not merely in managing material need, whose existence until then seemed entirely natural and inevitable, but in the elimination of the demand to conform to the principle by which material need is artificially maintained for the purposes of extracting surplus value. More generally, true progress would consist in breaking free of the belief in the naturality of social injustice as the inevitable expression of the survival of the species, even though the concept of species in no way entails the social injustices that have until now been one of the conditions of its survival. When progress *out of* this web of naturalized social relations becomes possible, as it does when material needs have been "potentially eliminated," then the false progress that takes place only *within* the self-perpetuating whole is unmasked.

To apply this to Heidegger now, one might say that the possibility of progress first arises when it becomes possible to free ourselves not only from metaphysics but also from the myth of an other beginning via the return to a unique forgotten origin. A form of progress worthy of the name would then require that we abandon every such limiting principle that acts as a screen and block before other potentialities. We would thereby put an end to the *myth* of progress—understood as the actualization of some fixed essence, be it the essence of beyng itself through the "step back" into the "not yet." The Adornian concept of progress is therefore intimately tied to a redemptive future that does not renounce or betray its futurity, as is the case with the Heideggerian "not yet" that is attainable only through a "step back."

What, then, does non-teleological progress in the name of humanity amount to? In summary, it means not falling prey, yet again, to the myth of some first principle of identity, even if the new first principle appears in the form of an answer to a legitimate criticism of some other first principle. It means not embracing anti-metaphysical being at the very moment that metaphysical being becomes untenable. It also means not fetishizing the meager progress that has already been accomplished—not fetishizing, for example, the exact terms of the Marxist answer to the contradictions of capitalism in a political dogmatism in an era of the historical failure of the mission of the proletariat. Ultimately, it means "resisting the danger of relapse," or, in other words, it is to resist falling "beneath the level of history"—to not merely subsist anachronistically in 1843 when Germany in 1843 had failed even to rise to the level of France in 1789 (to refer to Marx's example).[170] It is to create redemptive potentialities out of the ruins of those more static essences whose contradictions with existence can no longer be ignored or passed off as contingent. It is the "very production of humanity," where humanity has shown itself to be beneath the newly discovered potentiality that pits it against its former ideal. To actualize this potentiality is the redemption of humanity, its self-transcendence without leaving the scene of history.

This process is articulated in two stages. First, necessity ("nature" in Adorno's use of the term) must be shown to be contingent. Things could have and may yet be otherwise: "The rigidified institutions, the relations of production, are not being as such; rather, even in their omnipotence they are made by human beings and so revocable."[171] But contingency, the formal possibility of difference, is not yet a justification for anything in and of itself. It merely signals the discovery of non-inevitability. Thus, second, in the return of the pendulum, we must move beyond the formal possibility of difference towards a real ought that informs a remaking of second nature in the form of just customs and habits ("history" in Adorno's use of the term). In other words, the merely apparent necessity of the principle of the whole corresponds to the determinacy of *what ought not to exist:*

> We may not know what the human being should be, or what the right arrange-ment of human things should be, but what the human being should not be and which arrangement of human things is false, that we know, and it is only in the determinacy and concreteness of this knowing that something other, something positive opens up to us.[172]

The knowledge that Adorno has in mind is, of course, that of socially unneces-sary suffering, the shared suffering that we could but do not eliminate. The real, emphatic ought that structures his thinking is that of blocked real redemptive possibility, belonging to the historically developed potential of progress, the template of which is given by the social fact, denied by the society that pro-duced it, that material need has been "potentially eliminated." Progress would be the actualization of this anti-essentialist potentiality, the end of the injustice of the principle of identity that informs the social whole.

Heidegger's "Reply" to Adorno

Heidegger and Adorno seem to have met on only one occasion: Hermann Mörchen reports that Heidegger, in 1972, recalled having met Adorno (then Wiesengrund) in Frankfurt in 1925.[173] In terms of philosophical encounters, Heidegger never responded officially or directly to Adorno's criticisms, al-though he believed he knew their gist: "I was told that when Adorno returned to Germany, he said: 'Give me five years and I'll bring Heidegger down.' That's the sort of man we're dealing with."[174] Furthermore, Heidegger seems in general to have been kept informed by a number of people about Adorno's public and private references to him.

Adorno's presentation at the 1963 meeting of the Hölderlin Society, "Parataxis: On the Philosophical Interpretation of Hölderlin's Late Lyric Po-etry," brought certain issues to the fore in a quite public manner. Heidegger, whose influential readings of Hölderlin were the target of Adorno's paper, had supporters in the audience, one or perhaps several of whom caused some kind of commotion, according to a few reports.[175] In any case, the official summary of the meeting noted that "scarcely any other lecture provoked as impassioned a discussion as this one."[176] Two years later, in 1965, Robert Minder—who had invited Adorno to speak on Heidegger at the Collège de France in 1961—presented a paper at the annual meeting of the Hölderlin Society, which was "nearly more harsh" than Adorno's, according to one commentator.[177] Heidegger was aware of these events and chose to interpret them in the light of his own understanding of blocked possibility. In 1968, months after the sudden cancellation of his membership in the Hölderlin Society, Heidegger wrote to the president of the Society to say: "I consider the matter of Herr M[inder] closed, although I have heard that he has persisted in his uncalled-for polemic. The present age is no longer able to hear Hölderlin's voice."[178]

Although it is not entirely clear to what extent Heidegger also had Adorno in mind in this context, he was well aware of the connection between Minder and Adorno. Between the Minder paper at the Hölderlin Society meeting and the cancellation of Heidegger's membership, Ernst Jünger forwarded a letter to Heidegger from a French "disciple," in which the author of the letter apologized for Minder's polemic: "I genuinely feel ashamed opening the last issue of *Preuves*, which places [Jünger] side by side with the slanderous rantings of that 'rogue of culture' at the Collège de France, whose principal reason for existing is to direct his fury against the Socrates of Todtnauberg."[179] The text referred to is the French version of Minder's "Hölderlin und die Deutschen," the text he presented a year earlier at the meeting of the Hölderlin Society.[180] Heidegger replied to Jünger, leaving no doubt about how he understood things in 1966: "I have heard of the agitations of the gentleman of the Collège de France, but I have taken no further notice. A few years ago, the person in question summoned Wiesengrund-Adorno to the Collège de France in order to rail against me."[181] Heidegger knew, then, of Adorno's Collège de France lectures and of the connection with Minder and the Hölderlin Society.

Moreover, Heidegger also believed that there was a connection between Adorno and Günter Grass, who had published *Hundejahre* (*Dog Years*) in 1963. In it, in a way laying the groundwork for Bernhard's later satire, Grass mocks Heidegger's influence and language. Heidegger apparently did not take it well: shortly after *Jargon of Authenticity* was published in 1964, he wrote to his wife: "It now seems clear just *who* is behind the nastiness of [Grass's] *Dog Years*."[182] (Needless to say, Grass was in no way Adorno's messenger.)[183]

But perhaps the most sustained, though disappointing, response to Adorno is recorded in Richard Wisser's recollection of his televised interview with Heidegger, filmed in 1969, just a few weeks after Adorno's death. The official portion of the interview did not delve into Adorno's criticisms but instead only brought up the accusation that Heidegger was unconcerned with "concrete society and all its various responsibilities and worries, troubles and hopes."[184] He replied that such critiques were misunderstandings: "The openness of being *needs* human beings and, conversely, . . . human beings are human only insofar as they stand in the openness of being."[185] It is not clear in what sense this constitutes an answer to the question posed by Wisser. However, in the off-the-record portion of the interview, he was somewhat more forthcoming:

> "Do you think philosophy has a social mission?"
> In what was, for Heidegger, a characteristic gesture—as I would later notice—he brought his head up from a low, slanting position and, with a clear, expressive gaze, his eyes now opened wide, he replied: "No! I see none!"
> "Then could you at least *say* why that is the case? Could you be more explicit? Could you clear up the misunderstanding? Why does philosophy not have a social dimension?"
> "I would have to go way back to answer that question, back to Marx, and you know . . ."[186]

Heidegger trails off here. He may or may not have had Adorno in mind, but it seems unlikely that he would not have sensed the subtext of the question. One way or another, however, Wisser did not leave Heidegger in any doubt about what he was getting at: he soon mentions Adorno's *Jargon of Authenticity* explicitly, but Heidegger refuses to take the bait.[187] Wisser persists, though he does not seem able to formulate a question that Heidegger is willing to answer. Heidegger finally steps in, presumably to put an end to his persistence: "Heidegger remains on the topic of Adorno. He clearly wants to say something now in response to one of the questions that had been struck from the record: 'I have read nothing by him. Hermann Mörchen once tried to talk me into reading him. I never did.'"[188]

Somehow, Wisser takes this as an opening—and one really has to admire his persistence at this point—to talk about Adorno's "negative dialectic," at which point Heidegger raises the stakes: "'What does he take that to mean . . . *actually* [*eigentlich*]?' he asks, mischievously stretching out the contentious word."[189] (*Eigentlich* in this case just means "really" or "actually," but it is also the root of *Eigentlichkeit,* "authenticity.") Wisser is clearly unable to provide a convincing answer, so Heidegger comes to his aid: "So he's a sociologist, then, not a philosopher."[190] Is the architect not more important than the opportunistic cat burglar? With Wisser still unable to make a coherent point about Adorno's philosophy, Heidegger lets his disdain come to the surface more directly, as only an academic could:

> "With whom did he study?" I cannot answer the question, instead saying a word about his background, as I understand it, mostly to do with his publications. . . . He listens to me, but comes back to the question to which my explanations had provided no answer, only an adjournment: "But did he study with anyone at all?" "I don't know!"[191]

One might hope that the discomfort would have ended there, but the conversation continues a little longer. Nothing comes of it, but after a passing mention of Ernst Jünger, Heidegger makes his final point: "He takes the keyword 'Jünger' as an opportunity to change the subject."[192]

Possibility Read Backwards and Forwards

We have before us two models of redemptive possibility: one whose force is drawn from a forgotten source and another that stems from unriddling contradictory actuality here and now. But we would be mistaken if we thought that these were standpoints from which we might choose in the marketplace of ideas. Adorno himself warns us against viewing his criticisms as reflective of an unmediated opposition to Heidegger: "These are precisely not two brands from which one has to choose," he says, "as though one were choosing between two political parties, the CDU and the SPD for example."[193] Rather, we have to see them as utterly divergent in their belonging together. On the question of blocked possibility that is at the heart of both their philosophies, Heidegger is Adorno *in reverse,* as it were, stressing that the only future worthy of the name has to emerge from the other beginning, whereas Adorno takes this to be regressive and builds up his notion of the future, and of true progress, on the basis of a diagnosis and treatment of this regression—or relapse into the "superstitious belief in a first principle."

More specifically, they belong together in a dialectic of nature and history, in which Adorno seeks to counter the reified nature of Heidegger's "first possibility," precisely by way of a properly futural, *indicatively interpreted possibility of progress* that promises the elimination of socially unnecessary suffering in a renewed and redeemed second nature. Thus, however critically, Heidegger has a necessary role to play and the degree to which Adorno takes Heidegger seriously is the condition of relevance of his immanent critique. Heidegger is necessary because he represents the most influential philosophical attempt to break with the priority of metaphysical actuality over possibility, laying claim to a blocked possibility that must guide thinking and experience. And even though Heidegger's "treatment of relevant things lapsed into abstraction,"[194] he nevertheless provides a model of the sort of blocked possibility that must be avoided if we are to set things right.

It is this that explains the otherwise curious remark that Adorno makes in a letter to Horkheimer, written shortly after the publication of Heidegger's *Off the Beaten Track*: "I've been thinking a lot about Heidegger and will send you . . . a few more notes. In the meantime, his *Holzwege* [*Off the Beaten Track*] has appeared (he is *in favor* of occasional paths [*Holzwege*] in a way that's not very different from our own)."[195] This remark should not be read too concessively but rather as the sign that Heidegger's paths are both the promise of a redeemed actuality and the breaking of that promise. In this way, the immanence of Adorno's critique means that he has to follow certain threads in Heidegger's thinking in order to unravel the whole. Among these threads, the most important, philosophically speaking, is no doubt the critique of actuality as the suppression of the real possibility of its being set right.

What is at issue, then, is twofold. On the one hand, it is important not to underestimate the degree to which Adorno and Heidegger share a common premise; on the other hand, it is more important to chart the divergent paths they each take on the basis of this premise, lest we become too attached either to apparent similarities or to unqualified adversarial differences. The premise has been variously formulated above, for example, in terms of an attempt to reclaim a notion of an emphatic possibility that is neither fully real nor fully formal or in terms of a reversal of the metaphysical priority of actuality over possibility.

Indeed, it is on the basis of this shared premise that Adorno says in *Negative Dialectic* that "Heidegger gets as far as the borderline of the dialectical insight into the non-identity within identity."[196] Of course, he does not mean this positively. In the terms laid out here, he is acknowledging that Heidegger understands that metaphysically conceived actuality contains a contradiction: its first principle (for Heidegger, the interpretation of the being of beings as actuality) is not really "first" at all but just the illusion of firstness. However, from this starting point, he goes on to summarize the unbridgeable gap between his thought and Heidegger's, adding that

> he does not deal with the contradiction in the concept of being. He suppresses it. Whatever can be thought of under being flouts the identity of the concept with its correlate [i.e., actuality]; but Heidegger treats it as identity, as pure being itself, devoid of its otherness. He hushes up the non-identity in absolute identity as though it were a skeleton in the family closet.[197]

In other words, Heidegger leaves the contradiction between actuality and the heterogeneous possibility of interpreting being otherwise—which he quite correctly points out—entirely *intact* at the level of being itself, because the essence of being itself (that "beyng essences," as Heidegger says[198]) serves yet again as a principle of identity to which the human being is called upon to conform. But the non-identity between the human being and the essence of being (inauthenticity, the "danger," and so on) is not something from which we can or need to recover. The concept of being points not to the ever-same identity of existence and some essence more essential than any metaphysical essence but to the more general possibility that being *not be* what it purports to be. Thus, only "polemically" does being present itself to the human being, as that which does not conform to its purported essence.[199] The end of thinking and experience is not to be found in a more profound identity of existence and essence but in the end of identity qua end.

CHAPTER 5

ADORNO, BENJAMIN, AND WHAT WOULD BE DIFFERENT

> Everything in the process of becoming, possibility, necessarily contains a
> moment of abstractness as compared to the existent, violations of which
> will not go unpunished. There is no shortage of concretion, differentiation
> in that which is and has been. For that reason, differentiation has
> something *a priori* conservative about it, and all differentiation takes place
> within an experience that in a certain way sanctions that of which it is
> an experience. . . . But can one sacrifice differentiatedness? In so doing,
> does one not give up on the potential for something better in the midst of
> what exists, without that potential ever having realized itself? Is the rupture
> between possibility and actuality absolute?
>
> —Adorno[1]

> The gaslight that streams down upon the paving stones throws an
> equivocal light on this double ground.
>
> —Benjamin[2]

Idleness and the Ought

In the 1939 exposé of the *Arcades Project,* Benjamin says of the nineteenth century that "it was incapable of responding to the new technological possibilities
with a new social order."[3] It was, however, capable of producing an astonishing
number of images that indirectly present this impasse while evoking the vir-
tuosity of technological progress: arcades, boulevards, railroads, gas lighting,
the use of iron in construction, and so on. This impasse also leaves its traces on
figures such as the collector, the gambler, and the flaneur.

Such "dialectical images" are images of a historical dialectic that has come
to a standstill, as Benjamin famously says.[4] To put the issue in Hegelian terms—
contra Hegel, for whom the dialectic is "unhalting"[5]—the dialectic comes to a

standstill because the moment of the confrontation of what was in itself and what was for itself was missed: a concrete historical possibility of liberation was unable to disentangle itself from the defective way in which we represented it to ourselves and, therefore, from the way it played itself out. History did not produce what it could or ought to have produced. Accordingly, Benjaminian historiography is not concerned with presenting historical facts disinterestedly; it is an attempt to "rescue" what lies latent in dialectical images from oblivion and from the collective inhibitions that each one represents in its own particular manner. This rescue relies upon an ambiguity in history. Phenomena are not merely rescued from oblivion "but also from the catastrophe that so often characterizes how phenomena are handed down to us, their 'enshrinement as heritage.'—They are saved through the exposition of the fissure within them."[6]

If the phenomena of history are fissured or ambiguous, as Benjamin puts it, the reason is that history itself is equivocal, both "alluring and threatening."[7] Such ambiguities were always central to Benjamin's thought, of course. Here, the "fissure" that marks the dialectical image is the scar of the ongoing violence done to hope, but it is also, and for the same reason, the trace of that hope as constant and real, albeit as depicted in the instant of its disappointment and recuperation by the status quo. This is history as "primal history" (*Urgeschichte*, at least as the later Benjamin understands it): the repetition, in every century, of socially unnecessary suffering accompanied by the possibility of putting an end to it, despite the fact that this end is constantly deferred.[8] Thus, each of the images that Benjamin presents to the reader is a slight tear in the continuous fabric of social wrongs. Accordingly, writing the history of fissured phenomena is the attempt to save hope from the catastrophe of things "just carrying on" as ever.[9] The materialist historian's task is thereby to shed light on the equivocal past in order to recognize within experience "the sign of a messianic arrest of happening, or (to put it differently) a revolutionary chance in the fight for the suppressed past."[10] These relations of hope and loss are summarized in Benjamin's "basic historical concepts": "Catastrophe—to have missed the opportunity. Critical moment—the *status quo* threatens to be preserved. Progress—the first revolutionary measure taken."[11]

Benjamin's dialectical images, capturing as they do such historical moments of promise and betrayal, are essentially images of blocked possibility. In fact, one might say that they are the rightful alternatives to the "graven" images of liberation put forwards by Lukács and Bloch (although Adorno would no doubt have preferred it if Benjamin had been more openly critical of official Marxist discourse). Be that as it may, the power of dialectical images derives from their refusal of the myth of a unilinear, progressively unfolding story of liberation. Benjamin's materialism is one that "has annihilated within itself the idea of [te-leological or mere technological] progress,"[12] having understood that "history decays into images, not stories."[13] In this way, he participates in the construction of a new form of historical cognition, based on that which failed to occur or, what amounts to the same for him, the "repotentializing remembrance" (*Eingedenken*) of that which has yet to occur: "The past carries with it a secret index by which it is referred to redemption,"[14] hence "what [historical] science has 'established' repotentializing remembrance can modify. Such remembrance can make what is incomplete (happiness) into something complete, and what has been completed (suffering) into something incomplete."[15] Dialectical images are therefore not just a record of loss but the affirmation, however faint, of the possibility of one day not succumbing, yet again, to the ever-same.

The figure of the flaneur is one of the most developed of Benjamin's dialectical images. In the idle gaze of the flaneur is reflected the city's promise and its simultaneous betrayal: the potential of progress and its impossibility outside a narrow technological sense of the new. This gaze wants to see what the crowd cannot see. It waits for things to reveal what they conceal—what the street lamp simultaneously illuminates and throws into the shadows. Benjamin quotes Pierre Larousse: "His eyes open, his ears ready, searching for something entirely different from what the crowd gathers to see."[16] Yet the expectant gaze of the flaneur culminates in nothing, or merely in a pregnant pause and an inability to draw any decisive conclusions (*Unschlüssigkeit*) from that to which he is in any case merely a half-aware witness.[17] For the flaneur, the ambiguous character of urban phenomena remains at the level of suggestion.[18] The phenomena do not reveal the ground of their double nature, nor do they give rise to the new, although the flaneur's gaze is somehow drawn towards this vague promise.

However, the figure of the flaneur offers more to social theory than the mere suggestion of an otherness inherent in objectivity. For the flaneur too, in his persona, is an ambiguous figure—the subjective reflection of the vague "more" that urban objectivity suggests to his gaze. This is conveyed by the unintentional social dimension of the flaneur's idleness, which gives the appearance of not being immediately bound by the demands of labor: "The idleness of the flaneur is a demonstration against the division of labor."[19] Or again: "Basic to *flânerie*, among other things, is the idea that the fruits of idleness are more precious than the fruits of labor."[20] But the flaneur does not represent a true liberation from the demands of labor. He instead falls between the cracks of a rapidly advancing nineteenth century, incapable of understanding himself or of producing a real alternative to what he is and to what he bears witness. Nevertheless, he constitutes a counter-figure—however incomplete and equivocal— to the countless and nameless laborers of the crowd, whose rhythms of life are those of capitalism and not of an idleness that holds out the hope of "an experience that has not yet been honored by experience."[21]

Yet, because the flaneur's own ambiguous nature is lost on him and on those around him, he is powerless to escape his recuperation by the forces that formed his historical possibility:

> The very fact that the share of [the class from which the flaneur comes] could, at best, be enjoyment, but never power, made the period that history gave them a space for passing time. Anyone who sets out to while away time seeks enjoyment. It was self-evident, however, that the more this class wanted to have its enjoyment *in* this society, the more limited this enjoyment would be. The enjoyment promised to be less limited if this class found enjoyment *of* this society possible. If it wanted to achieve virtuosity in this kind of enjoyment, it could not spurn empathizing with commodities.[22]

On the basis of this distinction between momentary enjoyment and power, we might say that the social meaning of the figure of the flaneur lies in how it communicates to us a historical essence or potentiality that found expression only in *stunted* form and whose criterion of stuntedness—that is, its paradigm of complete expression—was never given in history. At the very moment that the critique of capitalism was formulating its call for the revolutionary overcoming of alienated labor, the forces of production had already produced the flaneur as a powerless by-product of history, the Pyrrhic victory of idleness that served only to foreshadow the continuing triumph of exchange value. In short, the flaneur merely suggests the possibility of a liberation from alienated labor in the era of its seemingly inevitable continuity.[23]

Consequently, the flaneur's powerlessness or lack of consequence made him an ephemeral figure that swiftly evolved away from the social potential at which his idleness hinted. In the end, the flaneur did not announce that society had finally provided us with the time required to decipher and mobilize in practice its inherent contradictions. On the contrary, the flaneur transformed into the detective, the journalist, or the sandwich-board man—the inevitable commodifications of the semblance of idleness that in the end proved to be no exception to the law of labor.[24] Benjamin quotes Paul-Ernest de Rattier in this regard: "The flaneur . . . became a farmer, a vintner, a linen manufacturer, a sugar refiner, a steel magnate."[25] Indeed, Benjamin says, "many [members of the petty bourgeoisie] would one day come up against the commodity nature of their labor power. But [in the era of the flaneur] this day had not yet come; until then, they were permitted (if one may put it this way) to while away the time."[26]

As indicative of socially blocked possibilities, such dialectical images are structured by a peculiar ought, to which Benjamin does not often call attention. However, in one passage there is a strong hint that he well understands the modality in play. He first quotes the young Marx, who writes that the social critic "can start from any form of theoretical and practical consciousness and develop true actuality out of the forms *inherent* within existing actuality as its ought and final goal."[27] The language that Marx uses here indicates both his proximity to and distance from the Hegelian dialectic: his ought is clearly that of true actuality winning its way through the contradictions of existing actuality by way of their dialectical negation—even if that means going beyond Hegel's view of contemporary history as already reflective of society's rational form.

Benjamin, however, seems to register the peculiarity of Marx's use of the ought, which for Hegel generally refers to unactualizable formal possibilities. At first glance, Marx's use of the ought may seem straightforward enough: is it not just a way of referring to that which history has not yet produced, that which, from the standpoint of theory, begins only at the moment Hegel's *Philosophy of Right* reaches its premature conclusion? Society *ought* to take on a form different from that of bourgeois civil society; it *ought* to achieve its hidden potential, which took shape only as the forces of production evolved. To this extent, Benjamin would no doubt agree. Unlike Marx, however, Benjamin thinks that the materialist historian has to confront the possibility that such oughts may well belong to "long-vanished epochs."[28] That is, they may have passed us by, or we may have failed to grasp them adequately; and so they slipped into near oblivion, becoming accessible again—or "legible"[29]—only once history has moved on. Accordingly, the materialist historian's aim is to make the oughts that lie hidden within things actual and relevant to history (what Benjamin calls *Aktualisierung*) rather than to chart the progress of reason within history.[30] Thus, whereas Marx sees history as rationally advancing towards true actuality (remaining Hegelian in this respect at least), Benjamin suggests that we might do better to reject this rationalistic, teleological vision of history progressing through stages, to focus instead on how history sketches and erases possibilities of progress. In this respect, every failed ought—which is to say, every dialectical image—is linked with every other one and each with a time when the catastrophic continuum of history would finally be broken:

> The starting point invoked here by Marx [i.e., existing actuality and its forms of consciousness as containing the germ of the next stage of history] need not necessarily be associated with the latest stage of development. It can be taken up from long-vanished epochs whose ought and whose final aim is then to be presented as a stage in its own right and as a preformation of the final aim of history—regardless of the [purported] next stage of development.[31]

For Benjamin, then, there is no dogmatically pre-determined next stage of development (although he was perhaps at one time hopeful in this regard).[32] There is, however, the possibility of presenting historical oughts as a "preformation of the final aim of history." This means not holding the actualization of an existing ought up as the prefiguration of an inevitable next and final stage when, on the contrary, history teaches us that such oughts frequently do *not* become actual. Rather than dismissing the ought, however, we should regard it—even as we grasp its historical powerlessness—precisely as the ephemeral image of a time *to come* when history's emergent potentialities would *no longer be suppressed* by the ongoing catastrophe of nothing ever changing, of the continual loss of what would be different. "Progress," says Benjamin—referring to *genuine* progress and not to what passes for it—"must be grounded in the idea of catastrophe,"[33] not in the teleological and inevitable actualization of unequivocal historical essences.

   In general, then, the materialist historian who has renounced graven images of redemption has to begin by seeking out those "deviations" from the historical continuum of perennial injustice, those "differentials of time" that allow us to penetrate beneath the hardened surface of history in order to grasp its contingency and thereby its mutability.[34] And as we have seen, dialectical images (e.g., the flaneur) and the oughts they stuntedly represent (e.g., a liberation from alienated labor) are precisely such "differentials," that is, phenomena that present themselves as slight deviations from the status quo—deviations whose non-identity (to speak Adornian) allows us to glimpse that of which society may yet be capable. It is through such empirical deviations that we can discover the forms they instantiate, such as the suppressed gap between the forces and relations of production or between the emancipatory promise of technology and how it is put to use to further the ends of capitalism. In short, "progress does not find its home in the continuity of passing time but in its interferences—where the truly new makes itself felt for the first time, with the sobriety of dawn."[35]

Of course, Benjamin is aware that the "truly new" has hitherto only been experienced as that which has been glimpsed and lost. Catastrophe, which continues to characterize human history, is "to have missed the moment" over and over again. But in the recognition of such moments, the possibility of *not* missing them is nevertheless sketched—and hence the possibility of truly revolutionary progress. To rescue such moments is already to give substantive content to what would be different.

Differences

Adorno's criticisms of Benjamin in the 1930s may seem harsh. More specifically, in relation to the notion of blocked possibility, it would seem that Benjamin has a great deal to say, as we have just seen. Why then does Adorno seem so critical? Perhaps, as with Bloch, Adorno's intellectual proximity to Benjamin led him to place great emphasis on what may initially look like small differences—although admittedly Adorno thinks that it is often such seemingly minor points of tension that force thinking to push itself beyond what has already been said and thought. As Adorno himself writes of Benjamin's relation to other philosophers: "The decisive differences between philosophers are always to be found tucked away in nuances; and [those positions] which are most irreconcilable are [precisely those which are] similar, but which thrive on different centers."[36]

While it is far from clear that Adorno's and Benjamin's "centers" are so very distant from each other, there is perhaps one telling difference, which has to do with how theoretical or metaphysical reflections are brought into play or kept in suspense. For present purposes, from among all of Adorno's criticisms, it is the absence of an explicit theory or metaphysics in Benjamin that is most relevant.

Already in 1935, commenting on the first exposé of the *Arcades Project*, Adorno says that Benjamin's theory of the dialectical image "seems in principle open even to the criticism of being *undialectical.*" This is due, among other things, to the impression such images give of being somewhat arbitrarily chosen and lacking in clear "objective liberating potential."[37] The problem is that it is not quite clear what their epistemic and social status amounts to. As things stand in 1935, Benjamin's dialectical images name experiences of ambiguity and of loss or decay. But to what liberation do they now contribute—and how? Or to put the issue in terms that Adorno himself admittedly does not use: If we are dealing with lost possibilities of liberation, then why are they not *just* lost? What theory of historical possibilities explains their expressive excess in such a way that they constitute not a catalogue of failures but a recovery of some "objective liberating potential"? Without an answer to such questions, dialectical images risk remaining bound to aspects of experience that are too subjective or psychological: the object of the flaneur's gaze or the *trouvaille* of the collector risk being mistaken for mere "facts of consciousness" and they themselves for enigmatically ambiguous but ultimately contingent "social products."[38] Adorno's worry seems to be that the *Arcades Project* would become a kind of cabinet of curiosities, and nothing more.

In 1938, after reading "The Paris of the Second Empire in Baudelaire," Adorno once again conveys his "disappointment": "Those parts of the study with which I am familiar do not constitute a model for the Arcades project so much as a prelude to the latter."[39] His criticisms are now sharper. The ideas that Benjamin seeks to convey remain "immured behind impenetrable layers of [historical] material."[40] What is lacking are "decisive theoretical answers" to the questions posed by dialectical images.[41] Indeed, the fact that Benjamin seems to refuse to make his theoretical framework explicit places him rather awkwardly "at the crossroads of magic and positivism"; that is, we seem faced with bewitched, partially undecipherable objective phenomena.[42] As Adorno had already put the issue in 1935, the ambiguous phenomena that Benjamin presents remain all too ambiguous and thereby render themselves powerless. Thus, whereas Benjamin says that "ambiguity [e.g., of the arcades as both house and street, of the flaneur as a figure of both idleness and labor] is the appearance of dialectic in images, the law of dialectic at a standstill,"[43] Adorno will reply that "it is not the translation of the dialectic into image that is ambiguous, but rather the 'trace' of that image [within history]—a trace that itself first has to be fully dialecticized by theory."[44] In short, Adorno thinks that Benjamin's dialectical images remain under a spell that "only theory would be able to break."[45]

But just what theory is it that Adorno is after? One might think, for example, that it is a question of Benjamin failing to remain faithful to the theoretical impulses of his own earlier work, especially *The Origin of the German Mourning Play*[46]—no doubt in part because that would have brought him closer to Adorno's own thought in the 1930s, itself in no small part based on a reading of Benjamin. However, Adorno also urges him to restore to the phenomena their embeddedness in "the entire social process" to avoid any recourse to a mythical "power of illumination" that is supposed to emanate from the phantasmagorical phenomena themselves.[47] It is in this specific regard that Adorno thinks that Benjamin should give freer rein to his original materialist theoretical insights rather than avoid theory or try to connect it to mainstream currents of materialist thought.

At one point, Adorno even invokes the Institute for Social Research's theoretical interests as a possible model for Benjamin.[48] However, it is far from clear what following this model would have entailed, for the Institute—though perhaps less Adorno himself—was at that time in the midst of a massive shift in theoretical focus. The failure of the proletarian revolution, the rise of fascism and of totalitarian socialism, among other factors, "lent impetus to the transition from the Critical Theory of the 1930s to the critique of instrumental reason during the 1940s, a critique which became at the same time theoretically more radical and practically more conservative."[49] Additionally, this situation led to a shift from economic to political and cultural questions, increased interest in psychoanalysis and the evolution of monopoly capitalism into state capitalism (leading also to various related divisions within the Institute), and a more central role for Adorno.[50] As Adorno later says, the world was heading towards something like what Aldous Huxley describes in *Brave New World* (except that Huxley ends up defending bourgeois culture, which for Adorno is complicit in the course of the world):

> The economic-political sphere as such recedes in importance. All that matters is
> a thoroughly rationalized class system on a planetary scale, a flawlessly planned
> state capitalism, in which total domination means total collectivization, while a
> money economy and the profit motive continue to exist.... [The situation is one
> of] degradation and regression in the midst of boundless possibility.[51]

All of these factors led Horkheimer and Adorno to one crucial issue, around which many others orbited: While the transition to a truly just society was still theoretically possible, it had become conjuncturally impossible. The world's resistance to change was hardening and deepening. It is this situation that called for *more* theory, "*more* dialectic,"[52] rather than a regressive reaffirmation of obsolete social analyses and a faith in a proletariat whose actual relevance was quickly fading. The problem of blocked possibilities of redemption began to loom large.

It is perhaps no wonder that the question of a qualified renewal of metaphysics also began to be posed. In the late 1930s, just around the time that Adorno was asking Benjamin to spell out a theory of dialectical images, even Horkheimer was planning a book on dialectical theory, which he described as "a material doctrine of categories" and which would present "the most important substantial categories of progressive consciousness in the present time." Examples of the categories he had in mind included "causality, tendency, progress, law, necessity, freedom, class, culture, value, ideology, [and] dialectic."[53] However, the book remained unwritten. Horkheimer was always less metaphysically inclined than Adorno: "The difference between us," he once said, "is that Teddie still retains a certain penchant for theology [i.e., a theory of redemption], whereas I would tend to say that good people are dying out. In the circumstances, planning would be the best option."[54]

In spite of Horkheimer's loss of interest in a material theory of categories, Adorno emphasized the need for such a work—he was, as Horkheimer suggests, unsatisfied with Pollock's call for political solutions and democratically organized economic planning.[55] In 1946, he made it clear what he thought was lacking:

> One should begin by analyzing logical and epistemological categories. The task would be to subject categories like concept, judgment, subject, substantiality, essence, and suchlike to the kind of examination that was already begun in the *Fragments* [i.e., *Dialectic of Enlightenment*]. This should include not only purely logical but also historical and social discussions. The historical and social substance of the categories and their present status should be determined from their immanent meanings, such that the analysis would lead to a judgment on the correct and false moments of the categories concerned. We should respond to Horkheimer's demand that we say what right thinking is through an examination of certain central categories of thought.[56]

It might be said that *Negative Dialectic* is the culmination of this need for a "material doctrine of categories," and Adorno himself saw it as taking up Benjamin's own challenge that one would have to "cross the frozen waste of abstraction to arrive at concise, concrete philosophizing."[57] But work in this direction had already begun in the period leading up to *Minima Moralia,* where it is a question of addressing the concept of the subject within the historical context of the obsolescence of its traditional philosophical concept (e.g., the Kantian free rational agent): "Individual experience necessarily bases itself on the old subject, now historically condemned, which is still for itself, but no longer in itself."[58] It is in such remarks that we can detect the need for a material doctrine of categories.

In general, and to return now to Adorno's criticisms of Benjamin, it is in the name of the theoretical legibility of the impasses of historical experience that Adorno demands from him an explicit theory. Experience is not just what it happens to be; it is structured by categories of thought and, more important, by the historical *failure* of some of these categories. Theory is called for at precisely the moment when our basic concepts begin to ring hollow.

In the 1930s, this takes the form of Adorno demanding from Benjamin a theory that he himself had yet to fully develop and that perhaps only really began to take shape in the 1947 edition of *Dialectic of Enlightenment.* However, Adorno soon came to see that at least some of what he wanted to find in Benjamin was perhaps already there all along—or was at least under development. (This may have been possible in a definitive way only once he was able, in the years leading up to the 1955 edition of Benjamin's writings, to survey all that he had accomplished.)[59] One way or another, Adorno eventually found a way to see the truth of the primary experiences that Benjamin so well described and, in fact, incarnated. Adorno wrote in 1950, ten years after Benjamin's death by suicide: "He sought to conceptualize the essence at those points where it could neither be distilled from its automatic deployment, nor dubiously intuited; he sought rather to methodically guess it from a configuration of elements that resist their meanings."[60]

Moreover, Adorno later praises what, in the 1930s, he had earlier taken to be potential weaknesses of Benjamin's dialectical images. Thus, against his initial insistence on the danger of remaining "at the crossroads of magic and positivism," he later claims that the "gentle irresistibility" of Benjamin's thought "resides neither in magical effects, which were not foreign to him, nor in an 'objectivity,' understood as a swallowing up of the subject in those constellations."[61] And whereas he had initially suspected Benjamin's dialectical images of being too subjective, he later concedes that they "are meant objectively, not psychologically."[62] (Of course, in the intervening years, Benjamin had developed and corrected certain concepts, in part in the wake of Adorno's criticisms.)[63] But perhaps most significant is the fact that Adorno himself puts the concept of dialectical image to work in the context of understanding the paradoxes of experience (such as alienated labor or nuclear energy): "Dialectical images: the historically-objective archetypes of that antagonistic unity of standstill and movement that defines the most universal bourgeois concept of progress."[64] The emancipatory promise of a technologically driven modernity is inseparable from its betrayal under conditions of the intensification of capitalism: the more technology advances, the closer society comes to its destruction. Adorno, thanks to Benjamin, knows that it is the riddle of the dialectical image of so-called historical progress that must be solved if we are ever to achieve true progress—which would amount to breaking free of the spell of barbarism.

Of course, this is not to say that Adorno had simply (or finally) merged into the Benjaminian currents that in any event had always been present in his thought. Adorno still regrets in the 1950s and 1960s, as he had in the 1930s, that Benjamin never "deigned" to write a metaphysics, for which the motto, as he says, would have been Kafka's "there is infinite hope, but not for us."[65] This motto is, of course, also the watchword of blocked possibility.

However, that Benjamin never wrote a metaphysics was not an oversight on his part. It was a deliberate omission that became an integral part of the *Arcades Project*. Benjamin aimed at a "*commentary* on actuality," not a *theory* thereof.[66] As Max Pensky puts it,

> Benjamin . . . grew increasingly unwilling to commit his project to a theoretical justification. He was convinced that theories in general remained too dependent upon the intentions of the theorist. All dialectical inversions notwithstanding, Benjamin was convinced that the historical truth of the nineteenth century was *objectively* present in his assembled fragments, and that this truth would be lost, not recovered, by the imposition of a theoretical superstructure upon them.[67]

We can well understand the point of this avoidance of theory. The temptation to hand over rapidly shifting historical phenomena to a schematic representation of their meaning would expose the whole enterprise to the danger of becoming disconnected from its material basis. The truth of history is precisely historical, not doctrinal: "Substantive truth-content [*Wahrheitsgehalt*] is only to be grasped through immersion in the most minute details of the substantive materiality of things [*Sachgehalt*]."[68] While Adorno clearly subscribes to this micrological "priority of the object,"[69] as he puts it, he maintains that it is essential that we make its "metaphysical" layer explicit instead of allowing it to "take the form of an 'impermissible "poetic" one.'" Adorno sees Benjamin's gesture as a "defeatism" and a "surrender" of sorts, but one that should push us to take up the challenge anew: "The fact that he could not bring himself to write out the definitive theory of the *Arcades Project* reminds us that philosophy is more than busy-work only where it runs the risk of total failure—this in reply to the absolute certainty that was traditionally obtained by fraudulent means."[70]

Of course, it is not that the theoretical moment is entirely absent from Benjamin's writings—on the contrary.[71] And in any case Adorno does not have in mind any traditional form of metaphysics and certainly nothing that would lay claim to any first principle of experience or "undialectical positivity." A material doctrine of categories would, as already mentioned, have to take into account the historical invalidation of certain apparently central categories, as well as the corresponding need to correct them. As he puts it in conversation with Horkheimer: "The really decisive questions of metaphysics can in fact only be answered negatively. To my mind, a determinate negation of the Hegelian position would be the optimum of theoretical truth."[72]

What, then, is lacking in Benjamin's work? It is obviously not the thought that the possibility of universal happiness and the redemption of past suffering is today—as ever—inextricably tangled up in the context of its apparent impossibility. Benjamin well delineates "the paradox of the impossible possibility."[73] What he does not provide, however, is the framework in which impossible possibilities make sense. Or to put it otherwise, the notion of dialectic at a standstill depends upon the theoretical elaboration of a modal category of real possibility in the mode of non-actualization. It is here that the notion of a material doctrine of categories takes on its meaning in relation to Adorno's work. In the absence of such a theory, the repotentialization of history risks being restricted to Marxist dogma (which, for Adorno, had in any case invalidated itself in becoming totalitarian and falling back into idealism). It is this missing theory of possibility that, in part at least, explains Adorno's remark to Gershom Scholem: "To salvage metaphysics is in fact the central aim of *Negative Dialectic.*"[74]

Solidarity with Metaphysics at the Moment of Its Fall

Of course, an Adornian "negative" metaphysics is not *reducible* to a theory of blocked possibility. As already mentioned, other categories also stand in need of revision. However, dialectic as the ontology of the wrong state of things at the very least requires, as we have seen throughout this book, a concrete grasping of *what would be different.* And this in turn requires *differentiation* within experience—the ability to name that which is non-identical with the basic presuppositions and principles of society as it is currently organized. In a way, one might say that for Adorno the only true "first" philosophy would be a philosophy of primary experience—that is, a philosophy organized around the "unregulated," expressive experience of "difference with respect to what merely exists," or to put it modally, the experience of blocked possibility or of a real— not fantastic—ought.[75]

This is what underpins Adorno's repeated complaint to Benjamin that he should pay more attention not to Marxist dogma but to Marx's initial theoretical insight into the fetish character of the commodity as a model for the presentation of dialectical images.[76] What he undoubtedly means is that the fetish character of the commodity resides not in the fact that some individual or group of individuals erroneously takes exchange-value to be an intrinsic quality of objects; it resides in the fact that contemporary experience *in general* is structured according to the principles of exchange and of the diversion of the forces of production into the extraction of surplus value. The theoretical formulation and interpretation of such false but socially prevalent "principles" of experience provide a prime example of the sort of negative metaphysics that Adorno had in mind. Another is provided by the reflection of the need to redraw the line separating formal from real possibility, starting from Hegel's typology of possibility and culminating in the real ought that legitimates the claim that "no one ought to go hungry anymore."

The point is not to found experience afresh on the ground of a static metaphysics of modality. As Marx knew (and it is partly from him that Benjamin inherits some of his misgivings), metaphysical concepts are not the absolute foundations of experience that we have often taken them to be. They are just theoretical *reflections or expressions of* experience—expressions to which we have the irritating ideological tendency to attribute exaggerated necessity and universality. Marx provides the crucial corrective insight: "Neither the thoughts nor the language [of philosophers] form a realm unto themselves; . . . they are merely the *outward expressions* of actual life."⁷⁷ Such expressions, when they are not mistaken for *absolute* or *first* principles, are an attempt to seize upon the forces that govern experience—and in that sense, they are legitimate. But they overstep their ambit when they become reified and immutable categories rather than a way of making sense of how historical experience is organized.

Thus, for Adorno, Marx's criticism of traditional philosophical thinking cannot mean that modal concepts are just fictions, purely expedient, or practically inert. They can and do play a central role in shaping and informing theory and practice. As noted in Chapter 2, Marx himself relies on a particularly complex modal vocabulary. But for them to take on this role, modal concepts must first be distilled from history and conceptually arranged in such a way that they can be used cogently and incisively in explanations and projections of experience. In light of this, the line separating formal from real possibility is not necessarily correctly drawn by Hegel. If experience contradicts Hegel's view decisively—for example, in the need to relocate a certain subset of oughts into a no-man's land separating formal from real possibility—then so be it. Marx, as much as Adorno, makes this clear in his insistence on the historical deactualization of the potential of the forces of production contra Hegel's philosophical adulation of bourgeois civil society. That the social potential of labor is obstructed by bourgeois consciousness and diverted into a false actualization is as much a problem for metaphysics as it is for sociology.

Taking this thought one step further, in part by liberating it from the constraints of a dogmatic Marxist philosophy of history, Adorno's attempt to "salvage metaphysics" in no way means to deny the vicissitudes of historical processes or their priority in terms of the formulation of theoretical concepts. The idea is instead to emphasize the bond between metaphysics and experience to the detriment of the usual categorial primacy of the former over the latter. Concretely, to understand historically blocked possibilities of happiness, we need to understand how they are related to actuality, to the apparent necessity of the present, and to other kinds of possibilities. For otherwise we may not see the nuance that separates blocked real possibility from mere formal possibility—the real ought from its unreal counterpart. Thinking that structures and understands itself in this way contributes something to redemption. It is what allows us to represent "what would be different" as "not having begun as yet."⁷⁸

All of this begins with primary experience or, what amounts to the same, the subjective capacity for what Adorno also calls differentiation: the ability to grasp, within the mass of existing conceptual distinctions and social differences, that which remains unthought and perhaps even structurally unthinkable until theory provides us with the concepts we need to think it. "The name 'dialectic' says no more," says Adorno, "than that objects do not simply disappear into their concepts, that they come to contradict the traditional norm of the *adaequatio*."[79] Put in other terms, even the most material of needs—including food, shelter, and medicine—is and has to be mediated by thinking. The expression of need and the criteria of its satisfaction require concepts; but at the same time, the eventual non-identity of need in relation to our socially mediated ways of conceiving it requires theory—metaphysics—to name and correct those basic presuppositions of historical experience that no longer hold. As Adorno puts it in the final lines of *Negative Dialectic:*

> Need wants to be negated [i.e., mediated] by thinking. It has to disappear within thinking if it is to be satisfied in reality. Need survives this negation and, in the innermost cells of thought, it becomes the representative of that which is unlike thought. The smallest inner-worldly impulses would be of relevance to the absolute, because it is the micrological gaze that cracks open the shell of what seems to be a helplessly isolated individual, [at least] according to the standard of the subsumptive higher concept. This gaze explodes the identity of concept and individual and thereby the delusion that the isolated individual is merely a specimen. There is solidarity between such thinking and metaphysics at the moment of its fall.[80]

This passage, in some ways the point of culmination of Adorno's thought and not merely of *Negative Dialectic,* says what it means to rescue what was hidden for so long within metaphysical thinking and its various misconceptions of the absolute. The absolute is neither that which stands above experience nor that which undergirds it as a foundation, nor is it actuality understood as a totality. It is instead that which asks to be "absolved," in the sense of *absolvere,* that which wants to be set free from the existing empirically given social totality. It is that which unsettles this totality from within by pointing towards what would be different. It is that which is grasped in micrological sensitivity to the smallest indices of redemption. Adorno here makes an interesting allusion to Max Weber's notion of "inner-worldly asceticism," the notion that salvation comes from a simultaneous participation in and opposition to the existing institutions of the world.[81] In the context of *Negative Dialectic,* this asceticism or refusal to simply assent to the way of the world is attributed to the individual who, instead of being passively assimilated into existing institutions, feels pressed to express the "more" of need that is held within the innermost cells of experience. This involves establishing the metaphysical and experiential status of blocked possibilities, which, while unactualized, nevertheless stand higher than certain other real possibilities—alienation, exploitation, hunger, poverty, and others—that serve to perpetuate the mere reality of socially unnecessary suffering.

Adorno's metaphysics of differentiation in this way tries to make explicit the theory that also drives Benjamin's need to rescue the dialectical images of primal history. To think according to non-identity and difference, rather than according to identity and assent, is to show solidarity with metaphysics at the moment of its fall. And to redraw the line between formal and real possibility is to actualize—in the sense intended by Adorno when he speaks of the "actuality" of philosophy—a "metaphysics beyond the Hegelian one."[82] To put the same thought more succinctly: "The idea of the 'different' is one whose time has come."[83]

NOTES

Chapter 1

1. Theodor W. Adorno, Correspondence with Arnold Gehlen, December 2, 1960, Theodor W. Adorno Archive, Frankfurt am Main, TWAA Br 0453. Compare Theodor W. Adorno, *Negative Dialectics*, trans. E. B. Ashton (London: Routledge, 1973), 106; Theodor W. Adorno, *Gesammelte Schriften*, ed. Rolf Tiedemann et al., 20 vols. (Frankfurt am Main: Suhrkamp Verlag, 1970–1986), 6:112. Existing translations of foreign-language texts have been cited where possible and tacitly emended where necessary. All other translations are my own.

2. See Adorno, *Negative Dialectics*, 145; GS, 6:148.

3. Theodor W. Adorno, *Minima Moralia: Reflections on a Damaged Life*, trans. E. F. N. Jephcott (London: Verso, 1978), § 18, 39; GS, 4:43. Adorno says, "Es gibt kein richtiges Leben im falschen." I retain Jephcott's translation, but a more literal alternative is "There is no correct life in the one that is false."

4. A number of approaches to Adorno's "negativism" are evidenced in the literature. See Michael Theunissen, "Negativität bei Adorno," in *Adorno-Konferenz 1983*, ed. Ludwig von Friedeburg and Jürgen Habermas (Frankfurt am Main: Suhrkamp Verlag, 1983); James Gordon Finlayson, "Adorno on the Ethical and the Ineffable," *European Journal of Philosophy* 10, no. 1 (2002): 1–25; Fabian Freyenhagen, *Adorno's Practical Philosophy: Living Less Wrongly* (Cambridge: Cambridge University Press, 2013); and James Gordon Finlayson, "Hegel, Adorno and the Origins of Immanent Criticism," *British Journal for the History of Philosophy* 22, no. 6 (2014): 1142–1166.

5. Theodor W. Adorno, "Opinion Delusion Society," in *Critical Models: Interventions and Catchwords*, trans. Henry W. Pickford (New York: Columbia University Press, 1998), 120; GS, 10.2:591.

6. Adorno, "Opinion Delusion Society," 120; GS, 10.2:591–592.

7. Adorno, *Negative Dialectics*, 204; GS, 6:204.

8. Adorno, *Minima Moralia*, § 6, 26; *GS*, 4:27.

9. Adorno, *Negative Dialectics*, 204–207; *GS*, 6:204–207. See also Max Horkheimer and Theodor W. Adorno, *Dialectic of Enlightenment: Philosophical Fragments*, trans. Edmund Jephcott (Stanford, CA: Stanford University Press, 2002), 18; Max Horkheimer, *Gesammelte Schriften,* ed. Alfred Schmidt and Gunzelin Schmid Noerr, 19 vols. (Frankfurt am Main: S. Fischer Verlag, 1985–1996), 5:46. See also the exchange between Bloch and Adorno on this question: Ernst Bloch and Theodor W. Adorno, "Something's Missing: A Discussion between Ernst Bloch and Theodor W. Adorno on the Contradictions of Utopian Longing," in *The Utopian Function of Art and Literature: Selected Essays*, by Ernst Bloch, trans. Jack Zipes and Frank Mecklenburg (Cambridge, MA: MIT Press, 1988), 10–14; Rainer Traub and Harald Wieser, eds., *Gespräche mit Ernst Bloch* (Frankfurt am Main: Suhrkamp Verlag, 1975), 68–73.

10. Adorno, *Negative Dialectics*, 205; *GS*, 6:205. The expression "theory based on images" (*Abbildtheorie*) alludes to Engels's or Lenin's "copy theory" of consciousness. However, in the present context, it is clear that Adorno is not limiting himself to such references but is attacking any theory that mistakes an "image" for objectivity.

11. Adorno, *Negative Dialectics*, 17; *GS*, 6:29.

12. Adorno, *Negative Dialectics*, 203; *GS*, 6:203.

13. Adorno, *Negative Dialectics*, 144; *GS*, 6:147.

14. Theodor W. Adorno, "Aldous Huxley and Utopia," in *Prisms*, trans. Samuel Weber and Shierry Weber (Cambridge, MA: MIT Press, 1981), 117; *GS*, 10.1:122.

15. G. W. F. Hegel, *The Encyclopaedia Logic: Part I of the Encyclopaedia of Philosophical Sciences, with the Zusätze,* trans. T. F. Geraets, W. A. Suchting, and H. S. Harris (Indianapolis, IN: Hackett, 1991), § 143, *Zusatz*, 216; G. W. F. Hegel, *Werke*, ed. Eva Moldenhauer and Karl Markus Michel, 20 vols. (Frankfurt am Main: Suhrkamp Verlag, 1969–1971), 8:283.

16. G. W. F. Hegel, *The Science of Logic*, trans. George di Giovanni (Cambridge: Cambridge University Press, 2010), 605, 716; *W*, 6:375, 524.

17. Hegel occasionally refers to the ought in a more generic and less critical manner, e.g., to characterize the moment in becoming in which something encounters a restriction placed on its development, which it has (or "ought") to transcend for it to become what it is. See Hegel, *Science of Logic*, 103–108; *W*, 5:142–148.

18. Immanuel Kant, *Critique of Practical Reason*, trans. Lewis White Beck (New York: Macmillan, 1956), 126–127; *Werke in zwölf Bänden*, 12 vols. (Frankfurt am Main: Suhrkamp Verlag, 1977), 7:252.

19. G. W. F. Hegel, *Hegel's Phenomenology of Spirit*, trans. A. V. Miller (Oxford: Oxford University Press, 1977), 369; *W*, 3:447 (emphasis added).

20. Hegel, *Phenomenology*, 369; *W*, 3:447.

21. Hegel, *Science of Logic*, 596; *W*, 6:363.

22. Hegel, *Science of Logic*, 113; *W*, 5:155.

23. Hegel, *Encyclopaedia Logic*, § 6, 30; *Werke*, 8:49.

24. Hegel, *Science of Logic*, 482; *W*, 6:208.

25. Bloch and Adorno, "Something's Missing," 6; Traub and Wieser, *Gespräche mit Ernst Bloch*, 64.

26. Theodor W. Adorno, "The Experiential Content of Hegel's Philosophy," in *Hegel: Three Studies*, trans. Shierry Weber Nicholsen (Cambridge, MA: MIT Press, 1993), 83; *GS*, 5:320.

27. Theodor W. Adorno, *Lectures on Negative Dialectics*, ed. Rolf Tiedemann, trans. Rodney Livingstone (Cambridge: Polity Press, 2008), 54; *Vorlesung über Negative Dialektik*, ed. Rolf Tiedemann (Frankfurt am Main: Suhrkamp Verlag, 2003), 84.

28. Adorno, *Negative Dialectics*, 52; *GS*, 6:62.

29. Theodor W. Adorno, "Why Still Philosophy," in *Critical Models: Interventions and Catchwords*, trans. Henry W. Pickford (New York: Columbia University Press, 1998), 16; *GS*, 10.2:472.

30. For an overview of the relation of Lukács and Bloch to Adorno, see Hans-Ernst Schiller, "Tod und Utopie: Ernst Bloch, Georg Lukács," in *Adorno-Handbuch: Leben— Werk—Wirkung*, ed. Richard Klein, Johann Kreuzer, and Stefan Müller-Doohm (Stuttgart: J. B. Metzler'sche Verlagsbuchhandlung und Carl Ernst Poeschel Verlag, 2011).

31. Georg Lukács, *History and Class Consciousness: Studies in Marxist Dialectics*, trans. Rodney Livingstone (Cambridge, MA: MIT Press, 1971), xviii; *Werke* (Neuwied: Luchterhand, 1962–1986), 2:20. See also Martin Jay, *Marxism and Totality: The Adventures of a Concept from Lukács to Habermas* (Berkeley: University of California Press, 1984), 112.

32. Max Weber, "Critical Studies in the Logic of the Cultural Sciences," in *Max Weber: Collected Methodological Writings*, ed. Hans Henrik Bruun and Sam Whimster, trans. Hans Henrik Bruun (Abingdon, UK: Routledge, 2012), 175; *Gesammelte Aufsätze zur Wissenschaftslehre*, ed. Johannes Winckelmann, 6th rev. ed. (Tübingen: Verlag J. C. B. Mohr [Paul Siebeck], 1985), 275.

33. Weber, "Critical Studies," 176; *Wissenschaftslehre*, 278.

34. Max Weber, "On Some Categories of Interpretive Sociology," in *Max Weber: Collected Methodological Writings*, ed. Hans Henrik Bruun and Sam Whimster, trans. Hans Henrik Bruun (Abingdon, UK: Routledge, 2012), 283; *Wissenschaftslehre*, 444.

35. Weber borrows much of this, including the example of the Battle of Marathon, from Eduard Meyer. See Weber, "Critical Studies," 174–177, 181; *Wissenschaftslehre*, 274–279, 286. See also Max Weber, *Economy and Society: An Outline of Interpretive Sociology*, ed. Guenther Roth and Claus Wittich, trans. Ephraim Fischoff, Hans Gerth, A. M. Henderson, Ferdinand Kolegar, C. Wright Mills, Talcott Parsons, Max Rheinstein, Guenther Roth, Edward Shils, and Claus Wittich (Berkeley: University of California Press, 1978), 11; *Wissenschaftslehre*, 550.

36. Weber, "On Some Categories of Interpretive Sociology," 281–282; *Wissenschaftslehre*, 441.

37. Weber, "On Some Categories of Interpretive Sociology," 284; *Wissenschaftslehre*, 444.

38. Max Weber, "The 'Objectivity' of Knowledge in Social Science and Social Policy," in *Max Weber: Collected Methodological Writings*, ed. Hans Henrik Bruun and Sam

Whimster, trans. Hans Henrik Bruun (Abingdon, UK: Routledge, 2012), 127; *Wissenschaftslehre*, 194. See, on this point, Gillian Rose, *Hegel contra Sociology* (London: Verso Books, 2009), 20–21.

39. Lukács, *History and Class Consciousness*, 51; *Werke*, 2:223–224.

40. Lukács, *History and Class Consciousness*, xviii–xix; *Werke*, 2:20–21. Lukács also owes his use of the verb *zurechnen* (to impute) to Weber.

41. Lukács, *History and Class Consciousness*, 73; *Werke*, 2:248.

42. Lukács, *History and Class Consciousness*, 80; *Werke*, 2:255.

43. Weber, "The 'Objectivity' of Knowledge," 132–133; *Wissenschaftslehre*, 205.

44. Lukács, *History and Class Consciousness*, 22; *Werke*, 2:196.

45. Lukács, *History and Class Consciousness*, 204; *Werke*, 2:392.

46. See Jay, *Marxism and Totality*, 141.

47. Lukács, *History and Class Consciousness*, 162; *Werke*, 2:346.

48. Lukács, *History and Class Consciousness*, 181; *Werke*, 2:366–367.

49. In a similar vein, Adorno remarks that Lukács subscribes to the "ideologically sanctioned copy theory [*Abbildtheorie*] of knowledge." See Theodor W. Adorno, "Extorted Reconciliation: On Georg Lukács' *Realism in Our Time*," in *Notes to Literature*, trans. Shierry Weber Nicholsen (New York: Columbia University Press, 1991), 1:236; *GS*, 11:274.

50. Adorno, *Negative Dialectics*, 191; *GS*, 6:191.

51. Adorno, *Negative Dialectics*, 191; *GS*, 6:192. The allusion is to Joseph von Eichendorff's poem "Schöne Fremde," in which "The distance speaks drunkenly, / As though of the great happiness to come."

52. Lukács, *History and Class Consciousness*, 161; *Werke*, 2:344.

53. Lukács, *History and Class Consciousness*, 184; *Werke*, 2:370.

54. Adorno, "Extorted Reconciliation," 239; *GS*, 11:278.

55. Adorno, *Negative Dialectics*, 205; *GS*, 6:205.

56. Adorno, *Negative Dialectics*, 192; *GS*, 6:193.

57. Adorno, *Negative Dialectics*, 5; *GS*, 6:17 (emphasis added).

58. Theodor W. Adorno, "Einleitung zu einer Diskussion über die 'Theorie der Halbbildung,'" in *Gesammelte Schriften* (Frankfurt am Main: Suhrkamp Verlag, 1972), 8:577.

59. Ernst Bloch, *Subjekt–Objekt: Erläuterungen zu Hegel* (Frankfurt am Main: Suhrkamp Verlag, 1962), 446–447.

60. Bloch, *Subjekt–Objekt*, 449.

61. Theodor W. Adorno, Correspondence with Joachim Günther, September 25, 1959, Theodor W. Adorno Archive, Frankfurt am Main, TWAA Ve 226.

62. Wolfgang Schopf, ed., *"So müßte ich ein Engel und kein Autor sein." Adorno und seine Frankurter Verleger. Der Briefwechsel mit Peter Suhrkamp und Siegfried Unseld* (Frankfurt am Main: Suhrkamp Verlag, 2003), November 10, 1958, 297–298.

63. Gunzelin Schmid Noerr, "Bloch und Adorno—bildhafte und bilderlose Utopie," *Zeitschrift für kritische Theorie*, no. 13 (2001): 34. See also Schopf, *Adorno und seine Frankurter Verleger*, November 10, 1958, 298, editorial note 3 on 301.

64. Theodor W. Adorno, "Ernst Bloch's *Spuren*: On the Revised Edition of 1959," in

Notes to Literature, trans. Shierry Weber Nicholsen (New York: Columbia University Press, 1991), 1:214; *GS,* 11:249.

65. Compare Ivan Boldyrev, *Ernst Bloch and His Contemporaries: Locating Utopian Messianism* (London: Bloomsbury, 2014), chap. 5.

66. Adorno, Correspondence with Joachim Günther, September 25, 1959.

67. Adorno, Correspondence with Joachim Günther, September 25, 1959. In the similar letter to Peter Suhrkamp, Adorno refers to Bloch's writings as the mere "ashes" of his living philosophical "genius." See Schopf, *Adorno und seine Frankurter Verleger,* November 10, 1958, 299.

68. Theodor W. Adorno and Max Horkheimer, *Briefwechsel,* 4 vols. (Frankfurt am Main: Suhrkamp Verlag, 2003–2006), September 22, 1937, 1:412–413.

69. Theodor W. Adorno, "Graeculus (II): Notizen zu Philosophie und Gesellschaft, 1943–1969," in *Frankfurter Adorno Blätter,* ed. Rolf Tiedemann (Munich: edition text + kritik, 2003), 8:29, 31. In *Negative Dialectics,* he writes that coldness is "the basic principle of bourgeois subjectivity, without which Auschwitz would not have been possible." See Adorno, *Negative Dialectics,* 363; *GS,* 6:356. Adorno had planned to write a book on coldness but did not live to realize the project. See Norbert Rath, "'Die Kraft zur Angst und die zum Glück sind das Gleiche': Das Konzept des Glücks in der Kritischen Theorie Adornos," in *Glücksvorstellungen: Ein Rückgriff in die Geschichte der Soziologie,* ed. Alfred Bellebaum and Klaus Barheier (Opladen: Westdeutscher Verlag, 1997), 184.

70. Theodor W. Adorno, "A Portrait of Walter Benjamin," in *Prisms,* trans. Samuel Weber and Shierry Weber (Cambridge, MA: MIT Press, 1981), 231; *GS,* 10.1:240.

71. Ernst Bloch, *The Principle of Hope,* trans. Neville Plaice, Stephen Plaice, and Paul Knight, 3 vols. (Cambridge: MIT Press, 1995), 1:197; *Das Prinzip Hoffnung,* 3 vols. (Frankfurt am Main: Suhrkamp Verlag, 2016), 1:226–227.

72. Bloch, *The Principle of Hope,* 1:200; *Das Prinzip Hoffnung,* 1:230. See also Schmid Noerr, "Bloch und Adorno," 40.

73. Bloch, *The Principle of Hope,* 1:235; *Das Prinzip Hoffnung,* 1:271.

74. Bloch, *The Principle of Hope,* 1:249; *Das Prinzip Hoffnung,* 1:288.

75. Bloch, *The Principle of Hope,* 1:17; *Das Prinzip Hoffnung,* 1:16.

76. For the reference to the "Stalinesque," see Schopf, *Adorno und seine Frankurter Verleger,* November 10, 1958, 300. Müller-Doohm comments concisely on the political view that Adorno himself held from the mid-1920s onward: "Collectivist ideologies did not have the slightest attraction for him." See Stefan Müller-Doohm, *Adorno: A Biography* (Cambridge: Polity Press, 2005), 80. See also Espen Hammer, *Adorno and the Political* (London: Routledge, 2005), esp. 13–14.

77. Adorno, "Ernst Bloch's *Spuren,*" 204; *GS,* 11:237.

78. Adorno, "Opinion Delusion Society," 108; *GS,* 10.2:577. See also Theodor W. Adorno, "Introduction," in *The Positivist Dispute in German Sociology,* trans. Glyn Adey and David Frisby (London: Heinemann, 1976), 35; *GS,* 8:319.

79. The "rescue of illusion" is an important aspect of Adorno's thought as well. See, e.g., Adorno, *Negative Dialectics,* 393; *GS,* 6:386.

80. Theodor W. Adorno, "The Handle, the Pot, and Early Experience," in *Notes*

to Literature, trans. Shierry Weber Nicholsen (New York: Columbia University Press, 1992), 2:219; *GS*, 11:566.

81. Adorno, "Ernst Bloch's *Spuren*," 211; *GS*, 11:245.

82. Adorno, "Ernst Bloch's *Spuren*," 213; *GS*, 11:248.

83. See, e.g., Theodor W. Adorno, *History and Freedom,* ed. Rolf Tiedemann, trans. Rodney Livingstone (Cambridge: Polity Press, 2006), 21; *Zur Lehre von der Geschichte und von der Freiheit,* ed. Rolf Tiedemann, 4th ed. (Frankfurt am Main: Suhrkamp Verlag, 2016), 32. Elsewhere, Adorno refers to primary experience as "unregulated spiritual experience." See Adorno, "A Portrait of Walter Benjamin," 237; *GS*, 10.1:247.

84. The expression "primary experience" refers to what Hegel calls *Erfahrung*—the experience that consciousness can undergo when "it spoils its own limited satisfaction" and is led to decisively transform its understanding of itself and the world. See Hegel, *Phenomenology,* 51; *W,* 3:74.

85. Compare Benjamin's well-known critique of Bloch's *Heritage of Our Times* in Walter Benjamin, *Briefe* (Frankfurt am Main: Suhrkamp Verlag, 1978), 2:648–649.

86. Adorno, "Ernst Bloch's *Spuren*," 215; *GS*, 11:249–250.

87. Adorno, "Ernst Bloch's *Spuren*," 213; *GS*, 11:248.

88. Bloch, *The Principle of Hope,* 1:241–246; *Das Prinzip Hoffnung,* 1:278–284.

89. Bloch, *The Principle of Hope,* 1:198–205; *Das Prinzip Hoffnung,* 1:227–235. "A Marxist," says Bloch, "does not have the right to be a pessimist." See Ernst Bloch, "'Ein Marxist hat nicht das Recht, Pessimist zu sein,'" in *Tagträume vom aufrechten Gang: Sechs Interviews mit Ernst Bloch,* ed. Arno Münster (Frankfurt am Main: Suhrkamp Verlag, 1977), 101.

90. Schopf, *Adorno und seine Frankurter Verleger,* November 10, 1958, 299. The comment is taken from an anecdote recounted to Peter Suhrkamp in the same letter: "Anton Bruckner once composed some choral piece or other and performed it in the poet's presence. The poet found that a certain turn of phrase came back too frequently in the composition. Bruckner barked back at him: 'You fool, you should've written more!' [*Hätt'st mehr dicht'*]. Something similar holds true for Bloch's *magnum opus*: 'You should've thought more!' [*Hätt'st mehr denkt*]."

91. Bloch, *The Principle of Hope,* 1:147; *Das Prinzip Hoffnung,* 1:167.

92. Adorno, *Lectures on Negative Dialectics,* 42; *Vorlesung über Negative Dialektik,* 68.

93. Karl Marx, *Critique of Hegel's "Philosophy of Right,"* trans. Annette Jolin and Joseph O'Malley (Cambridge: Cambridge University Press, 1970), 132–133; Karl Marx and Friedrich Engels, *Werke,* 43 vols. (Berlin: Dietz-Verlag, 1956–), 1:379–380. Bloch would of course deny the validity of Adorno's criticisms and in fact lays claim to a more nuanced view. See Bloch and Adorno, "Something's Missing," 1–17; Traub and Wieser, *Gespräche mit Ernst Bloch,* 58–77.

94. Adorno, *Minima Moralia,* § 100, 156; *GS*, 4:178.

95. Bloch and Adorno, "Something's Missing," 4; Traub and Wieser, *Gespräche mit Ernst Bloch,* 61.

96. Adorno says as much in *History and Freedom,* 67–68; *Zur Lehre von der Ge-*

schichte, 99–101. The term "objective possibility" occurs infrequently in Adorno's writings. When he does refer to it, it is generally quite clear that he means the objective possibility of what would be different, rather than adhering to its specifically Weberian or Lukácsian variants, as when he says explicitly that "the objective possibility of something better is blocked." See Theodor W. Adorno, "Culture and Administration," in *The Culture Industry: Selected Essays on Mass Culture*, ed. J. M. Bernstein, trans. Nicholas Walker (London: Routledge, 1991), 126; *GS*, 8:141.

97. Adorno, *History and Freedom*, 140; *Zur Lehre von der Geschichte*, 197.

98. Adorno, *Negative Dialectics*, 11; *GS*, 6:22.

99. Theodor W. Adorno, *Problems of Moral Philosophy*, trans. Rodney Livingstone (Stanford, CA: Stanford University Press, 2001), 167–168; *Probleme der Moralphilosophie*, ed. Thomas Schröder, 2nd ed. (Frankfurt am Main: Suhrkamp Verlag, 2015), 248–249.

Chapter 2

1. Hegel, *Science of Logic*, 33; *W*, 5:50.

2. Theodor W. Adorno, *Ontology and Dialectics*, trans. Nicholas Walker (Cambridge: Polity Press, 2019), 84, 43; *Ontologie und Dialektik*, ed. Rolf Tiedemann (Frankfurt am Main: Suhrkamp Verlag, 2002), 124, 67.

3. Adorno will sometimes use the expression *das Begriffslose*, in addition to the more common *das Nichtbegriffliche*, to convey his meaning. This clearly indicates that he has in mind that which is lacking an adequate concept, not that which is intrinsically non-conceptual. See, e.g., Adorno, *Negative Dialectics*, 10; *GS*, 6:21.

4. Adorno, *Negative Dialectics*, 8; *GS*, 6:20.

5. Martin Heidegger, "Hegel and the Greeks," in *Pathmarks*, ed. Will McNeill, trans. Robert Metcalf (Cambridge: Cambridge University Press, 1998), 335; Martin Heidegger, *Gesamtausgabe*, ed. Friedrich-Wilhelm von Herrmann (Frankfurt am Main: Vittorio Klostermann, 1975–), 9:444.

6. Adorno, *Ontology and Dialectics*, 85; *Ontologie und Dialektik*, 125.

7. Adorno, *Ontology and Dialectics*, 85; *Ontologie und Dialektik*, 125.

8. Adorno, *Ontology and Dialectics*, 86; *Ontologie und Dialektik*, 126.

9. Adorno, *Ontology and Dialectics*, 86; *Ontologie und Dialektik*, 126.

10. Adorno, *Ontology and Dialectics*, 85–86; *Ontologie und Dialektik*, 126.

11. Adorno, "Graeculus (II)," 11–12. Regarding "the ontological privilege of the ontic," see Martin Heidegger, *Being and Time*, trans. John Macquarrie and Edward Robinson (Oxford: Basil Blackwell, 1962), § 4, H12, H14, H16. (Page references to *Being and Time* are to the pagination of the German edition as reproduced in the margins of the translation and indicated by "H.")

12. Adorno's *Hegel: Three Studies* and the lecture course on *Ontology and Dialectics* date from about the same period. Textually, it seems very likely that Adorno had the same complaint in mind in both cases.

13. Theodor W. Adorno, "Skoteinos, or How to Read Hegel," in *Hegel: Three Studies*, trans. Shierry Weber Nicholsen (Cambridge, MA: MIT Press, 1993), 147; *GS*, 5:375.

14. Hegel, *Hegel's Phenomenology of Spirit*, 407; *W*, 3:492.

15. Hegel, *Science of Logic*, 416–417; *W*, 6:122. Tiedemann's comment on this passage is in Adorno, *Ontology and Dialectics*, 270n2; *Ontologie und Dialektik*, 368–369n108.

16. Michael Inwood also uses the example of hunger in his interpretation of ground. See Michael Inwood, *A Hegel Dictionary* (Oxford: Blackwell, 1992), 117.

17. Hegel, *Science of Logic*, 412; *W*, 6:116–117.

18. For Hegel, however, this general claim goes only so far, not least because it is limited by the metaphysics in which it takes part. See, e.g., Hegel, *Encyclopaedia Logic*, § 121, 188–192; *W*, 8:247–252.

19. Equivalently, Hegel says that *"the fact proceeds from ground."* See Hegel, *Science of Logic*, 416; *W*, 6:122.

20. Hegel, *Science of Logic*, 417; *W*, 6:122.

21. Søren Kierkegaard, *Philosophical Fragments, or A Fragment of Philosophy. Johannes Climacus, or De Omnibus Dubitandum Est: A Narrative*, trans. Howard V. Hong and Edna H. Hong (Princeton, NJ: Princeton University Press, 1985), 78; *Søren Kierkegaard's Skrifter*, ed. Niels Jørgen Cappelørn, Joakim Garff, Jette Knudsen, Johnny Kondrup, and Alastair McKinnon, 28 vols. (Copenhagen: Gads Forlag / Søren Kierkegaard Forskningscenteret, 1997–), 4:277–278n.

22. Hegel, *Science of Logic*, 322; *W*, 5:441.

23. Hegel, *Science of Logic*, 402; *W*, 6:103.

24. Hegel, *Science of Logic*, 416–417; *W*, 6:122.

25. Adorno, *Negative Dialectics*, 3; *GS*, 6:15.

26. See Theodor W. Adorno, "Diskussionsbeitrag zu 'Spätkapitalismus oder Industriegesellschaft?,'" in *GS*, 8:585. See also Theodor W. Adorno, "Late Capitalism or Industrial Society? The Fundamental Question of the Present Structure of Society," in *Can One Live after Auschwitz? A Philosophical Reader*, ed. Rolf Tiedemann, trans. Rodney Livingstone (Stanford, CA: Stanford University Press, 2003), 117; *GS*, 8:361–362.

27. G. W. F. Hegel, *Elements of the Philosophy of Right*, trans. H. B. Nisbet (Cambridge: Cambridge University Press, 1991), preface, 22; *W*, 7:26.

28. Hegel, *Encyclopaedia Logic*, § 121, 191; § 122, 192; *W*, 8:252–253.

29. Hegel, *Science of Logic*, 483; *W*, 6:210. See also Hegel, *Encyclopaedia Logic*, § 147, 221; *W*, 8:288.

30. Hegel, *Encyclopaedia Logic*, § 148, 224; *W*, 8:292. Compare Hegel, *Science of Logic*, 484; *W*, 6:210.

31. Hegel, *Science of Logic*, 484; *W*, 6:211.

32. Hegel, *Encyclopaedia Logic*, § 146, *Zusatz*, 219–220; *Science of Logic*, 484; *W*, 8:287, 6:211.

33. Hegel, *Science of Logic*, 484; *W*, 6:210–211.

34. Hegel affirms this thought in three key passages: Hegel, *Science of Logic*, 418; *Encyclopaedia Logic*, § 131, 199; and *The Philosophical Propaedeutic*, ed. Michael George and Andrew Vincent, trans. A. V. Miller (Oxford: Basil Blackwell, 1986), § 47, 84; see *W*, 6:124, 8:261, and 4:175, respectively.

35. Hegel, *Science of Logic*, 482; *W*, 6:208.

36. Hegel, *Propaedeutic*, § 47, 84; *W*, 4:175.

37. Hegel, *Science of Logic*, 479 (emphasis on "mere" added); *W*, 6:204.

38. For an overview of Hegel's wide-ranging understanding of actuality in relation to Kant and recent trends in Hegel interpretation, see Karen Ng, "Hegel's Logic of Actuality," *Review of Metaphysics* 63, no. 1 (2009): 139–172. See also Emmanuel Renault, *Connaître ce qui est: Enquête sur le présentisme hégélien* (Paris: Vrin, 2015).

39. G. W. F. Hegel, "The German Constitution," in *Hegel's Political Writings*, trans. T. M. Knox (Oxford: Oxford University Press), 145; *W*, 1:463.

40. Hegel, "The German Constitution," 145; *W*, 1:463–464.

41. G. W. F. Hegel, *Lectures on the Philosophy of World History: Introduction*, trans. H. B. Nisbet (Cambridge: Cambridge University Press, 1975), 33; *Vorlesungen über die Philosophie der Weltgeschichte*, 4 vols. (Hamburg: Felix Meiner Verlag, 1994), 1:36.

42. Karl Marx, *The Economic and Philosophic Manuscripts of 1844*, trans. Martin Milligan (New York: International Publishers, 1964), 175; Marx and Engels, *MEW*, 40:572. Compare the interpretation advanced here to what Adorno says about Hegel and Marx in lecture 15 of *History and Freedom*; *Zur Lehre von der Geschichte*.

43. Marx, *Economic and Philosophic Manuscripts of 1844*, 175; Marx and Engels, *MEW*, 40:581.

44. Marx, *Economic and Philosophic Manuscripts of 1844*, 175; Marx and Engels, *MEW*, 40:581.

45. Marx, *Critique of Hegel's "Philosophy of Right,"* introduction, 131; Marx and Engels, *MEW*, 1:378. See also Marx, *Economic and Philosophic Manuscripts of 1844*, 175; Marx and Engels, *MEW*, 40:581.

46. Marx, *Critique of Hegel's "Philosophy of Right,"* introduction, 131; Marx and Engels, *MEW*, 1:379.

47. Marx, *Critique of Hegel's "Philosophy of Right,"* introduction, 137, 142; Marx and Engels, *MEW*, 1:384, 391.

48. Marx, *Economic and Philosophic Manuscripts of 1844*, 184; Marx and Engels, *MEW*, 40:580.

49. Marx, *Critique of Hegel's "Philosophy of Right,"* introduction, 133; Marx and Engels, *MEW*, 1:380.

50. Marx, *Economic and Philosophic Manuscripts of 1844*, 184–185; Marx and Engels, *MEW*, 40:581.

51. Marx, *Economic and Philosophic Manuscripts of 1844*, 107; Marx and Engels, *MEW*, 40:511.

52. Karl Marx, *A Contribution to the Critique of Political Economy, Part One*, in *Marx–Engels Collected Works*, vol. 29, trans. Victor Schnittke (London: Lawrence and Wishart, 1987), preface, 263; Marx and Engels, *MEW*, 13:9.

53. Marx, *Economic and Philosophic Manuscripts of 1844*, 186; Marx and Engels, *MEW*, 40:582.

54. Hegel, *Philosophy of Right*, § 57, Zusatz, 88; *W*, 7:126.

55. Marx, *Economic and Philosophic Manuscripts of 1844*, 187; Marx and Engels, *MEW*, 40:583.

56. Marx, *Economic and Philosophic Manuscripts of 1844*, 187–188; Marx and Engels, *MEW*, 40:583–584. For the reference to "illusory essence," see Marx, *Economic and Philosophic Manuscripts of 1844*, 185; Marx and Engels, *MEW*, 40:581.

57. See Karl Marx, "Speech at the Anniversary of the People's Paper, April 14, 1856," in *Marx-Engels Collected Works* (London: Lawrence and Wishart, 1975), 14:655–656; Marx and Engels, *MEW*, 12:3–4.

58. Hegel, *Encyclopaedia Logic*, § 146, 219; *W*, 8:287.

59. Hegel, *Science of Logic*, 484; *W*, 6:211.

60. Hegel, *Encyclopaedia Logic*, § 146, *Zusatz*, 220; *W*, 8:287.

61. "The whole is the false," as Adorno puts it. See Adorno, *Minima Moralia*, § 29, 50; *GS*, 4:55.

62. Marx, *Economic and Philosophic Manuscripts of 1844*, 185; Marx and Engels, *MEW*, 40:581.

63. Adorno, *History and Freedom*, 68; *Zur Lehre von der Geschichte*, 100.

64. Hegel, *The Philosophical Propaedeutic*, § 47, 84; *W*, 4:175.

65. Adorno, "Graeculus (II)," 12.

66. See also Adorno, *History and Freedom*, 67–68; *Zur Lehre von der Geschichte*, 100.

67. Adorno, *History and Freedom*, 67; *Zur Lehre von der Geschichte*, 99–100.

68. Jürgen Habermas, "Toward a Reconstruction of Historical Materalism," in *Communication and the Evolution of Society,* trans. Thomas McCarthy (Boston: Beacon Press, 1979), 139; *Zur Rekonstruktion des historischen Materialismus* (Frankfurt am Main: Suhrkamp Verlag, 1976), 154.

69. See Karl Marx, *Capital: Volume 1*, trans. Ben Fowkes (Harmondsworth, UK: Penguin in association with *New Left Review*, 1976), 90–91; Marx and Engels, *MEW*, 23:12.

70. See, e.g., Friedrich Engels, *The Housing Question,* in *Marx-Engels Collected Works* (London: Lawrence and Wishart, 1988), 23: 324–325; Marx and Engels, *MEW*, 18:220–221.

71. Adorno, *Negative Dialectics*, 203–204; *GS*, 6:203.

72. Hegel, *Science of Logic*, 418; *W*, 6:124.

73. Hegel, *Encyclopaedia Logic*, § 234, *Zusatz,* 302; *W*, 8:387.

74. Hegel, *Science of Logic*, 731; *W*, 6:544.

75. Hegel, *Science of Logic*, 732; *W*, 6:545.

76. Hegel, *Encyclopaedia Logic*, § 234, *Zusatz,* 302; *W*, 8:387.

77. Hegel, *Science of Logic*, 732; *W*, 6:546.

78. Hegel, *Encyclopaedia Logic*, § 234, *Zusatz,* 302; *W*, 8:387. Compare Hegel, *Lectures on the Philosophy of World History*, 66; Hegel, *Vorlesungen über die Philosophie der Weltgeschichte*, 1:77.

79. Hegel, *Encyclopaedia Logic*, § 234, *Zusatz,* 302; *W*, 8:387.

80. Hegel, *Encyclopaedia Logic*, § 6, 30; *W*, 8:49.

81. Hegel, *Encyclopaedia Logic*, § 6, 30; *W*, 8:49.

82. Hegel, *Science of Logic*, 732–733; *W*, 6:546–547.

83. Hegel, "The German Constitution," 145; *W*, 1:463.

84. Adorno, *Negative Dialectics*, 335–336; *GS*, 6:329.

85. G. W. F. Hegel, *Hegel's Aesthetics: Lectures on Fine Art*, trans. T. M. Knox, 2 vols. (Oxford: Oxford University Press, 1975), 1:150; *W*, 13:199.

86. Adorno, "Graeculus (II)," 11–12.

87. Adorno, "Skoteinos," 147; *GS*, 5:375. Horkheimer completes the thought by suggesting that "good people" (i.e., those who could realize the idea of the good) are "dying out." See Theodor W. Adorno and Max Horkheimer, *Towards a New Manifesto*, trans. Rodney Livingstone, 2nd ed. (London: Verso, 2019), 14; Horkheimer, *HGS*, 19:41.

88. Adorno, *Negative Dialectics*, 159n; *GS*, 6, 161n.

89. Adorno, *Negative Dialectics*, 159–160; *GS*, 6:162.

90. Adorno, "Introduction," in *The Positivist Dispute*, 11–12; *GS*, 8:291–292.

91. Adorno, *History and Freedom*, 68; *Zur Lehre von der Geschichte*, 100–101.

92. Adorno, *Negative Dialectics*, 313; *GS*, 6:308.

Chapter 3

1. Ralf Dahrendorf, "Remarks on the Discussion of the Papers by Karl R. Popper and Theodor W. Adorno," in Adorno, *The Positivist Dispute*, 129; "Anmerkung zur Diskussion der Referate von Karl R. Popper und Theodor W. Adorno," in *Der Positivismusstreit in der deutschen Soziologie* (Darmstadt: Hermann Luchterhand Verlag, 1969), 151.

2. Adorno, *Negative Dialectics*, 52; *GS*, 6:62.

3. Jay M. Bernstein, *Adorno: Disenchantment and Ethics* (Cambridge: Cambridge University Press, 2001), 418, 435. See also Deborah Cook, "From the Actual to the Possible: Nonidentity Thinking," *Constellations* 12, no. 1 (2005): 21–35; and Deborah Cook, "Open Thinking: Adorno's Exact Imagination," *Philosophy and Social Criticism* 44, no. 8 (2018): 805–821.

4. See Tom Whyman, "Understanding Adorno on 'Natural-History,'" *International Journal of Philosophical Studies* 24, no. 4 (2016): 452–472.

5. See Hegel, *Science of Logic*, 631; *W*, 6:410.

6. Christoph Menke, "Hegel's Theory of Second Nature: The 'Lapse' of Spirit," *Symposium* 17, no. 1 (2013): 41.

7. Compare Alfred Schmidt, *The Concept of Nature in Marx*, trans. Ben Fowkes (London: New Left Books, 1971), 43; Alfred Schmidt, *Der Begriff der Natur in der Lehre von Marx*, 4th rev. and corr. ed. (Hamburg: Europäische Verlagsanstalt, 1993), 37.

8. Sophocles, *Sophocles: Plays. Antigone*, trans. R. C. Jebb (London: Bristol Classical Press, 2004), 454–457. Hegel occasionally refers to these lines. See, e.g., Hegel, *Hegel's Phenomenology of Spirit*, 261; *Elements of the Philosophy of Right*, § 144, *Zusatz*, 189; *W*, 3:322 and 7:294, respectively.

9. Theodor W. Adorno, "The Idea of Natural-History," in *Things beyond Resemblance: Collected Essays on Theodor W. Adorno*, ed. and trans. Robert Hullot-Kentor (New York: Columbia University Press, 2006), 253; *GS*, 1:346. I translate *Naturgeschichte* as "nature-history" and not as "natural-history" to underscore that what Adorno has in mind is not a history qualified by nature but rather the dialectical interrelation of the two moments of nature and history.

10. Adorno, "The Idea of Natural-History," 253; *GS*, 1:346.

11. Karl Marx, *The Poverty of Philosophy*, in *Marx–Engels Collected Works*, trans. Frida Knight (London: Lawrence and Wishart, 1976), 6:174; Marx and Engels, *MEW*, 4:139.

12. Georg Lukács, *The Theory of the Novel: A Historico-Philosophical Essay on the Forms of Great Epic Literature* (Cambridge, MA: MIT Press, 1971), 64; Georg Lukács, *Die Theorie des Romans: Ein geschichtsphilosophischer Versuch über die Formen der großen Epik* (Darmstadt: Hermann Luchterhand Verlag, 1971), 55.

13. Hegel, *Philosophy of Right*, preface, 23; *W*, 7:28. Compare Hegel, *Science of Logic*, 8; *W*, 5:15.

14. On this point, see also Adorno, *Minima Moralia*, § 14, 34; *GS*, 4:37.

15. Adorno, "The Idea of Natural-History," 262; *GS*, 1:357.

16. Adorno, "The Idea of Natural-History," 262; *GS*, 1:358.

17. In "The Idea of Natural-History," Adorno refers to the riddle-like nature of experience, but he makes more extensive use of this Benjaminian concept in the earlier paper "The Actuality of Philosophy." See, e.g., Theodor W. Adorno, "The Actuality of Philosophy," in *The Adorno Reader*, ed. Brian O'Connor, trans. Benjamin Snow (Oxford: Blackwell, 2000), 31–32; *GS*, 1:335.

18. Adorno, *Negative Dialectics*, 203; *GS*, 6:203. The allusion is to Friedrich Nietzsche, *Thus Spoke Zarathustra: A Book for Everyone and No One*, trans. R. J. Hollingdale (Harmondsworth, UK: Penguin, 1961), 244, 333; Friedrich Nietzsche, *Kritische Studienausgabe*, 15 vols. (Munich: dtv/de Gruyter, 1988), 4:286, 404.

19. The notion of blockage, in the form of the persistence of the current state of affairs, is more present in "The Actuality of Philosophy" but is almost reduced to the status of a methodological problem: with the correct form of dialectical critique, the blockage can be more or less directly overcome. For example, "Authentic philosophical interpretation does not aim for a fixed meaning that lies ready behind the question, but suddenly and instantaneously lights up [the riddle with which it is confronted], consuming it at the same time." This would seem to be a far more orthodox Hegelian view of determinate negation than is found in later writings, which emphasize the obstructive character of reality's riddles. See Adorno, "The Actuality of Philosophy," 31–32; *GS*, 1:335. For a more developed version of these issues, see in particular Adorno, *History and Freedom*, 120–121, 127–128; *Zur Lehre von der Geschichte*, 173–174, 184.

20. See, e.g., Walter Benjamin, *The Origin of German Tragic Drama*, trans. John Osborne (London: Verso, 1998), 223–224; Walter Benjamin, *Gesammelte Schriften*, ed. Rolf Tiedemann et al., 7 vols. (Frankfurt am Main: Suhrkamp Verlag, 1972–1989), 1.1:397–398. Except in references to the published translation, this work will be referred to as *The Origin of the German Mourning Play*.

21. Benjamin, *Origin of German Tragic Drama*, 81; *BGS*, 1.1:260.

22. Kafka is claimed to have said, "Oh, [there is] plenty of hope, an infinite amount of hope—but not for us." Quoted in Walter Benjamin, "Franz Kafka: On the Tenth Anniversary of His Death," in *Selected Writings*, ed. Michael W. Jennings and Howard Eiland (Cambridge, MA: Harvard University Press, 1999), 2.2:798; *BGS*, 2.2:414. See also Max

Brod, *Franz Kafka: A Biography*, trans. G. Humphreys Roberts and Richard Winston (New York: Schocken Books, 1960), 75; Max Brod, *Franz Kafka: Eine Biographie,* in *Über Franz Kafka* (Frankfurt am Main: Fischer Bücherei, 1966), 71.

23. "I am inclined to agree with your opinion that the souls of the just are asleep and that they do not know where they are, up to the Day of Judgement. . . . But I do not dare affirm that this is true for all souls in general, because of the ecstasy of Paul and the ascension of Elijah and Moses (who certainly did not appear as phantoms on Mount Tabor). Who knows how God deals with departed souls? . . . I think the same thing about condemned souls. . . . It is most probable, however, that, with few exceptions, all [departed souls] sleep without feeling." See Martin Luther, *Luther's Works,* ed. Helmut T. Lehmann and Jaroslav Pelikan, 55 vols. (St. Louis: Concordia Publishing House, 1955–1986), 48:360–361; Martin Luther, *D. Martin Luthers Werke: Kritische Gesamtausgabe—Briefwechsel* (Weimar: Verlag Hermann Böhlaus Nachfolger, 1931), 2:422.

24. Compare Theodor W. Adorno, "Progress," in *Critical Models: Interventions and Catchwords,* trans. Henry W. Pickford (New York: Columbia University Press, 1998), 155; *GS,* 10.2:631.

25. See Benjamin, *The Origin of German Tragic Drama,* 151–157; *BGS,* 1.1:329–334. See also Howard Caygill, *Walter Benjamin: The Colour of Experience* (London: Routledge, 1998), 53–54.

26. Benjamin, *Origin of German Tragic Drama,* 106; *BGS,* 1.1:285.

27. Benjamin, *Origin of German Tragic Drama,* 107; *BGS,* 1.1:285–286.

28. Benjamin, *Origin of German Tragic Drama,* 115; *BGS,* 1.1:294.

29. Benjamin, *Origin of German Tragic Drama,* 116–117; *BGS,* 1.1:296.

30. Benjamin, *Origin of German Tragic Drama,* 119; *BGS,* 1.1:298.

31. Benjamin, *Origin of German Tragic Drama,* 129; *BGS,* 1.1:308.

32. Among other things, Adorno gave a seminar on Benjamin's *Origin of the German Mourning Play* in Frankfurt in 1932. See Theodor W. Adorno, "Adornos Seminar vom Sommersemester 1932 über Benjamins *Ursprung des deutschen Trauerspiels,*" in *Frankfurter Adorno Blätter,* vol. 4, ed. Rolf Tiedemann (Munich: edition text + kritik, 1992). In particular, the seminar minutes for June 1 mention three forms of blockage at work in Benjamin's book: "at the level of individual action (as in Hamlet's case), at the level of heretical political action, and at the level of positive transcendence." The summary continues: "There is no possibility of gaining access to the sphere of grace [from within the immanence of the Baroque world]. . . . German Baroque drama does not know outward appearances [*Schein*] as the sphere of what is not actual, separated from what is actual." (See also the summary of the following session.) It is difficult to say from the minutes exactly how Adorno positioned himself with respect to these aspects of Benjamin's book, but it is clear that the group spent considerable time on them. In any case, the modal dimension of blockage, while mentioned, does not seem to have been developed in any detail.

33. Adorno, "The Idea of Natural-History," 259; *GS,* 1:353.

34. Adorno, "The Idea of Natural-History," 266; *GS,* 1:361.

35. Adorno retains this notion of discontinuity, essentially a way of speaking of the

driving force of non-identity, throughout his career. For example, "History is the unity of continuity and discontinuity." See Adorno, *Negative Dialectics*, 320; *GS*, 6:314.

36. "Myth is already enlightenment, and enlightenment reverts to mythology." See Horkheimer and Adorno, *Dialectic of Enlightenment*, xviii; Horkheimer, *HGS*, 5:21.

37. Adorno, "The Idea of Natural-History," 268; *GS*, 1:365.

38. Adorno, *Negative Dialectics*, 11; *GS*, 6:22.

39. It is perhaps from this vantage point that we can glimpse the real genius of Benjamin's gesture, of his insistence on a relegated and forgotten art form. For *The Origin of the German Mourning Play* is not as much a work of literary history as it is a kind of lens that can be used to gain a more precise view of the situation in Germany and in Europe in the mid-1920s and, indeed, of our situation today.

40. Adorno, "The Idea of Natural-History," 268; *GS*, 1:365.

41. Compare Jürgen Habermas, "Theodor Adorno: The Primal History of Subjectivity—Self-Affirmation Gone Wild," in *Philosophical-Political Profiles* (Cambridge, MA: MIT Press, 1983), 107; Jürgen Habermas, *Philosophisch-politische Profile*, enl. ed. (Frankfurt am Main: Suhrkamp Verlag, 1984), 176–177.

42. Theodor W. Adorno, *Introduction to Sociology*, ed. Christoph Gödde, trans. Edmund Jephcott (Cambridge: Polity Press, 2000), 64–65; Theodor W. Adorno, *Einleitung in die Soziologie*, ed. Christoph Gödde (Frankfurt am Main: Suhrkamp Verlag, 1993), 112.

43. Most of the extant materials are gathered in Horkheimer, *HGS*, 12:252–256, 12:559–586, and 19:21–27. Adorno's contribution appears in Adorno, *GS*, 8:392–396. While "Theses on Need" was not published during Adorno's lifetime, he incorporated some ideas and modified passages into "Aldous Huxley and Utopia"; *GS*, 10.1. In the latter text, he also quotes from Horkheimer's contribution to the seminar, as well as from Marcuse's presentation of *Brave New World*. See Adorno, *GS*, 10.2:839. For English translations of Adorno's and Horkheimer's contributions, see Theodor W. Adorno, "Theses on Need" and "On the Problem of Needs," in *Towards a New Manifesto*, by Theodor W. Adorno and Max Horkheimer, 2nd ed., trans. Iain Macdonald and Martin Shuster (London: Verso, 2019).

44. Richard Wolin, "Introduction to the Discussion of [Ludwig Marcuse's] 'Need and Culture in Nietzsche,'" *Constellations* 8, no. 1 (2001): 128.

45. Henry A. Wallace was US vice president under Franklin D. Roosevelt in 1942 and secretary of agriculture prior to that. The speech in question, from May 8 of that same year, made the following claim: "Modern science, which is a by-product and an essential part of the people's revolution, has made it technologically possible to see that all of the people of the world get enough to eat. Half in fun and half seriously, I said the other day to Madame Litvinov: 'The object of this war is to make sure that everybody in the world has the privilege of drinking a quart of milk a day.' She replied: 'Yes, even half a pint.' The peace must mean a better standard of living for the common man, not merely in the United States and England, but also in India, Russia, China and Latin America—not merely in the United Nations, but also in Germany and Italy and Japan." See Henry A. Wallace, "The Price of Free World Victory," in *Democracy Reborn*, ed. Russell Lord (New York: Reynal and Hitchcock, 1944), 193.

46. Adorno, "Theses on Need," 81; *GS*, 8:392.

47. Adorno, "Theses on Need," 81; *GS*, 8:392.

48. Recall Marx's remark: "Hunger is hunger, but the hunger satisfied by cooked meat eaten with a knife and fork is a different hunger from that which bolts down raw meat with the aid of hand, nail, and tooth." See Karl Marx, *Grundrisse: Foundations of the Critique of Political Economy (Rough Draft)*, trans. Martin Nicolaus (Harmondsworth, UK: Penguin in association with *New Left Review*, 1973), 92; Marx and Engels, *MEW*, 42:27.

49. Adorno, "Theses on Need," 84; *GS*, 8:393.

50. Adorno, "Theses on Need," 87; *GS*, 8:395.

51. Theodor W. Adorno, "Reflections on Class Theory," in *Can One Live after Auschwitz? A Philosophical Reader*, ed. Rolf Tiedemann, trans. Rodney Livingstone (Stanford, CA: Stanford University Press, 2003), 105; *GS*, 8:386.

52. See Horkheimer, *HGS*, 12:573.

53. Adorno, "Theses on Need," 88; *GS*, 8:395–396.

54. As Horkheimer puts it, "From the mouth of a government official, even the call for a pint of milk contains a number of unstated 'formal' elements: that the milk be delivered in a clean container, that it contain no harmful bacteria, that it have a certain fat content, and so on. If taken strictly verbatim, the demand for milk could be met and we would still have been duped. Dialectic recognizes that it is not merely the nutritional value and the kind of container that play a role in determining whether the child [who receives the milk] has been tricked, but also, e.g., that father and mother not suffer under the pressure of meaningless jobs and not live in constant fear of losing them, that they have appropriate housing, that a good doctor be available to them, that there exist no exploitative state of domination—a domination that can necessarily be seen in the faces and in the very essence of the parents, as well as in their surroundings, all of which in the long run spoils the milk far more than a dirty container ever could. The social order is contained within the milk, just as much as its fat content." See Horkheimer, "On the Problem of Needs," 93–94; *HGS*, 12:252–253.

55. Adorno, "Theses on Need," 88–89; *GS*, 8:396.

56. Compare Max Horkheimer, *Eclipse of Reason* (1974; repr., London: Continuum, 2004), 59, 104.

57. See Horkheimer, *HGS*, 12:578–579. It is not entirely clear to which of the seminar participants this passage should be attributed, but it is very close in meaning to what Adorno says at the end of the "Theses on Need."

58. Adorno, "Theses on Need," 89; *GS*, 8:396.

59. Theodor W. Adorno, *Erkenntnistheorie (1957/58)*, ed. Karel Markus (Frankfurt am Main: Suhrkamp Verlag, 2018), 9.

60. Theodor W. Adorno, "Society," trans. F. R. Jameson, *Salmagundi* 3, no. 10–11 (1969–1970): 144; *GS*, 8:9.

61. Adorno, "Society," 144; *GS*, 8:9.

62. Theodor W. Adorno, "On the Logic of the Social Sciences," in Adorno, *The Positivist Dispute*, 106; *GS*, 8:548.

63. Adorno, "On the Logic of the Social Sciences," 109; *GS*, 8:552.

64. See Axel Honneth, "Eine Physiognomie der kapitalistischen Lebensform: Skizze der Gesellschaftstheorie Adornos," in *Dialektik der Freiheit: Frankfurter Adorno-Konferenz 2003*, ed. Axel Honneth (Frankfurt am Main: Suhrkamp Verlag, 2005).

65. Adorno, "Society," 147; *GS*, 8:12.

66. See, e.g., Ralf Dahrendorf, "Herrschaft, Klassenverhältnis und Schichtung," in *Spätkapitalismus oder Industriegesellschaft? Verhandlungen des 16. Deutschen Soziologentages in Frankfurt am Main 1968*, ed. Theodor W. Adorno (Stuttgart: Ferdinand Enke, 1969), 91–92. Dahrendorf had been a close collaborator of Adorno and Horkheimer's at the Institute for Social Research, in whom Adorno in particular had "placed great hopes," according to Rolf Wiggershaus. But he left their ranks in 1954, unsatisfied with the approaches favored by the Institute. See Rolf Wiggershaus, *The Frankfurt School*, trans. Michael Robertson (Cambridge: Polity Press, 1994), 537, 471; Rolf Wiggershaus, *Die Frankfurter Schule*, 6th ed. (Munich: Deutscher Taschenbuch Verlag, 2001), 597, 525.

67. Ralf Dahrendorf, *Class and Class Conflict in Industrial Society* (Stanford, CA: Stanford University Press, 1959), 29.

68. Dahrendorf, *Class and Class Conflict in Industrial Society*, 60, 220.

69. Dahrendorf, *Class and Class Conflict in Industrial Society*, 30.

70. Dahrendorf, *Class and Class Conflict in Industrial Society*, 222.

71. "Conciliation, mediation, and arbitration, and their normative and structural prerequisites, are the outstanding mechanisms for reducing the violence of class conflict. Where these routines of relationship are established, group conflict loses its sting and becomes an institutionalized pattern of social life. For revolutionary upheavals to be transformed into evolutionary changes, there is, contrary to Marx's belief, no need for a classless society (that is, for a Utopian fiction); by effective regulation, class conflict may become the element of regularity in a continuously changing world. Even if the intensity of conflict remains undiminished its manifestations may be channeled in such a way as to protect the individual from the physical threat of a *bellum omnium contra omnes*." See Dahrendorf, *Class and Class Conflict in Industrial Society*, 230.

72. Dahrendorf, "Herrschaft, Klassenverhältnis und Schichtung," 99.

73. Theodor W. Adorno, "Diskussionsbeitrag zu 'Spätkapitalismus oder Industriegesellschaft?,'" in *GS*, 8:582.

74. Dahrendorf, *Class and Class Conflict in Industrial Society*, 224.

75. Adorno, "Diskussionsbeitrag zu 'Spätkapitalismus oder Industriegesellschaft?,'" *GS*, 8:584–585.

76. Adorno, "Introduction," in *The Positivist Dispute*, 57; *GS*, 8:342. This is one of the handful of references to Adornian "objective possibility," which should be understood as referring to blocked possibility, rather than to Weber's or Lukács's versions of the concept.

77. Adorno, "Diskussionsbeitrag zu 'Spätkapitalismus oder Industriegesellschaft?,'" *GS*, 8:582.

78. Marx, *Economic and Philosophic Manuscripts of 1844*, 107; Marx and Engels, *MEW*, 40:511.

79. Perhaps the most famous expression of this nature-like necessity is the follow-ing: "The capitalist mode of appropriation, which springs from the capitalist mode of production, produces capitalist private property. This is the first negation of individual private property, as founded on the labor of its proprietor. But capitalist production be-gets, with the necessity of a natural process, its own negation. This is the negation of the negation." See Marx, *Capital*, 1:929; Marx and Engels, *MEW*, 23:791.

80. It bears emphasizing that Adorno's critique of jazz has less to do with either the history of jazz or his defense of other art forms than with the charade of autonomy that cultural commodities promulgate.

81. Beethoven too can be packaged and served up on the radio, all the while leav-ing structural injustices intact: "[Both so-called deeper and superficial needs] have long been taken over by the [cultural] monopoly. The Beethoven symphony conducted by Toscanini is no better than the next popular film to come along, and the whole pro-cess is condensed into every single Bette Davis movie." See Adorno, "Theses on Need," 83–84; *GS*, 8:393. Compare the following passage on Toscanini, which implicitly refers to the nature-history dialectic: "People believe in Toscanini so as to have something to believe in, and this belief is a symptom of a mental state that is as much an obstacle to autonomy of judgement in artistic matters as it is elsewhere. To doubt Toscanini seems blasphemous, whereas in reality it is blasphemous to want to turn him into a god." See Theodor W. Adorno, "The Mastery of the Maestro," in *Sound Figures*, trans. Rodney Livingstone (Stanford, CA: Stanford University Press, 1999), 43; *GS*, 16:55. See also Adorno's critique of the revival of interest in Baroque music: "Der mißbrauchte Barock," in *GS*, 10.1:401–422. There are, of course, other examples of criticisms directed against so-called high culture in Adorno's writings.

82. See, e.g., Adorno, *Negative Dialectics*, 116; *GS*, 5:122.

83. Theodor W. Adorno, "Individuum und Organisation," in *GS*, 8:448.

84. Adorno, "Individuum und Organisation," *GS*, 8:451–452. "Social security" ap-pears in English in the text. Compare Adorno, "Reflections on Class Theory," 105; *GS*, 8:386.

85. Theodor W. Adorno, "Free Time," in *Critical Models: Interventions and Catch-words*, trans. Henry W. Pickford (New York: Columbia University Press, 1998), 169; *GS*, 10.2:647.

86. Franz Neumann, "Economics and Politics in the Twentieth Century," in *The Democratic and the Authoritarian State: Essays in Political and Legal Theory*, ed. Herbert Marcuse, trans. Peter Gay (Glencoe, IL: Free Press, 1957), 268; Franz Neumann, "Öko-nomie und Politik im zwanzigsten Jahrhundert," *Zeitschrift für Politik* 2, no. 1 (1955): 10.

87. Adorno, *Negative Dialectics*, 3; *GS*, 6:15.

88. Adorno, "Society," 153; *GS*, 8:19.

89. The term appears in two posthumously published texts from 1942 included in Adorno's collected writings. See "The Schema of Mass Culture," in *The Culture Industry: Selected Essays on Mass Culture*, ed. J. M. Bernstein, trans. Nicholas Walker (London: Routledge, 1991), 63; and "Reflections on Class Theory," 109; *GS*, 3:301 and 8:390, re-spectively. However, the concept of veil occurs frequently: "social veil," "individualis-

tic veil," and sometimes "monadological veil" or "ideological veil." Finally, it should be noted that Benjamin also uses the term fairly frequently.

90. Theodor W. Adorno, *Philosophical Elements of a Theory of Society*, ed. Tobias ten Brink and Marc Phillip Nogueira, trans. Wieland Hoban (Cambridge: Polity Press, 2019), 136; *Philosophische Elemente einer Theorie der Gesellschaft*, ed. Tobias ten Brink and Marc Phillip Nogueira (Frankfurt am Main: Suhrkamp Verlag, 2008), 210. See also Max Horkheimer, "The End of Reason," *Studies in Philosophy and Social Science* 9, no. 3 (1941): 384, 378; *HGS*, 5:345, 338. And see Theodor W. Adorno and Arnold Gehlen, "Ist die Soziologie eine Wissenschaft vom Menschen? Ein Streitgespräch," in *Adornos Philosophie in Grundbegriffen: Auflösung einiger Deutungsprobleme*, by Friedemann Grenz (Frankfurt am Main: Suhrkamp Verlag, 1974), 237.

91. Adorno, "The Schema of Mass Culture," 63; *GS*, 3:301. Compare: "People are inclined to take technology to be the thing itself, as an end in itself, a force of its own, and they forget that it is an extension of human dexterity. The means—and technology is the epitome of the means of self-preservation of the human species—are fetishized, because the ends—a life of human dignity—are concealed and removed from the consciousness of people." See Theodor W. Adorno, "Education after Auschwitz," in *Critical Models: Interventions and Catchwords*, trans. Henry W. Pickford (New York: Columbia University Press, 1998), 200; *GS*, 10.2:686.

92. Cicero, *De finibus bonorum et malorum*, trans. H. Rackham (London: William Heinemann, 1914), 5.74. Compare Aristotle, *Nicomachean Ethics*, trans. Terence Irwin, 2nd ed. (Indianapolis, IN: Hackett, 1999), VII.10, 1152a30–33.

93. Marx, *Capital*, 1:168–169; Marx and Engels, *MEW*, 23:90.

94. Adorno, *History and Freedom*, 121; *Zur Lehre von der Geschichte*, 174.

95. Adorno, "Late Capitalism or Industrial Society?," 118; *GS*, 8:362.

96. Adorno, "Diskussionsbeitrag zu 'Spätkapitalismus oder Industriegesellschaft?,'" *GS*, 8:585. Adorno here again invokes the apparently Weberian-Lukácsian concept of objective possibility. But it is equally clear from the reference to utopia that he is tacitly liberating it from Lukács's attempt to bind it to historical socialism, as well as from Weber's restriction of it to strictly sociological and historiographical interpretation.

97. Theodor W. Adorno, "Who's Afraid of the Ivory Tower? A Conversation with Theodor W. Adorno," in *Language without Soil: Adorno and Late Philosophical Modernity*, ed. and trans. Gerhard Richter (New York: Fordham University Press, 2010), 233; *GS*, 20.1:403.

98. See Immanuel Kant, "Idea for a Universal History with a Cosmopolitan Purpose," in *Kant's Political Writings*, ed. Hans Reiss, trans. H. B. Nisbet (Cambridge: Cambridge University Press, 1970), 44; *Gesammelte Schriften "Akademieausgabe"* (Berlin: Reimer/De Gruyter, 1900–), 8:20.

99. Adorno, "On the Logic of the Social Sciences," 112; *GS*, 8:554.

100. Adorno and Gehlen, "Ist die Soziologie eine Wissenschaft vom Menschen?," 246.

101. Adorno, "Late Capitalism or Industrial Society?," 119; *GS*, 8:364.

102. Adorno, "Late Capitalism or Industrial Society?," 120; *GS*, 8:364.

103. Theodor W. Adorno, "Theory of Pseudo-Culture," trans. Deborah Cook, *Telos* 95 (1993): 24; *GS*, 8:103.

104. For a discussion of Adorno's concept of autonomy in connection with issues raised here, see Iain Macdonald, "Cold, Cold, Warm: Autonomy, Intimacy and Maturity in Adorno," *Philosophy and Social Criticism* 37, no. 6 (2011): 669–689.

105. Theodor W. Adorno, *Aesthetic Theory*, trans. Robert Hullot-Kentor (Minneapolis: University of Minnesota Press, 1997), 121; *GS*, 7:183.

106. Adorno, *Aesthetic Theory*, 227; *GS*, 7:336–337.

107. Adorno, *Aesthetic Theory*, 236; *GS*, 7:351.

108. Adorno, *Aesthetic Theory*, esp. 5, 210, 225ff.; *GS*, 7:16, 312, 334ff.

109. Adorno, *Aesthetic Theory*, 158; *GS*, 7:236.

110. Compare Adorno, *Aesthetic Theory*, 2–3; *GS*, 7:11–12, 12.

111. Adorno frequently uses the Benjaminian word "intentionless" to suggest that artworks emerge from a historical situation in which the subject is most likely unconsciously embroiled and over which the arbitrary will of the artist has little direct control.

112. Adorno, *Aesthetic Theory*, 2; *GS*, 7:11.

113. "Rather no more art than socialist realism." See Adorno, *Aesthetic Theory*, 53; *GS*, 7:85.

114. Adorno, *Aesthetic Theory*, 321; *GS*, 7:475.

115. Adorno, *Aesthetic Theory*, 169; *GS*, 7:253.

116. Adorno, *Aesthetic Theory*, 228; *GS*, 7:339.

117. Adorno, *Aesthetic Theory*, 229; *GS*, 7:340.

118. Adorno, *Aesthetic Theory*, 95; *GS*, 7:146–147.

119. Adorno, *Aesthetic Theory*, 7; *GS*, 7:18.

120. Adorno, *Aesthetic Theory*, 34; *GS*, 7:57–58.

121. Adorno, *Aesthetic Theory*, 35; *GS*, 7:59.

122. Adorno, *Aesthetic Theory*, 156; *GS*, 7:233.

123. Adorno, *Aesthetic Theory*, 301; *GS*, 7:447.

124. Theodor W. Adorno, "On Some Relationships between Music and Painting," trans. Susan Gillespie, *Musical Quarterly* 79, no. 1 (1995): 72; *GS*, 16:635.

125. Theodor W. Adorno, "Ohne Leitbild," in *GS*, 10.1:294.

126. Adorno, *Aesthetic Theory*, 135; *GS*, 7:203.

127. Adorno, *Aesthetic Theory*, 231; *GS*, 7:343.

128. Compare Adorno and Gehlen, "Ist die Soziologie eine Wissenschaft vom Menschen?," 234. See also Adorno, *History and Freedom*, 143; *Zur Lehre von der Geschichte*, 202–203.

129. Adorno, *Aesthetic Theory*, 226; *GS*, 7:335.

130. Adorno, *Aesthetic Theory*, 83; *GS*, 7:129.

131. Adorno, *Aesthetic Theory*, 135; *GS*, 7:204.

132. The quoted expression is recurrent in Adorno. See, e.g., "Late Capitalism or Industrial Society?," 124; *GS*, 8:369.

133. Susan Buck-Morss underscores that each pole of the nature-history dialectic is itself dialectical. The dialectic of society and art is an illustration of this point. See Susan

Buck-Morss, *The Origin of Negative Dialectics: Theodor W. Adorno, Walter Benjamin, and the Frankfurt Institute* (New York: Free Press, 1977), 54.

134. Adorno, *Negative Dialectics*, 161; *GS*, 6:164.

135. Compare Bernstein, *Adorno*, 418, 435.

136. Adorno, "Diskussionsbeitrag zu 'Spätkapitalismus oder Industriegesellschaft?,'" *GS*, 8:586.

137. See Adorno, *Negative Dialectics*, 365; *GS*, 6:358.

138. See Adorno, "Theses on Need," 87; *GS*, 8:395; and Horkheimer, "On the Problem of Needs," 96; *HGS*, 12:254.

139. Adorno, *Negative Dialectics*, 203; *GS*, 6:203.

140. Adorno, *Negative Dialectics*, 11, 203; *GS*, 6:22, 203.

141. Adorno, *Negative Dialectics*, 203; *GS*, 6:203.

142. Adorno, *Negative Dialectics*, 203; *GS*, 6:203.

143. Hegel, *Encyclopaedia Logic*, § 143, *Zusatz*, 216; *W*, 8:283.

144. Hegel, *Science of Logic*, 479; *W*, 6:204.

145. Hegel, "The German Constitution," 145; *W*, 1:463.

146. See, e.g., Adorno, *Lectures on Negative Dialectics*, 103–108; *Vorlesung über Negative Dialektik*, 151–158.

147. Theodor W. Adorno, "Cultural Criticism and Society," in *Prisms*, trans. Samuel Weber and Shierry Weber (Cambridge, MA: MIT Press, 1981), 31; *GS*, 10.1:26.

148. On this issue, Adorno agrees with Bloch. See Bloch, *Subjekt-Objekt*, 446–447.

149. Bloch and Adorno, "Something's Missing," 4; Traub and Wieser, *Gespräche mit Ernst Bloch*, 61.

150. Adorno, *Negative Dialectics*, 52; *GS*, 6:62.

151. Adorno, *Negative Dialectics*, 393; *GS*, 6:385.

152. Adorno, *Negative Dialectics*, 56–57; *GS*, 6:66.

153. Andrew Buchwalter comes close to this reading by distinguishing primary real possibility from secondary real possibility in Adorno. However, it is untenable, I think, to oppose transcendence and immanence as he does. See Andrew Buchwalter, *Dialectics, Politics, and the Contemporary Value of Hegel's Practical Philosophy* (London: Routledge, 2012), 63–71.

154. Theodor W. Adorno, *An Introduction to Dialectics*, ed. Christoph Ziermann, trans. Nicholas Walker (Cambridge: Polity Press, 2017), 184; Theodor W. Adorno, *Einführung in die Dialektik*, ed. Christoph Ziermann (Frankfurt am Main: Suhrkamp Verlag, 2010), 261.

155. Marx, *Critique of Hegel's "Philosophy of Right,"* introduction, 133; Marx and Engels, *MEW*, 1:380.

156. Adorno, *Minima Moralia*, § 40, 65; *GS*, 4:72.

157. Adorno, *Minima Moralia*, § 22, 43–45; *GS*, 4:48–49. Compare Adorno, *Negative Dialectics*, 3; *GS*, 6:15. See also Karl Marx and Friedrich Engels, *The Communist Manifesto*, trans. Samuel Moore (Harmondsworth, UK: Penguin [Pelican], 1967), 94; Marx and Engels, *MEW*, 4:474.

158. Adorno, *History and Freedom*, 181–182; *Zur Lehre von der Geschichte*, 251.

159. Adorno, "Experiential Content of Hegel's Philosophy," 87; *GS*, 5:324.

Chapter 4

1. Jonathan Swift, "A Vindication of Mr. Gay, and the *Beggars Opera*," *The Intelligencer*, no. 3 (1728), 21–22. Reprint, 2nd ed. of 1730 (New York: AMS Press, 1967).

2. See Martin Heidegger, *Ponderings II–VI: Black Notebooks 1931–1938*, trans. Richard Rojcewicz (Bloomington: Indiana University Press, 2016), § 53, 16–17; *GA*, 94:21.

3. Heidegger, *Being and Time*, § 6, H22–23.

4. Heidegger, *Being and Time*, § 4, H12.

5. Heidegger, *Being and Time*, § 9, H42.

6. Heidegger, *Being and Time*, § 18, H84.

7. Heidegger, *Being and Time*, § 9, H43.

8. Heidegger, *Being and Time*, § 9, H42.

9. Heidegger, *Being and Time*, § 65, H329.

10. Heidegger, *Being and Time*, § 43, H201.

11. Heidegger, *Being and Time*, § 43, H207.

12. Heidegger, *Being and Time*, § 43, H209.

13. Heidegger, *Being and Time*, § 43, H211.

14. Heidegger, *Being and Time*, § 43, H212.

15. Heidegger, *Being and Time*, § 41, H191–192.

16. Heidegger, *Being and Time*, § 31, H143–144.

17. Heidegger, *Being and Time*, § 48, H242.

18. See also Francisco J. Gonzalez, "Whose Metaphysics of Presence? Heidegger's Interpretation of *Energeia* and *Dunamis* in Aristotle," *Southern Journal of Philosophy* 44, no. 4 (2006): 533–568; and Francisco J. Gonzalez, "Δύναμις and Dasein, 'Ενέργεια and Ereignis: Heidegger's (Re)Turn to Aristotle," *Research in Phenomenology* 48, no. 3 (2018): 409–432.

19. Heidegger, *Being and Time*, § 48, H244.

20. Heidegger, *Being and Time*, § 48, H244.

21. Heidegger, *Being and Time*, § 48, H261.

22. Martin Heidegger, *Contributions to Philosophy (Of the Event)*, trans. Richard Rojcewicz and Daniela Vallega-Neu (Bloomington: Indiana University Press, 2012), § 267, 374; *GA*, 65:475.

23. Heidegger, *Being and Time*, § 7, H38.

24. However, Husserl sets the correct tone by understanding phenomenology as a science of possibility, of essences: "The old ontological doctrine *that the cognition of 'possibilities' must precede the cognition of actualities* is, in my opinion, insofar as it is correctly understood and made useful in the right ways, a great truth." See Edmund Husserl, *Ideas pertaining to a Pure Phenomenology and to a Phenomenological Philosophy: First Book*, trans. F. Kersten (The Hague: Martinus Nijhoff, 1983), § 79, 190; Edmund Husserl, *Husserliana*, ed. S. Ijsseling et al. (The Hague: Martinus Nijhoff, 1950–), 3.1:159.

25. Martin Heidegger, *The Basic Problems of Phenomenology*, trans. Albert Hofstadter, rev. ed. (Bloomington: Indiana University Press, 1982), 308; *GA*, 24:438.

26. Herbert Spiegelberg, *The Phenomenological Movement: A Historical Introduction*, 3rd rev. and enl. ed. (The Hague: Martinus Nijhoff, 1982), 360.

27. See, e.g., Heidegger, *Ponderings II–VI*, § 184, 57; *GA*, 94:75–76.

28. Heidegger, *Contributions*, § 2, 8; *GA*, 65:6.

29. Heidegger, *Contributions*, § 81, 133; *GA*, 65:169.

30. Heidegger, *Contributions*, § 85, 136; *GA*, 65:172.

31. Heidegger, *Contributions*, § 173, 234; *GA*, 65:297.

32. Martin Heidegger, *Basic Questions of Philosophy: Selected "Problems" of "Logic,"* trans. Richard Rojcewicz and André Schuwer (Bloomington: Indiana University Press, 1994), § 13, 35; *GA*, 45:37. Heidegger elsewhere says that "no 'revolution' is 'revolutionary' enough." See Martin Heidegger, *The History of Beyng*, trans. William McNeill and Jeffrey Powell (Bloomington: Indiana University Press, 2015), § 21, 22; *GA*, 69:23. We should, however, recall that these lines are also indelibly marked by Heidegger's disappointment in National Socialism, which he considered a failed revolution. See, e.g., *GA*, 95:408.

33. Martin Heidegger, "Summary of a Seminar on 'Time and Being,'" in *On Time and Being*, trans. Joan Stambaugh (New York: Harper and Row, 1972), 53–54; *GA*, 14:63.

34. Heidegger, *Contributions*, § 158, 221; *GA*, 65:281.

35. Heidegger, *Contributions*, § 158, 221; *GA*, 65:281.

36. This is obviously not the only way to construe possibility and necessity, but what matters for Heidegger is the way in which actuality (that which is taken to be fully present and actual) primarily determines modality—whether in the form of a natural substance, a self-actualizing deity, or nature as exploitable resource. See also Heidegger, *Being and Time*, § 31, H143–144.

37. See Jaakko Hintikka, "Aristotle on the Realization of Possibilities in Time," in *Time and Necessity: Studies in Aristotle's Theory of Modality* (Oxford: Clarendon Press, 1973).

38. Heidegger, *Contributions*, § 34, 59; *GA*, 65:74.

39. Martin Heidegger, "Recollection in Metaphysics," in *The End of Philosophy*, trans. Joan Stambaugh (1973; repr., Chicago: University of Chicago Press, 2003), 80; *GA*, 6.2:445. Heidegger makes clear in a marginal note to the text that the term "machination" (*Machenschaft*) was the conceptual precursor to "enframing." See *GA*, 6.2:445, note a. See also Martin Heidegger, *Mindfulness*, trans. Parvis Emad and Thomas Kalary (London: Continuum, 2006), § 76, 257–258; *GA*, 66:289. There are many other passages in Heidegger that recount similar histories. See, e.g., Martin Heidegger, "Metaphysics as History of Being," in *The End of Philosophy*; *GA*, 6.2:363–416; or *Contributions*, § 55, 91–92; *GA*, 65:115.

40. The "future ones" are not only those of a future time but also those who, even today, have an inkling of and prepare the ground for the other beginning. Heidegger even uses the expression "we future ones" to speak of himself and those who may have an ear for the resonating of beyng in being. See Heidegger, *Contributions*, § 52, 89; *GA*, 65:112. Or again: "Today there are already a few of these future ones. Their surmising and seeking are hardly recognizable to *themselves* and to their genuine unrest." See Hei-

degger, *Contributions*, § 252, 317; *GA*, 65:400. There is no doubt an echo of Nietzsche here as well.

41. Heidegger, *Mindfulness*, § 76, 258; *GA*, 66:290. See also Heidegger, *Contributions*, § 149, 213; *GA*, 65:270.

42. For a more orthodox view of Heidegger on possibility, see Claudia Serban, *Phénoménologie de la possibilité: Husserl et Heidegger* (Paris: PUF, 2016).

43. Thomas Bernhard, *Old Masters: A Comedy*, trans. Ewald Osers (Chicago: University of Chicago Press, 1992), 42–43; Thomas Bernhard, *Alte Meister: Komödie* (Frankfurt am Main: Suhrkamp Verlag, 1985), 88–90. Reger seems to have been somewhat inspired by Günter Grass's *Dog Years* (first published in 1963), which, among other things, mocks Heidegger's "Alemannic stocking-cap." See Günter Grass, *Dog Years*, trans. Ralph Manheim (San Diego: Harcourt, 1965), 392–395; Günter Grass, *Hundejahre* (Darmstadt: Hermann Luchterhand Verlag, 1974), 330–332.

44. Bernhard, *Old Masters*, 151; *Alte Meister*, 302.

45. Bernhard, *Old Masters*, 31–32; *Alte Meister*, 67–68.

46. Heidegger, *Contributions*, § 29, 53; *GA*, 65:66.

47. See also Heidegger, *Contributions*, § 4, 11; *GA*, 65:10.

48. The reference to Faye, as a counterpart to the preceding reference to Bernhard, is meant to throw aspects of Adorno's philosophical criticisms of Heidegger into relief. The point is to see Adorno as a legitimate and compelling alternative to satirical and political dismissals of Heidegger. I do not take Faye's work to be representative of critical readings of Heidegger, of which there are many more philosophically substantial examples.

49. Peter E. Gordon, "Review of Emmanuel Faye, *Heidegger: The Introduction of Nazism into Philosophy in Light of the Unpublished Seminars of 1933–1935*," *Notre Dame Philosophical Reviews* (2010), last modified March 12, 2010, http://ndpr.nd.edu/news/24316/?id=19228.

50. See, e.g., Heidegger, *GA*, 96:262.

51. Heidegger, *GA*, 98:326.

52. Heidegger, *GA*, 95:408.

53. The literature on the topic is far too vast to list here, but a useful overview of the context in which Faye is writing is sketched in Tom Rockmore, "Foreword," in *Heidegger: The Introduction of Nazism into Philosophy in the Light of the Unpublished Seminars of 1933–1935*, by Emmanuel Faye, trans. Michael B. Smith (New Haven, CT: Yale University Press, 2009).

54. Heidegger, *GA*, 95:408.

55. Heidegger, *GA*, 95:408. Ernst Jünger later wrote of Heidegger: "Can one reproach him if the political powers disappointed his confidence in them?" See Martin Heidegger and Ernst Jünger, *Correspondence 1949–1975*, trans. Timothy Sean Quinn (London: Rowman and Littlefield, 2016), 38; Ernst Jünger and Martin Heidegger, *Briefe 1949–1975* (Stuttgart: Klett-Cotta, 2008), 59.

56. Heidegger, *GA*, 95:408. This "basis in thinking" of the promise of National Socialism is precisely what many of Heidegger's defenders have sought to deny. François Fédier provides an example: "Any convergence of [Heidegger's] thought with Nazism is

absurd on principle, first of all because the *idea* of Nazi thinking is something that simply does not exist. Nazism has no [basis in thinking, *denkerische Basis*], no basis. It's just affects, reactions, just, well, there is simply no such thing as a Nazi intellectual. These people were just con artists." In Walter Rüdel and Richard Wisser, "Martin Heidegger: Im Denken unterwegs . . ." (ZDF, 1969). (In the course of making this statement, Fédier pauses, searching for his words. The interviewer offers to complete his thought with the expression "basis in thinking," which Fédier accepts, repeating "no basis.")

57. Emmanuel Faye, *Heidegger: The Introduction of Nazism into Philosophy in the Light of the Unpublished Seminars of 1933–1935*, trans. Michael B. Smith (New Haven, CT: Yale University Press, 2009), 246; Emmanuel Faye, *Heidegger, l'introduction du nazisme dans la philosophie: Autour des séminaire inédits de 1933–1935* (Paris: Albin Michel, 2005), 399. Peter Gordon says that "it would be difficult to imagine a thesis more extreme than [Faye's]." See Gordon, "Review of Emmanuel Faye."

58. Faye, *Heidegger: The Introduction*, 319; *Heidegger*, 513.

59. Faye, *Heidegger: The Introduction*, 300; *Heidegger*, 484.

60. Faye, *Heidegger: The Introduction*, 320–321; *Heidegger*, 515–516.

61. Faye, *Heidegger: The Introduction*, 287, 300; *Heidegger*, 463, 484.

62. Dominique Pradelle was the first, to my knowledge, to make this point. See his review of *Heidegger: L'introduction du nazisme dans la philosophie*, by Emmanuel Faye, *Philosophie* 91, no. 4 (2006): 93.

63. Faye, *Heidegger: The Introduction*, 109; *Heidegger*, 181.

64. Faye, *Heidegger: The Introduction*, 238–239; *Heidegger*, 388.

65. Faye, *Heidegger: The Introduction*, 239; *Heidegger*, 389.

66. Adorno uses the somewhat comical and derogatory term *Heideggerei* (also translated as "the cult of Heidegger") in a letter to Robert Minder dated June 25, 1959, reprinted in part in the editorial note to *Ontology and Dialectics*, xv; *Ontologie und Dialektik*, 424.

67. Adorno, *GS*, 19:638.

68. The indications provided are in no way meant to be exhaustive.

69. *Bekenntnis der Professoren an den deutschen Universitäten und Hochschulen zu Adolf Hitler und dem nationalsozialistischen Staat* (Dresden: NS Lehrerbund Deutschland/Sachsen, 1933), 13–14. Adorno mentions Heidegger's participation in the profession of loyalty in a later letter to Hermann Mörchen. See Theodor W. Adorno, Correspondence with Hermann Mörchen, September 13, 1965, Theodor W. Adorno Archive, Frankfurt am Main, TWAA Br 1027.

70. See Adorno, *Negative Dialectics*, 130; *GS*, 6:135–136. See Karl Löwith, *Sämtliche Schriften* (Stuttgart: J. B. Metzler, 1981–1988), 8:169–170; Karl Löwith, "The Political Implications of Heidegger's Existentialism," in *The Heidegger Controversy*, ed. and trans. Richard Wolin (Cambridge, MA: MIT Press, 1993); and Guido Schneeberger, ed. *Nachlese zu Heidegger: Dokumente zu seinem Leben und Denken* (Bern: Suhr, 1962). Adorno's explicit references to Schneeberger are in Theodor W. Adorno, *The Jargon of Authenticity*, trans. Knut Tarnowski and Frederic Will (London: Routledge and Kegan Paul,

1973), 53–55; *GS*, 6:448–451; see also Theodor W. Adorno, *Philosophische Terminologie I und II*, ed. Henri Lonitz (Frankfurt am Main: Suhrkamp Verlag, 2016), 194.

71. Adorno, *Negative Dialectics*, 61; *GS*, 6:69.

72. The Nazi expression *alte Kämpfer* refers to individuals with an affiliation to the movement prior to 1933. Adorno, *Ontology and Dialectics*, 47; *Ontologie und Dialektik*, 74. Compare Adorno, *Jargon*, 40; *GS*, 6:440. For the reference to *Blut und Boden*, see Adorno, *Jargon*, 55; *GS*, 6:449.

73. Adorno, *Jargon*, 76, 102, 19; *GS*, 6:463, 481, 425.

74. Adorno, "Why Still Philosophy," 10; *GS*, 10.2:464. Adorno may be thinking of the *Bekenntnis der Professoren an den deutschen Universitäten und Hochschulen zu Adolf Hitler und dem nationalsozialistischen Staat*, 13–14, or perhaps texts from Schneeberger, *Nachlese zu Heidegger,* which appeared in 1962, the same year as Adorno's text.

75. Heidegger, *Being and Time*, § 36, H 173.

76. Adorno, *Jargon*, 113; *GS*, 6:488.

77. Adorno, *Jargon*, 81; *GS*, 6:467.

78. Adorno, *Jargon*, 87; *GS*, 6:470–471.

79. Adorno, *Ontology and Dialectics*, 68; *Ontologie und Dialektik*, 102–103. Compare Theodor W. Adorno, *Against Epistemology: A Metacritique*, trans. Willis Domingo (Oxford: Basil Blackwell, 1982), 37; *GS*, 5:44.

80. Adorno, *Jargon*, 18; *GS*, 6:425.

81. Adorno, *Jargon*, 53, 56, 59, 108; *GS*, 6:448, 450, 452, 485; *Ontology and Dialectics*, 194; *Ontologie und Dialektik*, 273. See also *Philosophische Terminologie*, 194.

82. Adorno, *Jargon*, 53, 15, 12; *GS*, 6:448, 423, 420.

83. Adorno, *Jargon*, 53; *GS*, 6:448.

84. Adorno, *Philosophische Terminologie*, 194–195.

85. Martin Heidegger, "Why Do I Stay in the Provinces?," in *Philosophical and Political Writings*, ed. Manfred Stassen, trans. Thomas Sheehan (New York: Continuum, 2003); *GA*, 13.

86. Adorno, *Philosophische Terminologie*, 203.

87. Adorno, *Philosophische Terminologie*, 212, 191, and 203, respectively.

88. Adorno, *Philosophische Terminologie*, 192.

89. Adorno, *Philosophische Terminologie*, 200.

90. Adorno, *Philosophische Terminologie*, 200. See also Adorno, *GS*, 10.1:302–309; and Theodor W. Adorno, *Kindheit in Amorbach: Bilder und Erinnerungen* (Frankfurt am Main: Insel Verlag, 2003).

91. Adorno, *Philosophische Terminologie*, 201–202 (emphasis added).

92. Lambert Zuidervaart characterizes Adorno and Heidegger as being "each other's reverse image," but on the more specific question of how they each "authenticate truth." See Lambert Zuidervaart, *Social Philosophy after Adorno* (Cambridge: Cambridge University Press, 2007), chap. 3.

93. Theodor W. Adorno and Walter Benjamin, *The Complete Correspondence 1928–1940*, trans. Nicholas Walker (Oxford: Polity Press, 1999), December, 17, 1934, 69;

Theodor W. Adorno and Walter Benjamin, *Briefwechsel 1928–1940*, ed. Henri Lonitz (Frankfurt am Main: Suhrkamp Verlag, 1994), 93.

94. But see Theodor W. Adorno, "Schubert," trans. Jonathan Dunsby and Beate Perrey, *19th-Century Music* 29, no. 1 (2005): 3–14, especially the translators' introduction, 4n3; *GS*, 17:18–33. For the original version, see Theodor W. Adorno, "Schubert," *Die Musik* 21, no. 1 (1928). When Adorno later republished that text, he noted that "only those passages were modified in which the author was too ashamed of his old shortcomings." See Adorno, *GS*, 17:9. See also Buck-Morss, *The Origin of Negative Dialectics*, 53, 53n78.

95. Theodor W. Adorno, *Kierkegaard: Construction of the Aesthetic*, trans. Robert Hullot-Kentor (Minneapolis: University of Minnesota Press, 1989); *GS*, 2. Adorno himself certainly thought that the book contained such a critique. With reference to the political context of 1933, the year in which the book appeared, he writes: "In particular, the critique of existential ontology that it carried out was intended, already at that time, to reach intellectuals in Germany opposed to the regime." See Adorno, *GS*, 2:261. See also Peter E. Gordon, *Adorno and Existence* (Cambridge, MA: Harvard University Press, 2016), chap. 1; Buck-Morss, *The Origin of Negative Dialectics*, 121; Müller-Doohm, *Adorno*, 128.

96. Theodor W. Adorno, *Die Transzendenz des Dinglichen und Noematischen in Husserls Phänomenologie*, in *GS*, 1:7–77.

97. Published in Adorno, *GS*, 5:7–245.

98. See Adorno, *Ontology and Dialectics*, xiv–xviii; *Ontologie und Dialektik*, 424–428.

99. Adorno, *Philosophische Terminologie*, esp. 189–218.

100. The longer, published version has a slightly different title. See Theodor W. Adorno, "Parataxis: On Hölderlin's Late Poetry," in *Notes to Literature*, vol. 2, trans. Shierry Weber Nicholsen (New York: Columbia University Press, 1992); *GS*, 11. The first appearance of the longer version of the paper was in Theodor W. Adorno, "Parataxis: Zur späten Lyrik Hölderlins," *Neue Rundschau* 75, no. 1 (1964).

101. Adorno, *Ontology and Dialectics*, 25, 46, 88; *Ontologie und Dialektik*, 42–43, 71–72, 128–129.

102. Karl Heinz Haag, *Kritik der neueren Ontologie*, in *Kritische Philosophie: Abhandlungen und Aufsätze*, ed. Rolf Tiedemann (Munich: edition text + kritik, 2012).

103. The term *Aktualität* generally refers, in Adorno, to the actual relevance of something (e.g., philosophy), often within a state of affairs that denies to the thing its relevance. See also Lydia Goehr, *Elective Affinities: Musical Essays on the History of Aesthetic Theory* (New York: Columbia University Press, 2008), 273.

104. Adorno, "The Actuality of Philosophy," 24 (emphasis added); *GS*, 1:325.

105. Adorno, "The Actuality of Philosophy," 24; *GS*, 1:325.

106. Adorno, "The Actuality of Philosophy," 29–30; *GS*, 1:332.

107. Adorno, "The Actuality of Philosophy," 25; *GS*, 1:325.

108. See, e.g., Adorno, *Negative Dialectics*, 119–122; *GS*, 6:125–128.

109. "The images of our life are guaranteed through history alone." See Adorno, "The Actuality of Philosophy," 24; *GS*, 1:325.

110. Martin Heidegger, "On the Essence of Truth," in *Pathmarks*, ed. William Mc-Neill, trans. John Sallis (Cambridge: Cambridge University Press, 1998), 145; *GA*, 9:190.

111. Adorno, "The Actuality of Philosophy," 35; *GS*, 1:339–340.

112. Heidegger, *Being and Time*, § 38, H176.

113. Stefan Müller-Doohm remarks that this reference must have irritated Horkheimer. See Müller-Doohm, *Adorno*, 137.

114. Adorno, "The Actuality of Philosophy," 35; *GS*, 1:340.

115. Hannah Arendt writes that notes to Heidegger's lectures were commonly circulated "among students everywhere" even before publication of *Being and Time*. See Hannah Arendt, "Martin Heidegger at Eighty," *New York Review of Books*, October 21, 1971, 50; Hannah Arendt, "Martin Heidegger zum achtzigsten Geburtstag," *Merkur* 10 (1969): 893–902. Adorno also seems to have been aware that Heidegger had given a lecture course on Hegel in Freiburg in 1930–1931. See Adorno, "The Idea of Natural-History," 259; *GS*, 1:354. See also Heidegger, *Hegel's Phenomenology of Spirit*; *GA*, 32.

116. Martin Heidegger, *The Fundamental Concepts of Metaphysics*, trans. William McNeill and Nicholas Walker (Bloomington: Indiana University Press, 1995), 261; *GA*, 29/30:379.

117. Heidegger, *Fundamental Concepts of Metaphysics*, 260; *GA*, 29/30:378.

118. Heidegger, *Fundamental Concepts of Metaphysics*, 261; *GA*, 29/30:379.

119. Martin Heidegger, "The End of Philosophy and the Task of Thinking," in *On Time and Being*, trans. Joan Stambaugh (New York: Harper and Row, 1972), 59; *GA*, 14:73.

120. It may seem that Adorno is drawing on Max Weber, for whom sociology involves "the interpretive understanding [*deutend verstehen*] of social action," especially since the relevance of sociology is at issue, as well as the concept of sense (*Sinn*), which Weber also uses. In some ways, Adorno, like Lukács before him, helps himself to Weberian concepts without committing himself to his broader positions. For the Weber quotation, see Weber, *Economy and Society*, 4.

121. The difference between these two kinds of interpretation relies mainly on the idea that *Interpretation* is generally more systematic or formal, whereas *Auslegung* is spontaneous, informal, and ontologically rooted in the disclosedness of *Dasein*. *Auslegung* describes the primordial or first "laying out" of beings in relation to *Dasein's* potentiality-for-being, prior to any formal investigation.

122. Heidegger, *Being and Time*, § 63, H315.

123. Heidegger, *Being and Time*, § 3, H10.

124. Heidegger, *Being and Time*, § 3, H11.

125. Heidegger, *Being and Time*, § 32, H149.

126. Adorno, "The Actuality of Philosophy," 31; *GS*, 1:334. Compare Adorno, *History and Freedom*, 127; *Zur Lehre von der Geschichte*, 183.

127. Adorno, "The Actuality of Philosophy," 31; *GS*, 1:334.

128. Adorno, "The Actuality of Philosophy," 31; *GS*, 1:334.

129. Adorno, "The Actuality of Philosophy," 31; *GS*, 1:334–335.

130. Marx, *Economic and Philosophic Manuscripts of 1844*, 107; Marx and Engels, *MEW*, 40:511.

131. Adorno, "The Actuality of Philosophy," 31ff.; *GS*, 1:334ff.

132. Adorno, "The Actuality of Philosophy," 34; *GS*, 1:338.

133. Karl Marx, "Theses on Feuerbach," in *Marx–Engels Collected Works*, trans. W. Lough (London: Lawrence and Wishart, 1975), 5:5; Marx and Engels, *MEW*, 3:7.

134. Adorno, *Negative Dialectics*, 3; *GS*, 6:15.

135. Richard Wisser, ed. *Martin Heidegger im Gespräch* (Freiburg: Verlag Karl Alber, 1970), 68–69.

136. Adorno, *History and Freedom*, 129; *Geschichte und Freiheit*, 186.

137. See, e.g., Hermann Mörchen, *Macht und Herrschaft im Denken von Heidegger und Adorno* (Stuttgart: Klett-Cotta, 1980); Hermann Mörchen, *Adorno und Heidegger: Untersuchung einer philosophischen Kommunikationsverweigerung* (Stuttgart: Klett-Cotta, 1981); Brian O'Connor, *Adorno's Negative Dialectic: Philosophy and the Possibility of Critical Rationality* (Cambridge, MA: MIT Press, 2005), chap. 5; Gordon, *Adorno and Existence*; Iain Macdonald and Krzysztof Ziarek, eds., *Adorno and Heidegger: Philosophical Questions* (Stanford, CA: Stanford University Press, 2008).

138. In 1965, Hermann Mörchen, the first person to devote substantial effort to understanding the Adorno-Heidegger conflict, wrote to Adorno, attaching a copy of his recent review of *Jargon of Authenticity*. Adorno responded by inviting Mörchen to visit him at the Institute for Social Research. Adorno writes: "I think I will be able to clear up a few misunderstandings at our meeting, though admittedly I do not hold out much hope that we will agree on the heart of the matter, since it is absolutely impossible for me to see Heidegger as a figure of outstanding significance; and by the way, my reaction immediately following the publication of *Being and Time*—therefore long before Heidegger's public profession of loyalty to fascism—was the same as it is today. But rest assured, I have always concerned myself exclusively with the facts of the matter and not with Heidegger as a private person. Also, allow me to say that I was pleased that an adversary such as yourself who, after all, seems to take the issue as seriously as I do should have taken it upon himself to contact me. I shall certainly come prepared to reply to you in detail, texts in hand—Heidegger's as well as my own. I should simply like to emphasize that in [the *Jargon of Authenticity*], I was concerned with a linguistic phenomenon, not with Heidegger himself, as is often mistakenly taken to be the case. Heidegger is only brought into it because his philosophy is a key to deciphering what is latent in the jargon of authenticity, which, to be sure, I take to be a highly dubious phenomenon. The phenomenon is philosophically deduced, as it were, in the third and fourth parts of my book, after it is physiognomically described and interpreted in the first part. It may help us to come to an understanding if you would bear this in mind." See Adorno, Correspondence with Hermann Mörchen, September 13, 1965; see also Hermann Mörchen, review of "Theodor W. Adorno, *Jargon der Eigentlichkeit*," *Zeitschrift für deutsches Altertum und deutsche Literatur* 94, no. 2 (1965): 89–95.

Mörchen tried to find a way to follow up on his interest in Adorno and Heidegger after Adorno's death in 1969, writing to Horkheimer in 1972 in the hope of finding a partner in dialogue. He received the following reply: "As I recall, Adorno's judgement related not least to Heidegger's style of thinking and expression, which was distant from ours. For that reason, it is only with difficulty that I can imagine a productive debate taking place between the two schools. I cannot even give you the name of anyone today who would be competent in this regard." See Horkheimer, *HGS*, March 16, 1972, 18:795. See also the two books that grew out of Mörchen's interest: Mörchen, *Macht und Herrschaft im Denken von Heidegger und Adorno* and *Adorno und Heidegger*.

139. Martin Heidegger, "The Question concerning Technology," in *The Question concerning Technology and Other Essays*, trans. William Lovitt (New York: Harper and Row, 1977), 24; *GA*, 7:25.

140. Heidegger, "The Question concerning Technology," 14, 17; *GA*, 7:15, 17.

141. Heidegger, "The Question concerning Technology," 23; *GA*, 7:24.

142. Heidegger, "The Question concerning Technology," 27; *GA*, 7:28.

143. Martin Heidegger, "The Turning," in *The Question concerning Technology and Other Essays*, trans. William Lovitt (New York: Harper and Row, 1977), 39; *GA*, 11:116.

144. Heidegger, "The Question concerning Technology," 28; *GA*, 7:29.

145. Heidegger, "The Question concerning Technology," 28; *GA*, 7:29. See also Friedrich Hölderlin, *Poems and Fragments*, trans. Michael Hamburger, 3rd, bilingual ed. (London: Anvil Press Poetry, 1994), 482–483.

146. Heidegger, "The Question concerning Technology," 33; *GA*, 7:34.

147. Heidegger, "The Turning," 41; *GA*, 11:118.

148. Heidegger, "The Question concerning Technology," 28; *GA*, 7:29.

149. Heidegger, "The Question concerning Technology," 26; *GA*, 7:26–27 (emphasis added).

150. Peter Trawny instead sees in Heidegger an anarchy, an *absence* of ἀρχαί, but for reasons already discussed, the problem is that the absence of a *metaphysical* first principle is not the same as an absence of principles. See Peter Trawny, *Freedom to Fail: Heidegger's Anarchy*, trans. Ian Alexander Moore and Christopher Turner (Cambridge: Polity Press, 2015). As Reiner Schürmann puts it, "Still a principle, but a principle of anarchy." I do not think Trawny successfully sidesteps this claim by saying that Heidegger's anarchy is a freedom from principles. See Reiner Schürmann, *Heidegger on Being and Acting: From Principles to Anarchy*, trans. Christine-Marie Gros and Reiner Schürmann (Bloomington: Indiana University Press, 1987), 6. (Trawny refers to this passage in a note to page 36 of his book.)

151. Heidegger, "The Question concerning Technology," 22; *GA*, 7:23.

152. Heidegger, "Hegel and the Greeks," 335–336; *GA*, 9:444.

153. Heidegger, "The Turning," 48–49; *GA*, 11:123.

154. Adorno, "Progress," 143–144; *GS*, 10.2:617. See also Amy Allen, *The End of Progress: Decolonizing the Normative Foundations of Critical Theory* (New York: Columbia University Press, 2015), esp. 163–176.

155. Adorno, "Progress," 160; *GS*, 10.2:638.

156. Theodor W. Adorno, "Trying to Understand *Endgame*," in *Notes to Literature*, trans. Shierry Weber Nicholsen (New York: Columbia University Press, 1991), 1:270; *GS*, 11:315.

157. Adorno, *Negative Dialectics*, 320; *GS*, 6:314. Compare Adorno, "Progress," 153; *GS*, 10.2:629.

158. Martin Heidegger, "Conversation on a Country Path about Thinking," in *Discourse on Thinking*, trans. John M. Anderson and E. Hans Freund (New York: Harper and Row, 1966), 79; *GA*, 13:61.

159. Martin Heidegger, "Letter on 'Humanism,'" in *Pathmarks*, ed. Will McNeill, trans. Frank A. Capuzzi (Cambridge: Cambridge University Press, 1998), 255; *GA*, 9:335.

160. Martin Heidegger, "The Onto-Theo-Logical Constitution of Metaphysics," in *Identity and Difference*, trans. Joan Stambaugh (Chicago: University of Chicago Press, 1969), 50–52; *GA*, 11:59–61.

161. Adorno, "Progress," 153; *GS*, 10.2:628–629.

162. Adorno, "Progress," 144; *GS*, 10.2:617. The expression *das lösende Wort* is a reference to Goethe's poem "Die Metamorphose der Pflanzen."

163. Adorno, "Progress," 144; *GS*, 10.2:618.

164. Adorno, "Progress," 145; *GS*, 10.2:619–620. Adorno is referring to one of Kafka's "Zürau aphorisms": "Believing in progress does not mean believing that some progress has already taken place. That would not be a belief." See Franz Kafka, *Nachgelassene Schriften und Fragmente II*, ed. Jost Schillemeit (Frankfurt am Main: S. Fischer Verlag, 1992), § 48, 123. For an English translation of the aphorisms, see Franz Kafka, *The Zürau Aphorisms*, trans. Michael Hofmann (London: Harvill Secker, Random House, 2006).

165. Heidegger, "The Question concerning Technology," 22; *GA*, 7:23.

166. Adorno, *Negative Dialectics*, 72; *GS*, 6:79.

167. Adorno, "Progress," 149; *GS*, 10.2:623.

168. See Christoph Menke, "Hegel's Theory of Liberation: Law, Freedom, History, Society," *Symposium* 17, no. 1 (2013): 10–30.

169. Adorno, "Progress," 150; *GS*, 10.2:625.

170. Marx, *Critique of Hegel's "Philosophy of Right,"* introduction, 132–133; Marx and Engels, *MEW*, 1:379–380.

171. Adorno, "Progress," 156; *GS*, 10.2:632.

172. Adorno, "Individuum und Organisation," *GS*, 8:456.

173. Mörchen, *Adorno und Heidegger*, 13.

174. Richard Wisser, "Das Fernseh-Interview," in *Erinnerung an Martin Heidegger*, ed. Günther Neske (Pfullingen: Verlag Günther Neske, 1977), 283. Heidegger recounted the same story to Hermann Mörchen in a letter from 1965. See Mörchen, *Adorno und Heidegger*, 13.

175. See Robert Savage, *Hölderlin after the Catastrophe: Heidegger—Adorno—Brecht* (Rochester, NY: Camden House, 2008), 96–99.

176. Wolfgang Binder, "Bericht über die Diskussion," *Hölderlin-Jahrbuch* 13 (1963–1964): 178. See also Klaus Betzen, "Bericht über die über die Jahresversammlung in Berlin 7.–9. Juni 1963," *Hölderlin-Jahrbuch* 13 (1963–1964): 172–184.

177. Thomas Pfizer, "'Die Ausnahme,'" in *Erinnerung an Martin Heidegger*, ed. Günther Neske (Pfullingen: Verlag Günther Neske, 1977), 194.

178. Pfizer, "'Die Ausnahme,'" 194–195.

179. Heidegger and Jünger, *Correspondence 1949–1975*, August 26, 1966, 36; Jünger and Heidegger, *Briefe 1949–1975*, 57. Heidegger's French "disciple" was Jean Reboul, who wrote to Jünger on August 10, 1966.

180. Robert Minder, "Hölderlin und die Deutschen," *Hölderlin-Jahrbuch* 14 (1965–1966): 1–19; "Hölderlin chez les allemands," *Preuves* 16, no. 186–187 (1966): 24–32.

181. Heidegger and Jünger, *Correspondence 1949–1975*, August 27, 1966, 37; Jünger and Heidegger, *Briefe 1949–1975*, 58.

182. Martin Heidegger, *Letters to His Wife, 1915–1970*, ed. Gertrud Heidegger, trans. Rupert Glasgow (Cambridge: Polity Press, 2008), June 14, 1964, 290; *"Mein liebes Seelchen!": Briefe Martin Heideggers an seine Frau Elfride, 1915–1970*, ed. Gertrud Heidegger (Munich: Deutsche Verlags-Anstalt, 2005), 352.

183. Müller-Doohm, *Adorno*, 460–461; Lorenz Jäger, *Adorno: A Political Biography*, trans. Stewart Spencer (New Haven, CT: Yale University Press, 2004), 200–201.

184. Wisser, *Martin Heidegger im Gespräch*, 69.

185. Wisser, *Martin Heidegger im Gespräch*, 69.

186. Wisser, "Das Fernseh-Interview," 260–261. The transcript of the televised interview makes it clear exactly what Heidegger said: "No! One cannot speak of a social mission in this sense!" Heidegger had, of course, ascribed a different kind of social mission to philosophy in the 1930s. See Wisser, *Martin Heidegger im Gespräch*, 68.

187. Wisser, "Das Fernseh-Interview," 268–269.

188. Wisser, "Das Fernseh-Interview," 283–284.

189. Wisser, "Das Fernseh-Interview," 284.

190. Wisser, "Das Fernseh-Interview," 284.

191. Wisser, "Das Fernseh-Interview," 284.

192. Wisser, "Das Fernseh-Interview," 285.

193. Adorno, *Ontology and Dialectics,* 2; *Ontologie und Dialektik,* 10.

194. Adorno, *Negative Dialectics*, 63; *GS*, 6:71.

195. Adorno and Horkheimer, *Briefwechsel*, November 26, 1949, 3:351. Adorno thought that Horkheimer might write a review of *Holzwege*. See also Wiggershaus, *The Frankfurt School*, 593. A few months later, in a letter to Peter von Haselberg, he is a little more explicit: "Compared to [Lukács's *The Young Hegel*, Heidegger's essay on "Hegel's Concept of Experience"] in *Holzwege* at least shows the labor of the concept, though naturally the conversion of Hegel into an ontologist is just as absurd as the attempt [by Lukács] to construe the economic factor as Hegel's central concern. But Heidegger at least goes to the heart of the matter, instead of just pigeonholing." See Theodor W. Adorno, Correspondence with Peter von Haselberg, May 23, 1950, Theodor W. Adorno Archive, Frankfurt am Main, TWAA Br 0559.

196. Adorno, *Negative Dialectics*, 104; *GS*, 6:110.

197. Adorno, *Negative Dialectics*, 104; *GS*, 6:110–111.

198. Heidegger, *Contributions*, § 10, 26; *GA*, 65:30.

199. Compare Adorno, "The Actuality of Philosophy," 24; *GS*, 1:325.

Chapter 5

1. Adorno, "Graeculus (II)," March 24, 1968, 30–31. Compare Adorno, *History and Freedom*, 141; *Zur Lehre von der Geschichte*, 199.

2. Walter Benjamin, *The Arcades Project*, trans. Howard Eiland and Kevin McLaughlin (Cambridge, MA: Belknap Press of Harvard University Press, 1999), [M1,2], 416; *BGS*, 5:524.

3. Benjamin, *Arcades Project*, "Exposé of 1939," 26; *BGS*, 5:76.

4. For the notion of dialectic at a standstill, see in particular Benjamin, *Arcades Project*, "Exposé of 1935," 10; [N2a,3], 462; [N3,1], 463; and [N10a,3], 475; *BGS*, 5:55, 577, 578, and 595, respectively. For detailed discussions of the concept of dialectical image, see Susan Buck-Morss, *The Dialectics of Seeing: Walter Benjamin and the Arcades Project* (Cambridge, MA: MIT Press, 1989); Rolf Tiedemann, "Dialectics at a Standstill: Approaches to the *Passagen-Werk*," in *On Walter Benjamin: Critical Essays and Reflections*, ed. Gary Smith, trans. Gary Smith and André Lefevere (Cambridge, MA: MIT Press, 1988); Michael W. Jennings, *Dialectical Images: Walter Benjamin's Theory of Literary Criticism* (Ithaca, NY: Cornell University Press, 1987); and Eli Friedlander, *Walter Benjamin: A Philosophical Portrait* (Cambridge, MA: Harvard University Press, 2012). The Tiedemann piece is reprinted at the end of the English edition of the *Arcades Project*.

5. Hegel writes: "Progress towards [the point where knowledge no longer needs to go beyond itself] is . . . unhalting [*unaufhaltsam*], and short of it no satisfaction is to be found at any of the stations on the way." See Hegel, *Hegel's Phenomenology of Spirit*, 51; *W*, 3:74.

6. Benjamin, *Arcades Project*, [N9,4], 473; *BGS*, 5:591.

7. Benjamin, *Arcades Project*, [K2a,1], 393; *BGS*, 5:496.

8. "Blanqui's theory as a *répétition du mythe*—my fundamental example of the primal history of the nineteenth century. In every century, humanity has to stay after school in detention." See Benjamin, *Arcades Project*, [D10,2], 118; *BGS*, 5:177. For the Blanqui reference, see Benjamin, *Arcades Project*, "Exposé of 1939," 25–26; *BGS*, 5:76.

9. Benjamin, *Arcades Project*, [N9a,1], 473; *BGS*, 5:592.

10. Walter Benjamin, "On the Concept of History," in *Selected Writings*, vol. 4, ed. Michael W. Jennings and Howard Eiland, trans. Harry Zohn (Cambridge, MA: Harvard University Press, 2003), XVII, 4:396; *BGS*, 1:703.

11. Benjamin, *Arcades Project*, [N10,2], 474; *BGS*, 5:593.

12. Benjamin, *Arcades Project*, [N2,2], 460; *BGS*, 5:574.

13. Benjamin, *Arcades Project*, [N11,4], 476; *BGS*, 5:596.

14. Benjamin, "On the Concept of History," II, 4:390; *BGS*, 1:693. See also Benjamin, *Arcades Project*, [N13a,1], 479; *BGS*, 5:600.

15. Benjamin, *Arcades Project*, [N8,1], 471; *BGS*, 5:589.

16. Benjamin, *Arcades Project*, [M20a,1], 453; *BGS*, 5:567.

17. Benjamin, *Arcades Project*, [M4a,1], 425; *BGS*, 5:535.

18. Benjamin, *Arcades Project*, [M6a,1], 429; *BGS*, 5:540.

19. Benjamin, *Arcades Project*, [M5,8], 427; *BGS*, 5:538.

20. Benjamin, *Arcades Project*, [M20a,1], 453; *BGS*, 5:567.

21. Adorno, "Ernst Bloch's *Spuren,*" 204; *GS,* 11:237.

22. Walter Benjamin, "The Paris of the Second Empire in Baudelaire," in *Selected Writings,* ed. Michael W. Jennings and Howard Eiland, trans. Harry Zohn (Cambridge, MA: Harvard University Press, 2003), 4:34; *BGS,* 1:561.

23. As Tiedemann remarks concerning the arcades, the flaneur too "owed [his] existence to and served the industrial order of production, while at the same time containing ... something unfulfilled, never to be fulfilled within the confines of capitalism." See Tiedemann, "Dialectics at a Standstill," 268; Benjamin, *BGS,* 5:17.

24. For references to the detective, the journalist, and the sandwich-board man, see Benjamin, *Arcades Project,* [M13a2], 442; [M16,4] and [M16a,1], 446–447; [M17a,2] and [M19,2], 448 and 451; *BGS,* 5:554, 559–560, 562, and 565, respectively. For the sandwich-board man, see also Adorno and Benjamin, *Correspondence,* February 23, 1939, 310; *Briefwechsel 1928–1940,* 404.

25. Benjamin, "The Paris of the Second Empire in Baudelaire," 31; *BGS,* 1:557. See also Benjamin, *Arcades Project,* [M8,1], 432; *BGS,* 5:543.

26. Benjamin, "The Paris of the Second Empire in Baudelaire," 34; *BGS,* 1:561.

27. Karl Marx, "An Exchange of Letters," in *Writings of the Young Marx on Philosophy and Society,* ed. and trans. Loyd D. Easton and Kurt H. Guddat (Indianapolis, IN: Hackett, 1997), Marx to Ruge, September 1843, 213; Marx and Engels, *MEW,* 1:345. Benjamin's reference is in *Arcades Project,* [N5,3], 466; *BGS,* 5:582–583.

28. Benjamin, *Arcades Project,* [N5,3], 466; *BGS,* 5:583.

29. Benjamin, *Arcades Project,* [N3,1], 462–463; *BGS,* 5:577–578.

30. Benjamin, *Arcades Project,* [N2,2], 460; *BGS,* 5:574.

31. Benjamin, *Arcades Project,* [N5,3], 466; *BGS,* 5:583.

32. As in the "Exposé of 1935," which draws Adorno's criticism on precisely this point. See Benjamin, *Arcades Project,* 4–5; *BGS,* 5:46–47; and Adorno and Benjamin, *Correspondence,* August 2–4, 1935, 105; *Briefwechsel,* 139.

33. Benjamin, *Arcades Project,* [N9a,1], 473; *BGS,* 5:592.

34. Benjamin, *Arcades Project,* [N1,2], 456; *BGS,* 5:570.

35. Benjamin, *Arcades Project,* [N9a,7], 474; *BGS,* 5:593.

36. Adorno, "A Portrait of Walter Benjamin," 231; *GS,* 10.1:240.

37. Adorno and Benjamin, *Correspondence,* August 2–4, 1935, 105; *Briefwechsel,* 139.

38. Adorno and Benjamin, *Correspondence,* August 2–4, 1935, 105, 110; *Briefwechsel,* 139, 145.

39. Adorno and Benjamin, *Correspondence,* November 10, 1938, 281; *Briefwechsel,* 365.

40. Adorno and Benjamin, *Correspondence,* November 10, 1938, 281; *Briefwechsel,* 365.

41. Adorno and Benjamin, *Correspondence,* November 10, 1938, 281; *Briefwechsel,* 365.

42. Adorno and Benjamin, *Correspondence,* November 10, 1938, 283; *Briefwechsel,* 368.

43. Benjamin, *Arcades Project,* "Exposé of 1935," 10; *BGS,* 5:55.

44. Adorno and Benjamin, *Correspondence,* August 2–4, 1935, 113; *Briefwechsel,* 149.

45. Adorno and Benjamin, *Correspondence,* November 10, 1938, 283; *Briefwechsel,* 368. As he puts it in another letter, what Benjamin needs, according to Adorno, is "*more* dialectic." See Adorno and Benjamin, *Correspondence,* March 18, 1936, 131; *Briefwechsel,* 173.

46. See, e.g., Adorno and Benjamin, *Correspondence*, August 2–4, 1935, 108; *Briefwechsel*, 142–143.

47. Adorno and Benjamin, *Correspondence*, November 10, 1938, 281, 284; *Briefwechsel*, 366, 369.

48. Adorno and Benjamin, *Correspondence*, November 10, 1938, 284; *Briefwechsel*, 370.

49. Gunzelin Schmid Noerr, "Editor's Afterword: The Position of 'Dialectic of Enlightenment' in the Development of Critical Theory," in *Dialectic of Enlightenment: Philosophical Fragments*, by Max Horkheimer and Theodor W. Adorno, trans. Edmund Jephcott (Stanford, CA: Stanford University Press, 2002), 228; Horkheimer, *HGS*, 5:434.

50. In addition to the previous reference to Schmid Noerr, see Willem van Reijen and Jan Bransen, "The Disappearance of Class History in 'Dialectic of Enlightenment': A Commentary on the Textual Variants (1947 and 1944)," in *Dialectic of Enlightenment: Philosophical Fragments*, by Max Horkheimer and Theodor W. Adorno, trans. Edmund Jephcott (Stanford, CA: Stanford University Press, 2002), 248ff.; Horkheimer, *HGS*, 5:453ff.

51. Adorno, "Aldous Huxley and Utopia," 99, 101; *GS*, 10.1:100, 101–102. Adorno's essay on Huxley is based in part on a discussion of Huxley's *Brave New World* that took place in 1942, involving members of the Institute for Social Research, as well as Bertolt Brecht and some of his circle. This was precisely the period during which the Institute's theoretical focus was shifting in different ways. See Adorno, "Theses on Need"; *GS*, 8:392–396; and Horkheimer, "On the Problem of Needs"; *HGS*, 12:252–256, 12:559–586, 19:22–27.

52. Adorno and Benjamin, *Correspondence*, March 18, 1936, 131; *Briefwechsel*, 173.

53. Horkheimer, *HGS*, 12:156–157; also quoted and discussed in Schmid Noerr, "Editor's Afterword," 225–226; *HGS*, 5:431–432.

54. Adorno and Horkheimer, *Towards a New Manifesto*, 14; Horkheimer, *HGS*, 19:41.

55. Frederick Pollock, "State Capitalism: Its Possibilities and Limitations," *Studies in Philosophy and Social Science* 9, no. 2 (1941): 225.

56. Horkheimer, *HGS*, 12:600; quoted in part in Schmid Noerr, "Editor's Afterword," 241; *HGS*, 5:447.

57. Adorno, *Negative Dialectics*, xix; *GS*, 6:9.

58. Adorno, *Minima Moralia* 15–16; *GS*, 4:14.

59. Walter Benjamin, *Schriften*, ed. Theodor W. Adorno, Gretel Adorno, and Friedrich Podszus, 2 vols. (Frankfurt am Main: Suhrkamp Verlag, 1955).

60. Adorno, "A Portrait of Walter Benjamin," 229–230; *GS*, 10.1:239.

61. Adorno, "A Portrait of Walter Benjamin," 230; *GS*, 10.1:239.

62. Theodor W. Adorno, "Introduction to Benjamin's *Schriften*," in *On Walter Benjamin: Critical Essays and Reflections*, ed. Gary Smith, trans. Robert Hullot-Kentor (Cambridge, MA: MIT Press, 1988), 10; *GS*, 11:575.

63. See Tiedemann, "Dialectics at a Standstill," 284–285; Benjamin, *BGS*, 5:34–35.

64. Adorno, "Progress," 159–160; *GS*, 10.2:637.

65. Adorno, "A Portrait of Walter Benjamin," 231; *GS*, 10.1:240. "Oh, [there is] plenty of hope, an infinite amount of hope—but not for us." Quoted in Benjamin, "Franz Kafka," 2.2:798; *BGS*, 2.2:414. See also Brod, *Franz Kafka: A Biography*, 75; Brod, *Franz Kafka. Eine Biographie*, 71.

66. Benjamin, *Arcades Project*, "First Sketches: Paris Arcades <1>," <O°,9>, 858; Benjamin, *BGS*, 5:1028 (emphasis added).

67. Max Pensky, "Method and Time: Benjamin's Dialectical Images," in *The Cambridge Companion to Walter Benjamin*, ed. David S. Ferris (Cambridge: Cambridge University Press, 2004), 180.

68. Benjamin, *Origin of German Tragic Drama*, 27–29; *BGS*, 1:207–209.

69. Adorno, *Negative Dialectics*, 183; *GS*, 6:184.

70. Adorno, *Negative Dialectics*, 18–19; *GS*, 6:29–30. Adorno quotes from a letter from Benjamin to Gretel Karplus (later Gretel Adorno). See Adorno and Benjamin, *Correspondence*, August 16, 1935, 116–119; *Briefwechsel*, 154–157. As suggested in an editorial note to the letter of August 2–4, 1935, the "original draft" to which Adorno refers seems to be "<The Arcades of Paris>: <Paris Arcades II>," in Benjamin, *Arcades Project*, 873–884; *BGS*, 5:1044–1059. See Adorno and Benjamin, *Correspondence*, 115, 105n2; *Briefwechsel*, 152, 140n2.

71. Numerous works provide us with theoretical forms (including the epistemo-critical preface to *The Origin of the German Mourning Play* and the sketch of a methodological introduction to the planned book on Baudelaire), not to mention a philosophy of language. Also, in a well-known letter to Max Rychner, Benjamin writes that "there is a point of mediation between my very particular stance on the philosophy of language and the perspective of dialectical materialism, however strained and problematic that mediation may be." See Walter Benjamin, *Correspondence 1910–1940*, trans. M. R. Jacobson and E. M. Jacobson (Chicago: University of Chicago Press, 1994), March 7, 1931, 372; *Briefe*, 2:523. (Of course, Adorno worried that Benjamin's theoretical inclinations had led him to stray too close to Marxist orthodoxy, which for him was a betrayal of the dialectic of theory and practice.) Additionally, Adorno gives indications of where to search for the traces of theory in Benjamin in his "Introduction to Benjamin's *Schriften*," 11; *GS*, 11:576.

72. Max Horkheimer and Theodor W. Adorno, "[Diskussionen über die Differenz zwischen Positivismus und materialistischer Dialektik] (1939)," in Max Horkheimer, *Gesammelte Schriften* (Frankfurt am Main: S. Fischer Verlag, 1985), 12:489. Adorno says elsewhere that metaphysics has to be transformed into history and thereby "into the secular category *par excellence,* that of decay." See Adorno, *History and Freedom*, 126; *Zur Lehre von der Geschichte*, 181.

73. Adorno, "A Portrait of Walter Benjamin," 241; *GS*, 10.1:252.

74. Theodor W. Adorno and Gershom Scholem, *Briefwechsel 1939–1969*, ed. Asaf Angermann (Frankfurt am Main: Suhrkamp Verlag, 2015), March 14, 1967, 413.

75. Adorno, *Negative Dialectics*, 31, 313; *GS*, 6:42, 308.

76. For example: "The fetish character of the commodity is not a fact of consciousness; it is rather dialectical in character, in the eminent sense that it produces conscious-

ness. . . . Our task is to polarize and dissolve this 'consciousness' dialectically in terms of society and singular subjects, not to galvanize it as the imagistic correlate of the commodity character." See Adorno and Benjamin, *Correspondence*, August 2–4, 1935, 105, 107; *Briefwechsel*, 139, 141–142. Tiedemann notes that Horkheimer and Adorno had in all likelihood insisted, already in 1929, that "it was impossible to speak sensibly about the nineteenth century without considering Marx's analysis of capital." See Tiedemann, "Dialectics at a Standstill," 275–276; Benjamin, *BGS*, 5:24–25. Adorno reminds Benjamin of this in the letter just quoted (see 111; 147 in the German edition).

77. Karl Marx and Friedrich Engels, *The German Ideology,* in *Marx–Engels Collected Works,* trans. Clemens Dutt, W. Lough, and C. P. Magill (London: Lawrence and Wishart, 1975), 5:447; *MEW*, 3:432–433.

78. Adorno, *Negative Dialectics*, 145; *GS*, 6:148.

79. Adorno, *Negative Dialectics*, 5; *GS*, 6:16–17.

80. Adorno, *Negative Dialectics*, 408; *GS*, 6:399–400.

81. In contrast to a "world-rejecting asceticism" (*weltablehnende Askese*), Weber notes that "the concentration of human behavior on activities leading to salvation may require participation within the world (or more precisely: within the institutions of the world but in opposition to them) on the basis of the religious individual's piety and his qualifications as the elect instrument of god. This is 'inner-worldly asceticism' [*innerweltliche Askese*]. In this case the world is presented to the religious virtuoso as his responsibility. He may have the obligation to transform the world in accordance with his ascetic ideals, in which case the ascetic will become a rational reformer or revolutionary on the basis of a theory of natural rights." See Weber, *Economy and Society*, 542; Max Weber, *Wirtschaft und Gesellschaft: Grundriß der verstehenden Soziologie,* ed. Johannes Winckelmann, 5th rev. ed. (Tübingen: Verlag J. C. B. Mohr [Paul Siebeck], 1980), 329.

82. Adorno, *Negative Dialectics*, 159n; *GS*, 6:161n.

83. Adorno and Horkheimer, *Towards a New Manifesto*, 58; Horkheimer, *HGS*, 19:63.

BIBLIOGRAPHY

Adorno, Theodor W. "The Actuality of Philosophy." In *The Adorno Reader*, edited by Brian O'Connor, translated by Benjamin Snow, 23–39. Oxford: Blackwell, 2000.

———. "Adornos Seminar vom Sommersemester 1932 über Benjamins *Ursprung des deutschen Trauerspiels*." In *Frankfurter Adorno Blätter*, edited by Rolf Tiedemann, 4:52–77. Munich: edition text + kritik, 1992.

———. *Aesthetic Theory*. Translated by Robert Hullot-Kentor. Minneapolis: University of Minnesota Press, 1997.

———. *Against Epistemology: A Metacritique*. Translated by Willis Domingo. Oxford: Basil Blackwell, 1982.

———. "Aldous Huxley and Utopia." In *Prisms*, translated by Samuel Weber and Shierry Weber, 95–117. Cambridge, MA: MIT Press, 1981.

———. Correspondence with Arnold Gehlen. Theodor W. Adorno Archive, Frankfurt am Main, TWAA Br 0453.

———. Correspondence with Hermann Mörchen. Theodor W. Adorno Archive, Frankfurt am Main, TWAA Br 1027.

———. Correspondence with Joachim Günther. Theodor W. Adorno Archive, Frankfurt am Main, TWAA Ve 226.

———. Correspondence with Peter von Haselberg. Theodor W. Adorno Archive, Frankfurt am Main, TWAA Br 0559.

———. "Cultural Criticism and Society." In *Prisms*, translated by Samuel Weber and Shierry Weber, 17–34. Cambridge, MA: MIT Press, 1981.

———. "Culture and Administration." In *The Culture Industry: Selected Essays on Mass Culture*, edited by J. M. Bernstein, translated by Nicholas Walker, 107–131. London: Routledge, 1991.

———. "Der mißbrauchte Barock." In *Gesammelte Schriften*, 10.1:401–422. Frankfurt am Main: Suhrkamp Verlag, 1977.

——. *Die Transzendenz des Dinglichen und Noematischen in Husserls Phänomenologie.* In *Gesammelte Schriften*, vol. 1. Frankfurt am Main: Suhrkamp Verlag, 1973.

——. "Diskussionsbeitrag zu 'Spätkapitalismus oder Industriegesellschaft?'" In *Gesammelte Schriften*, 8:578–587. Frankfurt am Main: Suhrkamp Verlag, 1972.

——. "Education after Auschwitz." In *Critical Models: Interventions and Catchwords*, translated by Henry W. Pickford, 191–204. New York: Columbia University Press, 1998.

——. *Einführung in die Dialektik.* Edited by Christoph Ziermann. Frankfurt am Main: Suhrkamp Verlag, 2010.

——. *Einleitung in die Soziologie.* Edited by Christoph Gödde. Frankfurt am Main: Suhrkamp Verlag, 1993.

——. "Einleitung zu einer Diskussion über die 'Theorie der Halbbildung.'" In *Gesammelte Schriften*, 8:574–577. Frankfurt am Main: Suhrkamp Verlag, 1972.

——. *Erkenntnistheorie (1957/58).* Edited by Karel Markus. Frankfurt am Main: Suhrkamp Verlag, 2018.

——. "Ernst Bloch's *Spuren*: On the Revised Edition of 1959." In *Notes to Literature*, translated by Shierry Weber Nicholsen, 1:200–215. New York: Columbia University Press, 1991.

——. "The Experiential Content of Hegel's Philosophy." In *Hegel: Three Studies*, translated by Shierry Weber Nicholsen, 53–88. Cambridge, MA: MIT Press, 1993.

——. "Extorted Reconciliation: On Georg Lukács' *Realism in Our Time*." In *Notes to Literature*, translated by Shierry Weber Nicholsen, 1:216–240. New York: Columbia University Press, 1991.

——. "Free Time." In *Critical Models: Interventions and Catchwords*, translated by Henry W. Pickford, 167–175. New York: Columbia University Press, 1998.

——. *Gesammelte Schriften.* Edited by Rolf Tiedemann, Gretel Adorno, Susan Buck-Morss, and Klaus Schultz. 20 vols. Frankfurt am Main: Suhrkamp Verlag, 1970–1986.

——. "Graeculus (II): Notizen zu Philosophie und Gesellschaft, 1943–1969." In *Frankfurter Adorno Blätter*, edited by Rolf Tiedemann, 8:9–41. Munich: edition text + kritik, 2003.

——. "The Handle, the Pot, and Early Experience." In *Notes to Literature*, translated by Shierry Weber Nicholsen, 2:211–219. New York: Columbia University Press, 1992.

——. *History and Freedom.* Edited by Rolf Tiedemann. Translated by Rodney Livingstone. Cambridge: Polity Press, 2006.

——. "The Idea of Natural-History." In *Things beyond Resemblance: Collected Essays on Theodor W. Adorno*, edited and translated by Robert Hullot-Kentor, 252–269. New York: Columbia University Press, 2006.

——. "Individuum und Organisation." In *Gesammelte Schriften*, 8:440–456. Frankfurt am Main: Suhrkamp Verlag, 1972.

——. "Introduction [to *The Positivist Dispute in German Sociology*]." In *The Positivist: Dispute in German Sociology*, translated by Glyn Adey and David Frisby, 1–67. London: Heinemann, 1976.

———. "Introduction to Benjamin's *Schriften*." In *On Walter Benjamin: Critical Essays and Reflections*, edited by Gary Smith, translated by Robert Hullot-Kentor, 2–17. Cambridge, MA: MIT Press, 1988.

———. *An Introduction to Dialectics*. Edited by Christoph Ziermann. Translated by Nicholas Walker. Cambridge: Polity Press, 2017.

———. *Introduction to Sociology*. Edited by Christoph Gödde. Translated by Edmund Jephcott. Cambridge: Polity Press, 2000.

———. *The Jargon of Authenticity*. Translated by Knut Tarnowski and Frederic Will. London: Routledge, 1973.

———. *Kierkegaard: Construction of the Aesthetic*. Translated by Robert Hullot-Kentor. Minneapolis: University of Minnesota Press, 1989.

———. *Kindheit in Amorbach: Bilder und Erinnerungen*. Frankfurt am Main: Insel Verlag, 2003.

———. "Late Capitalism or Industrial Society? The Fundamental Question of the Present Structure of Society." In *Can One Live after Auschwitz? A Philosophical Reader*, edited by Rolf Tiedemann, translated by Rodney Livingstone, 111–125. Stanford, CA: Stanford University Press, 2003.

———. *Lectures on Negative Dialectics*. Edited by Rolf Tiedemann. Translated by Rodney Livingstone. Cambridge: Polity Press, 2008.

———. "The Mastery of the Maestro." In *Sound Figures*, translated by Rodney Livingstone, 40–53. Stanford, CA: Stanford University Press, 1999.

———. *Minima Moralia: Reflections on a Damaged Life*. Translated by E. F. N. Jephcott. London: Verso, 1978.

———. *Negative Dialectics*. Translated by E. B. Ashton. London: Routledge, 1973.

———. "Ohne Leitbild." In *Gesammelte Schriften*, 10.1:291–301. Frankfurt am Main: Suhrkamp Verlag, 1997.

———. "On Some Relationships between Music and Painting." Translated by Susan Gillespie. *Musical Quarterly* 79, no. 1 (1995): 66–79.

———. "On the Logic of the Social Sciences." In *The Positivist Dispute in German Sociology*, translated by Glyn Adey and David Frisby, 105–122. London: Heinemann, 1976.

———. *Ontologie und Dialektik*. Edited by Rolf Tiedemann. Frankfurt am Main: Suhrkamp Verlag, 2002.

———. *Ontology and Dialectics*. Edited by Rolf Tiedemann. Translated by Nicholas Walker. Cambridge: Polity Press, 2019.

———. "Opinion Delusion Society." In *Critical Models: Interventions and Catchwords*, translated by Henry W. Pickford, 105–122. New York: Columbia University Press, 1998.

———. "Parataxis: On Hölderlin's Late Poetry." In *Notes to Literature*, translated by Shierry Weber Nicholsen, 2:109–149. New York: Columbia University Press, 1992.

———. "Parataxis: Zur späten Lyrik Hölderlins." *Neue Rundschau* 75, no. 1 (1964): 15–46.

———. *Philosophical Elements of a Theory of Society*. Edited by Tobias ten Brink and

Marc Phillip Nogueira. Translated by Wieland Hoban. Cambridge: Polity Press, 2019.

———. *Philosophische Elemente einer Theorie der Gesellschaft*. Edited by Tobias ten Brink and Marc Phillip Nogueira. Frankfurt am Main: Suhrkamp Verlag, 2008.

———. *Philosophische Terminologie I und II*. Edited by Henri Lonitz. Frankfurt am Main: Suhrkamp Verlag, 2016.

———. "A Portrait of Walter Benjamin." In *Prisms*, translated by Samuel Weber and Shierry Weber, 227–241. Cambridge, MA: MIT Press, 1981.

———. *Probleme der Moralphilosophie*. Edited by Thomas Schröder. 2nd ed. Frankfurt am Main: Suhrkamp Verlag, 2015.

———. *Problems of Moral Philosophy*. Translated by Rodney Livingstone. Stanford, CA: Stanford University Press, 2001.

———. "Progress." In *Critical Models: Interventions and Catchwords*, translated by Henry W. Pickford, 143–160. New York: Columbia University Press, 1998.

———. "Reflections on Class Theory." In *Can One Live after Auschwitz? A Philosophical Reader*, edited by Rolf Tiedemann, translated by Rodney Livingstone, 93–110. Stanford, CA: Stanford University Press, 2003.

———. "The Schema of Mass Culture." In *The Culture Industry: Selected Essays on Mass Culture*, edited by J. M. Bernstein, translated by Nicholas Walker, 61–97. London: Routledge, 1991.

———. "Schubert." Translated by Jonathan Dunsby and Beate Perrey. *19th-Century Music* 29, no. 1 (2005): 3–14.

———. "Schubert." *Die Musik* 21, no. 1 (1928): 1–12.

———. "Skoteinos, or How to Read Hegel." In *Hegel: Three Studies*, translated by Shierry Weber Nicholsen, 89–148. Cambridge, MA: MIT Press, 1993.

———. "Society." Translated by F. R. Jameson. *Salmagundi* 3, no. 10–11 (1969–1970): 144–153.

———. "Theory of Pseudo-Culture." Translated by Deborah Cook. *Telos* 95 (1993): 15–38.

———. "Theses on Need." In *Towards a New Manifesto*, by Theodor W. Adorno and Max Horkheimer, 2nd ed., translated by Iain Macdonald and Martin Shuster, 79–89. London: Verso, 2019.

———. "Trying to Understand *Endgame*." In *Notes to Literature*, translated by Shierry Weber Nicholsen, 1:241–275. New York: Columbia University Press, 1991.

———. *Vorlesung über Negative Dialektik*. Edited by Rolf Tiedemann. Frankfurt am Main: Suhrkamp Verlag, 2003.

———. "Who's Afraid of the Ivory Tower? A Conversation with Theodor W. Adorno." In *Language without Soil: Adorno and Late Philosophical Modernity*, edited and translated by Gerhard Richter, 227–238. New York: Fordham University Press, 2010.

———. "Why Still Philosophy." In *Critical Models: Interventions and Catchwords*, translated by Henry W. Pickford, 5–17. New York: Columbia University Press, 1998.

———. *Zur Lehre von der Geschichte und von der Freiheit*. Edited by Rolf Tiedemann. 4th ed. Frankfurt am Main: Suhrkamp Verlag, 2016.

Adorno, Theodor W., and Walter Benjamin. *Briefwechsel 1928–1940*. Edited by Henri Lonitz. Frankfurt am Main: Suhrkamp Verlag, 1994.

———. *The Complete Correspondence 1928–1940*. Translated by Nicholas Walker. Oxford: Polity Press, 1999.

Adorno, Theodor W., and Arnold Gehlen. "Ist die Soziologie eine Wissenschaft vom Menschen? Ein Streitgespräch." In *Adornos Philosophie in Grundbegriffen: Auflösung einiger Deutungsprobleme*, by Friedemann Grenz, 225–251. Frankfurt am Main: Suhrkamp Verlag, 1974.

Adorno, Theodor W., and Max Horkheimer. *Briefwechsel*. 4 vols. Frankfurt am Main: Suhrkamp Verlag, 2003–2006.

———. *Towards a New Manifesto*. Translated by Rodney Livingstone. 2nd ed. London: Verso, 2019.

Adorno, Theodor W., and Gershom Scholem. *Briefwechsel 1939–1969*. Edited by Asaf Angermann. Frankfurt am Main: Suhrkamp Verlag, 2015.

Allen, Amy. *The End of Progress: Decolonizing the Normative Foundations of Critical Theory*. New York: Columbia University Press, 2015.

Arendt, Hannah. "Martin Heidegger at Eighty." *New York Review of Books*, October 21, 1971, 50–54.

———. "Martin Heidegger zum achtzigsten Geburtstag." *Merkur* 10 (1969): 893–902.

Aristotle. *Nicomachean Ethics*. Translated by Terence Irwin. 2nd ed. Indianapolis, IN: Hackett, 1999.

Bekenntnis der Professoren an den deutschen Universitäten und Hochschulen zu Adolf Hitler und dem nationalsozialistischen Staat. Dresden: NS Lehrerbund Deutschland/ Sachsen, 1933.

Benjamin, Walter. *The Arcades Project*. Translated by Howard Eiland and Kevin McLaughlin. Cambridge, MA: Belknap Press of Harvard University Press, 1999.

———. *Briefe*. Frankfurt am Main: Suhrkamp Verlag, 1978.

———. *Correspondence 1910–1940*. Translated by M. R. Jacobson and E. M. Jacobson. Chicago: University of Chicago Press, 1994.

———. "Franz Kafka: On the Tenth Anniversary of His Death." In *Selected Writings*, edited by Michael W. Jennings and Howard Eiland, translated by Harry Zohn, 2.2:794–818. Cambridge, MA: Harvard University Press, 1999.

———. *Gesammelte Schriften*. Edited by Rolf Tiedemann, Hermann Schweppenhäuser, Hella Tiedemann-Bartels, and Tillman Rexroth. 7 vols. Frankfurt am Main: Suhrkamp Verlag, 1972–1989.

———. "On the Concept of History." In *Selected Writings*, edited by Michael W. Jennings and Howard Eiland, translated by Harry Zohn, 4:389–400. Cambridge, MA: Harvard University Press, 2003.

———. *The Origin of German Tragic Drama*. Translated by John Osborne. London: Verso, 1998.

———. "The Paris of the Second Empire in Baudelaire." In *Selected Writings*, edited by Michael W. Jennings and Howard Eiland, translated by Harry Zohn, 4:3–92. Cambridge, MA: Harvard University Press, 2003.

———. *Schriften*. Edited by Theodor W. Adorno, Gretel Adorno, and Friedrich Podszus. 2 vols. Frankfurt am Main: Suhrkamp Verlag, 1955.

Bernhard, Thomas. *Alte Meister: Komödie*. Frankfurt am Main: Suhrkamp Verlag, 1985.

———. *Old Masters: A Comedy*. Translated by Ewald Osers. Chicago: University of Chicago Press, 1992.

Bernstein, Jay M. *Adorno: Disenchantment and Ethics*. Cambridge: Cambridge University Press, 2001.

Betzen, Klaus. "Bericht über die über die Jahresversammlung in Berlin 7.–9. Juni 1963." *Hölderlin-Jahrbuch* 13 (1963–1964): 172–184.

Binder, Wolfgang. "Bericht über die Diskussion." *Hölderlin-Jahrbuch* 13 (1963–1964): 185–186.

Bloch, Ernst. *Das Prinzip Hoffnung*. 3 vols. Frankfurt am Main: Suhrkamp Verlag, 2016.

———. "'Ein Marxist hat nicht das Recht, Pessimist zu sein.'" In *Tagträume vom aufrechten Gang: Sechs Interviews mit Ernst Bloch*, edited by Arno Münster, 101–120. Frankfurt am Main: Suhrkamp Verlag, 1977.

———. *The Principle of Hope*. Translated by Neville Plaice, Stephen Plaice, and Paul Knight. 3 vols. Cambridge, MA: MIT Press, 1995.

———. *Subjekt–Objekt: Erläuterungen zu Hegel*. Frankfurt am Main: Suhrkamp Verlag, 1962.

Bloch, Ernst, and Theodor W. Adorno. "Something's Missing: A Discussion between Ernst Bloch and Theodor W. Adorno on the Contradictions of Utopian Longing." In *The Utopian Function of Art and Literature: Selected Essays*, by Ernst Bloch, translated by Jack Zipes and Frank Mecklenburg, 1–17. Cambridge, MA: MIT Press, 1988.

Boldyrev, Ivan. *Ernst Bloch and His Contemporaries: Locating Utopian Messianism*. London: Bloomsbury, 2014.

Brod, Max. *Franz Kafka: A Biography*. Translated by G. Humphreys Roberts and Richard Winston. New York: Schocken Books, 1960.

———. *Franz Kafka: Eine Biographie*. In *Über Franz Kafka*. Frankfurt am Main: Fischer Bücherei, 1966.

Buchwalter, Andrew. *Dialectics, Politics, and the Contemporary Value of Hegel's Practical Philosophy*. London: Routledge, 2012.

Buck-Morss, Susan. *The Dialectics of Seeing: Walter Benjamin and the Arcades Project*. Cambridge, MA: MIT Press, 1989.

———. *The Origin of Negative Dialectics: Theodor W. Adorno, Walter Benjamin, and the Frankfurt Institute*. New York: Free Press, 1977.

Caygill, Howard. *Walter Benjamin: The Colour of Experience*. London: Routledge, 1998.

Cicero. *De finibus bonorum et malorum*. Translated by H. Rackham. London: William Heinemann, 1914.

Cook, Deborah. "From the Actual to the Possible: Nonidentity Thinking." *Constellations* 12, no. 1 (2005): 21–35.

———. "Open Thinking: Adorno's Exact Imagination." *Philosophy and Social Criticism* 44, no. 8 (2018): 805–821.

Dahrendorf, Ralf. "Anmerkung zur Diskussion der Referate von Karl R. Popper und Theodor W. Adorno." In *Der Positivismusstreit in der deutschen Soziologie*, 145–153. Darmstadt: Hermann Luchterhand Verlag, 1969.

———. *Class and Class Conflict in Industrial Society*. Stanford, CA: Stanford University Press, 1959.

———. "Herrschaft, Klassenverhältnis und Schichtung." In *Spätkapitalismus oder Industriegesellschaft? Verhandlungen des 16. Deutschen Soziologentages in Frankfurt am Main 1968*, edited by Theodor W. Adorno, 88–99. Stuttgart: Ferdinand Enke, 1969.

———. "Remarks on the Discussion of the Papers by Karl R. Popper and Theodor W. Adorno." In *The Positivist Dispute in German Sociology*, translated by Glyn Adey and David Frisby, 123–130. London: Heinemann, 1976.

Engels, Friedrich. *The Housing Question*. In *Marx-Engels Collected Works*, 23:317–391. London: Lawrence and Wishart, 1988.

Faye, Emmanuel. *Heidegger, l'introduction du nazisme dans la philosophie: Autour des séminaires inédits de 1933–1935*. Paris: Albin Michel, 2005.

———. *Heidegger: The Introduction of Nazism into Philosophy in the Light of the Unpublished Seminars of 1933–1935*. Translated by Michael B. Smith. New Haven, CT: Yale University Press, 2009.

Finlayson, James Gordon. "Adorno on the Ethical and the Ineffable." *European Journal of Philosophy* 10, no. 1 (2002): 1–25.

———. "Hegel, Adorno and the Origins of Immanent Criticism." *British Journal for the History of Philosophy* 22, no. 6 (2014): 1142–1166.

Freyenhagen, Fabian. *Adorno's Practical Philosophy: Living Less Wrongly*. Cambridge: Cambridge University Press, 2013.

Friedlander, Eli. *Walter Benjamin: A Philosophical Portrait*. Cambridge, MA: Harvard University Press, 2012.

Goehr, Lydia. *Elective Affinities: Musical Essays on the History of Aesthetic Theory*. New York: Columbia University Press, 2008.

Gonzalez, Francisco J. "Whose Metaphysics of Presence? Heidegger's Interpretation of *Energeia* and *Dunamis* in Aristotle." *Southern Journal of Philosophy* 44, no. 4 (2006): 533–568.

———. "Δύναμις and Dasein, ’Ενέργεια and Ereignis: Heidegger's (Re)Turn to Aristotle." *Research in Phenomenology* 48, no. 3 (2018): 409–432.

Gordon, Peter E. *Adorno and Existence*. Cambridge, MA: Harvard University Press, 2016.

———. "Review of Emmanuel Faye, *Heidegger: The Introduction of Nazism into Philosophy in Light of the Unpublished Seminars of 1933–1935*." *Notre Dame Philosophical Reviews* (2010). Last modified March 12, 2010. http://ndpr.nd.edu/news/24316/?id=19228.

Grass, Günter. *Dog Years*. Translated by Ralph Manheim. San Diego: Harcourt, 1965.

———. *Hundejahre*. Darmstadt: Hermann Luchterhand Verlag, 1974.

Haag, Karl Heinz. *Kritik der neueren Ontologie*. In *Kritische Philosophie: Abhandlungen und Aufsätze*, edited by Rolf Tiedemann. Munich: edition text + kritik, 2012.

Habermas, Jürgen. *Philosophisch-politische Profile*. Enl. ed. Frankfurt am Main: Suhrkamp Verlag, 1984.

———. "Theodor Adorno: The Primal History of Subjectivity—Self-Affirmation Gone Wild." In *Philosophical-Political Profiles*, by Jürgen Habermas, 99–109. Cambridge, MA: MIT Press, 1983.

———. "Toward a Reconstruction of Historical Materialism." In *Communication and the Evolution of Society*, translated by Thomas McCarthy, 130–177. Boston: Beacon Press, 1979.

———. *Zur Rekonstruktion des historischen Materialismus*. Frankfurt am Main: Suhrkamp Verlag, 1976.

Hammer, Espen. *Adorno and the Political*. London: Routledge, 2005.

Hegel, G. W. F. *Elements of the Philosophy of Right*. Translated by H. B. Nisbet. Cambridge: Cambridge University Press, 1991.

———. *The Encyclopaedia Logic: Part I of the Encyclopaedia of Philosophical Sciences, with the Zusätze*. Translated by T. F. Geraets, W. A. Suchting, and H. S. Harris. Indianapolis, IN: Hackett, 1991.

———. "The German Constitution." In *Hegel's Political Writings*, translated by T. M. Knox, 143–242. Oxford: Oxford University Press, 1964.

———. *Hegel's Aesthetics: Lectures on Fine Art*. Translated by T. M. Knox. 2 vols. Oxford: Oxford University Press, 1975.

———. *Hegel's Phenomenology of Spirit*. Translated by A. V. Miller. Oxford: Oxford University Press, 1977.

———. *Lectures on the Philosophy of World History: Introduction*. Translated by H. B. Nisbet. Cambridge: Cambridge University Press, 1975.

———. *The Philosophical Propaedeutic*. Edited by Michael George and Andrew Vincent. Translated by A. V. Miller. Oxford: Basil Blackwell, 1986.

———. *The Science of Logic*. Translated by George di Giovanni. Cambridge: Cambridge University Press, 2010.

———. *Vorlesungen über die Philosophie der Weltgeschichte*. 4 vols. Hamburg: Felix Meiner Verlag, 1994.

———. *Werke*. Edited by Eva Moldenhauer and Karl Markus Michel. 20 vols. Frankfurt am Main: Suhrkamp Verlag, 1969–1971.

Heidegger, Martin. *The Basic Problems of Phenomenology*. Translated by Albert Hofstadter. Rev. ed. Bloomington: Indiana University Press, 1982.

———. *Basic Questions of Philosophy: Selected "Problems" of "Logic."* Translated by Richard Rojcewicz and André Schuwer. Bloomington: Indiana University Press, 1994.

———. *Being and Time*. Translated by John Macquarrie and Edward Robinson. Oxford: Basil Blackwell, 1962.

———. *Contributions to Philosophy (Of the Event)*. Translated by Richard Rojcewicz and Daniela Vallega-Neu. Bloomington: Indiana University Press, 2012.

———. "Conversation on a Country Path about Thinking." In *Discourse on Thinking*, translated by John M. Anderson and E. Hans Freund, 58–90. New York: Harper and Row, 1966.

———. "The End of Philosophy and the Task of Thinking." In *On Time and Being*, translated by Joan Stambaugh, 55–73. New York: Harper and Row, 1972.

———. *The Fundamental Concepts of Metaphysics*. Translated by William McNeill and Nicholas Walker. Bloomington: Indiana University Press, 1995.

———. *Gesamtausgabe*. Edited by Friedrich-Wilhelm von Herrmann. Frankfurt am Main: Vittorio Klostermann, 1975–.

———. "Hegel and the Greeks." In *Pathmarks*, edited by Will McNeill, translated by Robert Metcalf, 323–336. Cambridge: Cambridge University Press, 1998.

———. *Hegel's Phenomenology of Spirit*. Translated by Parvis Emad and Kenneth Maly. Bloomington: Indiana University Press, 1988.

———. *The History of Beyng*. Translated by William McNeill and Jeffrey Powell. Bloomington: Indiana University Press, 2015.

———. "Letter on 'Humanism.'" In *Pathmarks*, edited by Will McNeill, translated by Frank A. Capuzzi, 239–276. Cambridge: Cambridge University Press, 1998.

———. *Letters to His Wife, 1915–1970*. Edited by Gertrud Heidegger. Translated by Rupert Glasgow. Cambridge: Polity Press, 2008.

———. *"Mein liebes Seelchen!" Briefe Martin Heideggers an seine Frau Elfride, 1915–1970*. Edited by Gertrud Heidegger. Munich: Deutsche Verlags-Anstalt, 2005.

———. "Metaphysics as History of Being." In *The End of Philosophy*, translated by Joan Stambaugh, 1–54. 1973. Reprint, University of Chicago Press, 2003.

———. *Mindfulness*. Translated by Parvis Emad and Thomas Kalary. London: Continuum, 2006.

———. "On the Essence of Truth." In *Pathmarks*, edited by William McNeill, translated by John Sallis, 136–154. Cambridge: Cambridge University Press, 1998.

———. "The Onto-Theo-Logical Constitution of Metaphysics." In *Identity and Difference*, translated by Joan Stambaugh, 42–74. Chicago: University of Chicago Press, 1969.

———. *Ponderings II–VI: Black Notebooks 1931–1938*. Translated by Richard Rojcewicz. Bloomington: Indiana University Press, 2016.

———. "The Question concerning Technology." In *The Question concerning Technology and Other Essays*, translated by William Lovitt, 3–35. New York: Harper and Row, 1977.

———. "Recollection in Metaphysics." In *The End of Philosophy*, translated by Joan Stambaugh, 75–83. 1973. Reprint, University of Chicago Press, 2003.

———. "Summary of a Seminar on 'Time and Being.'" In *On Time and Being*, translated by Joan Stambaugh, 25–54. New York: Harper and Row, 1972.

———. "The Turning." In *The Question concerning Technology and Other Essays*, translated by William Lovitt, 36–49. New York: Harper and Row, 1977.

———. "Why Do I Stay in the Provinces?" In *Philosophical and Political Writings*, edited by Manfred Stassen, translated by Thomas Sheehan, 16–18. New York: Continuum, 2003.

Heidegger, Martin, and Ernst Jünger. *Correspondence 1949–1975*. Translated by Timothy Sean Quinn. London: Rowman and Littlefield, 2016.

Hintikka, Jaakko. "Aristotle on the Realization of Possibilities in Time." In *Time and Necessity: Studies in Aristotle's Theory of Modality*, by Jaakko Hintikka, 93–113. Oxford: Clarendon Press, 1973.

Hölderlin, Friedrich. *Poems and Fragments*. Translated by Michael Hamburger. 3rd, bilingual ed. London: Anvil Press Poetry, 1994.

Honneth, Axel. "Eine Physiognomie der kapitalistischen Lebensform: Skizze der Gesellschaftstheorie Adornos." In *Dialektik der Freiheit: Frankfurter Adorno-Konferenz 2003*, edited by Axel Honneth, 165–187. Frankfurt am Main: Suhrkamp Verlag, 2005.

Horkheimer, Max. *Eclipse of Reason*. 1974. Reprint, London: Continuum, 2004.

———. "The End of Reason." *Studies in Philosophy and Social Science* 9, no. 3 (1941): 366–388.

———. *Gesammelte Schriften*. Edited by Alfred Schmidt and Gunzelin Schmid Noerr. 19 vols. Frankfurt am Main: S. Fischer Verlag, 1985–1996.

———. "On the Problem of Needs." In *Towards a New Manifesto*, by Theodor W. Adorno and Max Horkheimer, 2nd ed., translated by Iain Macdonald, 91–101. London: Verso, 2019.

Horkheimer, Max, and Theodor W. Adorno. *Dialectic of Enlightenment: Philosophical Fragments*. Translated by Edmund Jephcott. Stanford, CA: Stanford University Press, 2002.

———. "[Diskussionen über die Differenz zwischen Positivismus und materialistischer Dialektik] (1939)." In *Gesammelte Schriften*, by Max Horkheimer, 12:436–492. Frankfurt am Main: S. Fischer Verlag, 1985.

Husserl, Edmund. *Husserliana*. Edited by Sam Ijsseling et al. The Hague: Martinus Nijhoff, 1950–.

———. *Ideas pertaining to a Pure Phenomenology and to a Phenomenological Philosophy: First Book*. Translated by F. Kersten. The Hague: Martinus Nijhoff, 1983.

Inwood, Michael. *A Hegel Dictionary*. Oxford: Blackwell, 1992.

Jäger, Lorenz. *Adorno: A Political Biography*. Translated by Stewart Spencer. New Haven, CT: Yale University Press, 2004.

Jay, Martin. *Marxism and Totality: The Adventures of a Concept from Lukács to Habermas*. Berkeley: University of California Press, 1984.

Jennings, Michael W. *Dialectical Images: Walter Benjamin's Theory of Literary Criticism*. Ithaca, NY: Cornell University Press, 1987.

Jünger, Ernst, and Martin Heidegger. *Briefe 1949–1975*. Stuttgart: Klett-Cotta, 2008.

Kafka, Franz. *Nachgelassene Schriften und Fragmente II*. Edited by Jost Schillemeit. Frankfurt am Main: S. Fischer Verlag, 1992.

———. *The Zürau Aphorisms*. Translated by Michael Hofmann. London: Harvill Secker, 2006.

Kant, Immanuel. *Critique of Practical Reason*. Translated by Lewis White Beck. New York: Macmillan, 1956.

———. *Gesammelte Schriften "Akademieausgabe."* Berlin: Reimer/De Gruyter, 1900–.

———. "Idea for a Universal History with a Cosmopolitan Purpose." In *Kant's Political*

Writings, edited by Hans Reiss, translated by H. B. Nisbet, 41–53. Cambridge: Cambridge University Press, 1970.

———. *Werke in zwölf Bänden*. 12 vols. Frankfurt am Main: Suhrkamp Verlag, 1977.

Kierkegaard, Søren. *Philosophical Fragments, or A Fragment of Philosophy. Johannes Climacus, or De Omnibus Dubitandum Est: A Narrative*. Translated by Howard V. Hong and Edna H. Hong. Princeton, NJ: Princeton University Press, 1985.

———. *Søren Kierkegaard's Skrifter*. Edited by Niels Jørgen Cappelørn, Joakim Garff, Jette Knudsen, Johnny Kondrup, and Alastair McKinnon. 28 vols. Copenhagen: Gads Forlag / Søren Kierkegaard Forskningscenteret, 1997–.

Löwith, Karl. "The Political Implications of Heidegger's Existentialism." In *The Heidegger Controversy*, edited and translated by Richard Wolin, 167–185. Cambridge, MA: MIT Press, 1993.

———. *Sämtliche Schriften*. Stuttgart: J. B. Metzler, 1981–1988.

Lukács, Georg. *Die Theorie des Romans: Ein geschichtsphilosophischer Versuch über die Formen der großen Epik*. Darmstadt: Hermann Luchterhand Verlag, 1971.

———. *History and Class Consciousness: Studies in Marxist Dialectics*. Translated by Rodney Livingstone. Cambridge, MA: MIT Press, 1971.

———. *The Theory of the Novel: A Historico-Philosophical Essay on the Forms of Great Epic Literature*. Cambridge, MA: MIT Press, 1971.

———. *Werke*. Neuwied: Luchterhand, 1962–1986.

Luther, Martin. *D. Martin Luthers Werke: Kritische Gesamtausgabe—Briefwechsel*. Weimar: Verlag Hermann Böhlaus Nachfolger, 1931.

———. *Luther's Works*. Edited by Helmut T. Lehmann and Jaroslav Pelikan. 55 vols. St. Louis, MO: Concordia Publishing House, 1955–1986.

Macdonald, Iain. "Cold, Cold, Warm: Autonomy, Intimacy and Maturity in Adorno." *Philosophy and Social Criticism* 37, no. 6 (2011): 669–689.

Macdonald, Iain, and Krzysztof Ziarek, eds. *Adorno and Heidegger: Philosophical Questions*. Stanford, CA: Stanford University Press, 2008.

Marx, Karl. *Capital: Volume 1*. Translated by Ben Fowkes. Harmondsworth, UK: Penguin in association with *New Left Review*, 1976.

———. *A Contribution to the Critique of Political Economy, Part One*. In *Marx-Engels Collected Works*, vol. 29, translated by Victor Schnittke. London: Lawrence and Wishart, 1987.

———. *Critique of Hegel's "Philosophy of Right."* Translated by Annette Jolin and Joseph O'Malley. Cambridge: Cambridge University Press, 1970.

———. *The Economic and Philosophic Manuscripts of 1844*. Translated by Martin Milligan. New York: International Publishers, 1964.

———. "An Exchange of Letters." In *Writings of the Young Marx on Philosophy and Society*, edited and translated by Loyd D. Easton and Kurt H. Guddat, 203–215. Indianapolis, IN: Hackett, 1997.

———. *Grundrisse: Foundations of the Critique of Political Economy (Rough Draft)*. Translated by Martin Nicolaus. Harmondsworth, UK: Penguin in association with *New Left Review*, 1973.

———. *The Poverty of Philosophy.* In *Marx-Engels Collected Works,* vol. 6, translated by Frida Knight. London: Lawrence and Wishart, 1976.

———. "Speech at the Anniversary of the People's Paper, April 14, 1856." In *Marx-Engels Collected Works,* 14:655–656. London: Lawrence and Wishart, 1980.

———. "Theses on Feuerbach." In *Marx-Engels Collected Works,* translated by W. Lough, 5:3–5. London: Lawrence and Wishart, 1975.

Marx, Karl, and Friedrich Engels. *The Communist Manifesto.* Translated by Samuel Moore. Harmondsworth, UK: Penguin, 1967.

———. *The German Ideology.* In *Marx-Engels Collected Works,* vol. 5, translated by Clemens Dutt, W. Lough, and C. P. Magill. London: Lawrence and Wishart, 1975.

———. *Werke.* 43 vols. Berlin: Dietz-Verlag, 1956–.

Menke, Christoph. "Hegel's Theory of Liberation: Law, Freedom, History, Society." *Symposium* 17, no. 1 (2013): 10–30.

———. "Hegel's Theory of Second Nature: The 'Lapse' of Spirit." *Symposium* 17, no. 1 (2013): 31–49.

Minder, Robert. "Hölderlin chez les allemands." *Preuves* 16, no. 186–187 (1966): 24–32.

———. "Hölderlin und die Deutschen." *Hölderlin-Jahrbuch* 14 (1965–1966): 1–19.

Mörchen, Hermann. *Adorno und Heidegger: Untersuchung einer philosophischen Kommunikationsverweigerung.* Stuttgart: Klett-Cotta, 1981.

———. *Macht und Herrschaft im Denken von Heidegger und Adorno.* Stuttgart: Klett-Cotta, 1980.

———. Review of Theodor W. Adorno, *Jargon der Eigentlichkeit. Zeitschrift für deutsches Altertum und deutsche Literatur* 94, no. 2 (1965): 89–95.

Müller-Doohm, Stefan. *Adorno: A Biography.* Cambridge: Polity Press, 2005.

Neumann, Franz. "Economics and Politics in the Twentieth Century." In *The Democratic and the Authoritarian State: Essays in Political and Legal Theory,* edited by Herbert Marcuse, translated by Peter Gay, 257–269. Glencoe, IL: Free Press, 1957.

———. "Ökonomie und Politik im zwanzigsten Jahrhundert." *Zeitschrift für Politik* 2, no. 1 (1955): 1–11.

Ng, Karen. "Hegel's Logic of Actuality." *Review of Metaphysics* 63, no. 1 (2009): 139–172.

Nietzsche, Friedrich. *Kritische Studienausgabe.* 15 vols. Munich: dtv/de Gruyter, 1988.

———. *Thus Spoke Zarathustra: A Book for Everyone and No One.* Translated by R. J. Hollingdale. Harmondsworth, UK: Penguin, 1961.

O'Connor, Brian. *Adorno's Negative Dialectic: Philosophy and the Possibility of Critical Rationality.* Cambridge, MA: MIT Press, 2005.

Pensky, Max. "Method and Time: Benjamin's Dialectical Images." In *The Cambridge Companion to Walter Benjamin,* edited by David S. Ferris, 177–198. Cambridge: Cambridge University Press, 2004.

Pfizer, Thomas. "'Die Ausnahme.'" In *Erinnerung an Martin Heidegger,* edited by Günther Neske, 191–196. Pfullingen, Germany: Verlag Günther Neske, 1977.

Pollock, Frederick. "State Capitalism: Its Possibilities and Limitations." *Studies in Philosophy and Social Science* 9, no. 2 (1941): 200–225.

Pradelle, Dominique. Review of *Heidegger: L'introduction du nazisme dans la philosophie*, by Emmanuel Faye. *Philosophie* 91, no. 4 (2006): 91–93.

Rath, Norbert. "'Die Kraft zur Angst und die zum Glück sind das Gleiche': Das Konzept des Glücks in der Kritischen Theorie Adornos." In *Glücksvorstellungen: Ein Rückgriff in die Geschichte der Soziologie*, edited by Alfred Bellebaum and Klaus Barheier, 177–196. Opláden, Germany: Westdeutscher Verlag, 1997.

Renault, Emmanuel. *Connaître ce qui est: Enquête sur le présentisme hégélien*. Paris: Vrin, 2015.

Rockmore, Tom. "Foreword." In *Heidegger: The Introduction of Nazism into Philosophy in the Light of the Unpublished Seminars of 1933–1935*, by Emmanuel Faye, translated by Michael B. Smith, vii–xxi. New Haven, CT: Yale University Press, 2009.

Rose, Gillian. *Hegel contra Sociology*. London: Verso Books, 2009.

Rüdel, Walter, and Richard Wisser. "Martin Heidegger: Im Denken unterwegs...." ZDF, 1969.

Savage, Robert. *Hölderlin after the Catastrophe: Heidegger—Adorno—Brecht*. Rochester, NY: Camden House, 2008.

Schiller, Hans-Ernst. "Tod und Utopie: Ernst Bloch, Georg Lukács." In *Adorno-Handbuch: Leben—Werk—Wirkung*, edited by Richard Klein, Johann Kreuzer, and Stefan Müller-Doohm, 25–35. Stuttgart: J. B. Metzler'sche Verlagsbuchhandlung und Carl Ernst Poeschel Verlag, 2011.

Schmid Noerr, Gunzelin. "Bloch und Adorno—bildhafte und bilderlose Utopie." *Zeitschrift für kritische Theorie*, no. 13 (2001): 25–55.

———. "Editor's Afterword: The Position of 'Dialectic of Enlightenment' in the Development of Critical Theory." In *Dialectic of Enlightenment: Philosophical Fragments*, by Max Horkheimer and Theodor W. Adorno, translated by Edmund Jephcott, 217–247. Stanford, CA: Stanford University Press, 2002.

Schmidt, Alfred. *The Concept of Nature in Marx*. Translated by Ben Fowkes. London: New Left Books, 1971.

———. *Der Begriff der Natur in der Lehre von Marx*. 4th rev. and corr. ed. Hamburg: Europäische Verlagsanstalt, 1993.

Schneeberger, Guido, ed. *Nachlese zu Heidegger: Dokumente zu seinem Leben und Denken*. Bern: Suhr, 1962.

Schopf, Wolfgang, ed. *"So müßte ich ein Engel und kein Autor sein": Adorno und seine Frankurter Verleger. Der Briefwechsel mit Peter Suhrkamp und Siegfried Unseld*. Frankfurt am Main: Suhrkamp Verlag, 2003.

Schürmann, Reiner. *Heidegger on Being and Acting: From Principles to Anarchy*. Translated by Christine-Marie Gros and Reiner Schürmann. Bloomington: Indiana University Press, 1987.

Serban, Claudia. *Phénoménologie de la possibilité: Husserl et Heidegger*. Paris: PUF, 2016.

Sophocles. *Sophocles: Plays. Antigone*. Translated by R. C. Jebb. London: Bristol Classical Press, 2004.

Spiegelberg, Herbert. *The Phenomenological Movement: A Historical Introduction*. 3rd rev. and enl. ed. The Hague: Martinus Nijhoff, 1982.

Swift, Jonathan. "A Vindication of Mr. Gay, and the *Beggars Opera.*" *The Intelligencer*, no. 3 (1728): 17–29. Reprint, 2nd ed. of 1730, New York: AMS Press, 1967.

Theunissen, Michael. "Negativität bei Adorno." In *Adorno-Konferenz 1983*, edited by Ludwig von Friedeburg and Jürgen Habermas, 41–65. Frankfurt am Main: Suhrkamp Verlag, 1983.

Tiedemann, Rolf. "Dialectics at a Standstill: Approaches to the *Passagen-Werk.*" In *On Walter Benjamin: Critical Essays and Reflections*, edited by Gary Smith, translated by Gary Smith and André Lefevere, 260–291. Cambridge, MA: MIT Press, 1988.

Traub, Rainer, and Harald Wieser, eds. *Gespräche mit Ernst Bloch*. Frankfurt am Main: Suhrkamp Verlag, 1975.

Trawny, Peter. *Freedom to Fail: Heidegger's Anarchy*. Translated by Ian Alexander Moore and Christopher Turner. Cambridge: Polity Press, 2015.

Van Reijen, Willem, and Jan Bransen. "The Disappearance of Class History in 'Dialectic of Enlightenment': A Commentary on the Textual Variants (1947 and 1944)." In *Dialectic of Enlightenment: Philosophical Fragments*, by Max Horkheimer and Theodor W. Adorno, translated by Edmund Jephcott, 248–252. Stanford, CA: Stanford University Press, 2002.

Wallace, Henry A. "The Price of Free World Victory." In *Democracy Reborn*, edited by Russell Lord, 190–195. New York: Reynal and Hitchcock, 1944.

Weber, Max. "Critical Studies in the Logic of the Cultural Sciences." In *Max Weber: Collected Methodological Writings*, edited by Hans Henrik Bruun and Sam Whimster, translated by Hans Henrik Bruun, 139–184. Abingdon, UK: Routledge, 2012.

———. *Economy and Society: An Outline of Interpretive Sociology*. Edited by Guenther Roth and Claus Wittich. Translated by Ephraim Fischoff, Hans Gerth, A. M. Henderson, Ferdinand Kolegar, C. Wright Mills, Talcott Parsons, Max Rheinstein, Guenther Roth, Edward Shils, and Claus Wittich. Berkeley: University of California Press, 1978.

———. *Gesammelte Aufsätze zur Wissenschaftslehre*. Edited by Johannes Winckelmann. 6th rev. ed. Tübingen: Verlag J. C. B. Mohr (Paul Siebeck), 1985.

———. "The 'Objectivity' of Knowledge in Social Science and Social Policy." In *Max Weber: Collected Methodological Writings*, edited by Hans Henrik Bruun and Sam Whimster, translated by Hans Henrik Bruun, 100–138. Abingdon, UK: Routledge, 2012.

———. "On Some Categories of Interpretive Sociology." In *Max Weber: Collected Methodological Writings*, edited by Hans Henrik Bruun and Sam Whimster, translated by Hans Henrik Bruun, 273–301. Abingdon, UK: Routledge, 2012.

———. *Wirtschaft und Gesellschaft: Grundriß der verstehenden Soziologie*. Edited by Johannes Winckelmann. 5th rev. ed. Tübingen: Verlag J. C. B. Mohr (Paul Siebeck), 1980.

Whyman, Tom. "Understanding Adorno on 'Natural-History.'" *International Journal of Philosophical Studies* 24, no. 4 (2016): 452–472.

Wiggershaus, Rolf. *Die Frankfurter Schule*. 6th ed. Munich: Deutscher Taschenbuch Verlag, 2001.

———. *The Frankfurt School.* Translated by Michael Robertson. Cambridge: Polity Press, 1994.

Wisser, Richard. "Das Fernseh-Interview." In *Erinnerung an Martin Heidegger*, edited by Günther Neske, 257–287. Pfullingen, Germany: Verlag Günther Neske, 1977.

———, ed. *Martin Heidegger im Gespräch.* Freiburg: Verlag Karl Alber, 1970.

Wolin, Richard. "Introduction to the Discussion of [Ludwig Marcuse's] 'Need and Culture in Nietzsche.'" *Constellations* 8, no. 1 (2001): 127–129.

Zuidervaart, Lambert. *Social Philosophy after Adorno.* Cambridge: Cambridge University Press, 2007.

INDEX